Sparring with
Smokin' Joe

Sparring with Smokin' Joe

Joe Frazier's Epic Battles and Rivalry with Ali

GLENN LEWIS

ROWMAN & LITTLEFIELD
Lanham • Boulder • New York • London

Published by Rowman & Littlefield
An imprint of The Rowman & Littlefield Publishing Group, Inc.
4501 Forbes Boulevard, Suite 200, Lanham, Maryland 20706
www.rowman.com

86-90 Paul Street, London EC2A 4NE, United Kingdom

Distributed by NATIONAL BOOK NETWORK

British Library Cataloguing in Publication Information Available

Library of Congress Cataloging-in-Publication Data
Names: Lewis, Glenn, 1947– author.
Title: Sparring with Smokin' Joe : Joe Frazier's epic battles and rivalry with Ali / Glenn Lewis.
Description: Lanham : Rowman & Littlefield, [2021] | Includes bibliographical references and index. | Summary: "This book aims to rectify the imbalance in coverage between Joe Frazier and Muhammad Ali just in time for the 50th anniversary of The Fight of the Century. It is based on several months the author spent in the gym, on the road, and in verbal tussles with the legendary champion and gives new insight into Frazier"— Provided by publisher.
Identifiers: LCCN 2020031150 (print) | LCCN 2020031151 (ebook) | ISBN 9781538136799 (cloth) | ISBN 9781538199046 (paperback) ISBN 9781538136805 (ebook)
Subjects: LCSH: Frazier, Joe, 1944-2011. | Ali, Muhammad, 1942-2016. | African American boxers—United States. | Boxers (Sports)—United States. | Boxing—United States—History. | Sports rivalries—United States—History.
Classification: LCC GV1132.F7 L49 2021 (print) | LCC GV1132.F7 (ebook) | DDC 796.83/092 [B]—dc23
LC record available at https://lccn.loc.gov/2020031150
LC ebook record available at https://lccn.loc.gov/2020031151

♾™ The paper used in this publication meets the minimum requirements of American National Standard for Information Sciences—Permanence of Paper for Printed Library Materials, ANSI/NISO Z39.48-1992.

For my wife, Francine,
who helped define the arc of this book and my life—
and made both so much better all along the way.

For my daughters, Lindsay (the lawyer) and Caroline (the journalist),
who every day display the fighting spirit, concern for others,
and intellect needed to make the world a better place.

Contents

Acknowledgments

Most authors begin their long journey wondering what it will take to write *my* book. The more aware ones end up thanking a whole crowd of kind, talented souls for helping to bring *our* book to fruition.

Given that the reporting for this book dates back four decades, before two recent years of research and writing, the contributors to *our* book are plentiful. Yet, due to limited space, here is my thanks to a small part of that group. I hope those left out know the role they played and the depth of my gratitude.

To my wife Francine Fialkoff, a superb editor-writer and the best person I ever met, thanks for your love and support on this project dating back to 1980. Every step, and word, along the way I benefited from your ability as a pitch-perfect sounding board.

To my wonderful agent Rita Rosenkranz, thanks for the comfort in knowing I was always represented by the smartest person in the room. I appreciate your expertise, experience, and sensitive appraisal of the publishing terrain.

To my editor Christen Karniski at Rowman & Littlefield, thanks for your unerring vision and willingness to see the potential in this project from the first time we spoke. It's editors like you who make authors want to keep writing.

To the publisher Julie Kirsch, my undying gratitude for jumping in at the height of the pandemic to put everything on track and in the best possible place. Your leadership inspires confidence, enthusiasm, and a sense that everything will be even better than expected.

Thanks as well to Erinn Slanina, Kate Powers, Jessica McCleary, Jackie Hicks, and the rest of the dedicated team at Rowman & Littlefield.

To Susan Schulman and Linda Migalti, thanks for your warm response to the book and quick decision to work on selling key sub rights.

To my friend Bernie Starr, a fine journalist and knowledgeable advisor, thanks for introducing me to Rita and constantly steering me to my next best opportunity.

To Cheryl and Richard Fialkoff, family, and friends, thanks for the uncommon bravery shown in reading the earliest draft of the book and providing an unflinching critique. Medals have been won for less.

To Caroline, Lindsay, and Jordan, my three points of pride, thanks for your constant support and feedback as well. It takes a family to make it through anything worthwhile.

To my supportive colleagues at York College, thanks Donna Chirico, Panayotis Meleties, and Heather Robinson for helping me secure the sabbatical to write the book and signaling your support while I was gone.

To Bill Hughes and Tom Moore, my brothers in journalism at York, thanks for keeping the program vibrant and thriving in my absence. You guys always have my back.

To Marcia Moxam Comrie, a dear friend and former student, thanks for spearheading the publicity effort for the book at the college—and for your unswerving support over the years.

To my fellow journalists and friends at the Journalism School, thanks Amy Dunkin, Andy Mendelson, and Errol Louis for your strong support. And thanks to Judy Watson for years of encouragement and camaraderie that spilled over to this book.

I want to finish off by acknowledging my special debt to those who helped me back in 1980. After all these years, some are gone but none have been forgotten.

To Ken Johnson, thanks for befriending me and acting as my rock on the road.

To the "Professor" George Benton, thanks for the open dialogue, insights into the darker side of boxing's past, and candor in discussing the challenges of the day.

To Gil Clancy, boxing trainer and commentator extraordinaire, thanks for taking me to boxing school ringside at MSG. It was an experience I'll never forget.

To Joey Goldstein, immortal sports publicist, thanks for taking a young writer under your wing and introducing him to Joe Frazier, the U.S. Olympic team, and so many other stars of the day.

To Morty Holtzer, thanks for the stories that made great events come alive.

To Florence Smith Frazier, as I knew her then, thanks for your honesty, quick wit, and kind heart. It was always a pleasure talking to you. And thanks to the rest of the Frazier family and inner circle for the candid talks and welcoming gestures back then.

To Marvis Frazier, thanks for sharing your special, amazingly sophisticated view of the boxing world and life at age nineteen. Your courage and skill in the ring, more than you ever got credit for, was only matched by your compassion and dedication to others outside the ring. It was a privilege spending time with you.

Finally, to Smokin' Joe Frazier, your determination and punching power made you a legend in the ring. However, your generosity of spirit, homespun wisdom, and joyous nature made you "the Greatest" in my book.

MAIN EVENT

1

Up in Joe's Lair

Joe Frazier's three-story boxing gym, sandwiched between a gas station and a nondescript industrial building, remained trapped in the shadows of the North Philadelphia elevated train station. The grimy burgundy façade blended in with the bleak urban neighborhood and made the place seem even more forbidding to a casual visitor. The dark, shade-covered windows certainly didn't help.

The only bright spot was the name "Joe Frazier" in large white letters, adorned with a crown insignia, just above the door. "Cloverlay Gymnasium" appeared in smaller letters as a tribute to the syndicate that had originally owned part of Frazier's boxing contract and had guided him to a title. Joe had bought the syndicate out several years before to finish off his career as his own man. He had also become the sole owner of the gym—known as "the boss" to all who trained or worked there.

It was March 10, 1980, two months after an initial interview session for a short article with the 36-year-old Frazier and his son Marvis, age 19. I was there now to begin work on a much longer piece that would involve several months of shadowing Joe and, along the way, his son. The aim was to capture the pair at a crossroads of their fighting careers and personal lives. Joe had promised me the kind of blanket access that neither man was used to providing nor normally condoned. Yet, after much discussion, the invasive coverage was finally set to begin that day.

I had heard unsubstantiated rumors that the older Frazier was seriously considering getting back in the ring in the not-too-distant future, while looking to pursue a successful music career. Those long-range plans were likely a response to the comeback announcement just made by his old nemesis, Muhammad Ali. "The Greatest" was in the early stages of putting together a title shot against the current World Boxing Council (WBC) heavyweight champ Larry Holmes for sometime in the following year. And, historically, Joe Frazier's career moves were closely tied to Ali's boxing decisions.

At the same time, the younger Frazier was putting the finishing touches on a stellar stint as an amateur boxer. His more immediate agenda included a run at both the National AAU Heavyweight Boxing Championship and an Olympic gold medal to match the one his dad had won in the 1964 Tokyo Games. Joe then envisioned preparing his son for a pro debut just over the horizon and perhaps even a heavyweight championship bout further down the line. Both fighters' grand plans fed into Joe's burning desire to solidify his ring legacy and continue his lofty place in the boxing world.

Joe Frazier had retired in 1976 after a historic 11-year professional career with a 32–4 record (27 of those wins by knockouts). But it had all ended on a terribly sour note for the legendary champion. His final couple of bouts had been brutal defeats by the only two men who had ever beaten him—Muhammad Ali and George Foreman. It was an ending Joe still yearned to rewrite.

First, Ali had barely outlasted Frazier in their epic third meeting dubbed the Thrilla in Manila on October 1, 1975. It had been their rubber match after splitting the first two bouts at Madison Square Garden. Both fighters were totally exhausted and badly hurt after 14 rounds of body-crunching blows, a relentless pace, and suffocating Philippine heat.

One of Joe's eyes had been swollen closed and the other headed that way. Joe's trainer, Eddie Futch, afraid for his fighter's health, had stopped the match before the 15th and final round began. It had been questionable in retrospect whether Ali himself could have fought on if the bout had continued. According to a 2011 ESPN story announcing Frazier's death, Ali admitted after the fight that it was "the closest thing to dying I know of."

Neither Frazier nor Ali ever seemed to be the same after that battle. The next year an apparently diminished Frazier lost for a second time to George Foreman. He fought a more subdued, tentative fight—a dramatic departure from the trademark free-throwing style of Smokin' Joe. After a pair of knockdowns, the fight was abruptly stopped in the fifth round. Shortly after the defeat, Joe Frazier announced his retirement.

———

I opened the door of the gym to an explosion of noise and a relatively small, dimly lit area covered in dark blue carpeting. A swinging wooden gate led to the main workout space and sported a sign that read "Admission $1/No Smoking." The gym was dominated by a patriotically designed, full-size boxing ring replete with red and white ropes and a blue canvas. The patriotic theme was augmented by small American flags that hung all around the walls.

Two young fighters exchanged cautious blows in the center of the ring while a trainer yelled out a stream of instructions. Nearby a boxer pummeled a heavy bag while others skipped rope or churned out a steady *rat-a-tat* on speed bags. The wall opposite the ring was covered end to end with a five-foot-high mirror that reflected the work of three shadowboxers down in a crouch and throwing punches from a variety of angles.

Behind the ring, there was a red brick wall encrusted with framed photographs taken from Joe's boxing career and the fights of those he admired. A close-up of a smiling, fresh-faced Joe topped the wall, and just below a fit Frazier got weighed in for his first championship bout with Muhammad Ali. Joe Louis was caught struggling with Max Schmeling, Floyd Patterson exchanged blows with the Swede Ingemar Johansson, and then a dazed Patterson appeared to be overmatched by a towering, younger Ali. Farther down the wall, Joe wore his championship belt in a color photo from *Jet* after beating the enormous Buster Mathis for his first pro title in 1968. Amid all the boxing glory, there was a haunting black-and-white photo of a solitary Joe Frazier running down a seemingly endless country road with a small white dog trailing behind.

Before heading up the stairs to the second floor, I was particularly taken with a painted portrait of a middle-aged guy, looking older than his years, seated in a simple chair. It depicted a weary, serious-looking Yancey "Yank" Durham. He had been flagging a bit before later dying of a stroke at age 52 in August 1973. Joe stood proudly next to Yank with a comforting hand resting on his shoulder. This light-skinned black man had been Joe's original trainer/manager and latter-day father figure—and Joe's affection for his mentor radiated from the painting.

At the top of the stairs, there was a fairly large outer office with an over-sized window looking out over the hubbub of the gym below. Some of Joe's many trophies lined the window as a sort of glorious picket fence to be viewed by those gazing up from the workout area. Boxing gloves hung along one wall. Each carried the name of an opponent and the date of a professional fight. Surprisingly, they featured the four painful losses as well as the many victories. There was also a plaque representing Joe's induction into the then newly formed World Boxing Hall of Fame.

On an adjacent wall was a black-and-white framed photograph of Joe's wife Florence and his four children. Joe was holding the youngest of his three daughters, then an infant, and a 10-year-old Marvis stood nearby. This was the only picture of his family anywhere in the gym. Beneath the family photo, I found a number of faded news clippings that went back to Joe's early career and the years before.

One old headline read "Joe Too Was Marked." It told the story of how Joe Frazier had grown up the second youngest of 13 children in a four-room shack on a farm in Beaufort County, South Carolina. On the day Joe was born, his father Rubin supposedly prophesied that the infant would one day become his "famous son." When Joe was old enough to tend the hogs and plant okra, he decided to stuff a feed bag with rags, corncobs, moss, and a brick for stability. He hung it on an oak tree and began to occupy every spare moment punching away at the makeshift heavy bag.

"Ya all gonna laugh," young Joe had allegedly told his brothers and sisters. "But I'm gonna be the next Joe Louis."

Another article mounted on the wall was from March 8, 1971. It was a *Time* magazine report on Joe Frazier's first fight with Muhammad Ali. It contained a pithy description of Frazier in Smokin' Joe mode.

"No amount of bluster will deter Smokin' Joe—a ragin', bobbin', weavin', rollin' swarmer who moves in one basic direction, right into his opponent's gut," read the *Time* piece. "A kind of motorized [Rocky] Marciano, he works his short arms like pistons, pumping away with such mechanical precision that he consistently throws between 54 and 58 punches each round."

After a while, I was ushered into a smaller, cluttered inner office by Joe's trusted secretary Rochelle Bacon. The attractive, mocha-skinned woman chatted easily with me in between answering the phone and tending to paper-work. This was as far as I had gotten on my first visit in January. It was where

I had previously interviewed both Joe and Marvis. At that time, I had not yet earned the right to enter Joe's private sanctuary.

"The lair," as all referred to it, was Joe's exclusive, tricked-out man cave. Only Marvis seemed to come and go on a regular basis. All others from his inner circle had to be specifically invited in. The lair occupied a long, somewhat narrow space beyond a sliding door at the far end of the inner office. As a mark of my new privileged status, I was scheduled to hold my initial interviews today up in Joe's lair.

––––––––

The door to the lair slid open, and I instinctively took a step back. There, on a too-close opposite wall, loomed the image of a larger-than-life Joe Frazier, with left glove cocked, hulking over a flat-on-his-back Muhammad Ali. The nine-year-old black-and-white photo, blown up to a startling full-wall mural, caught the bloodlust in Joe's eyes as he stared down at a prone Ali, just daring him to get up. For his part, Ali's swollen face and bewildered gaze indicated the end was near whether or not he made it back to his feet. Nobody in the vast Madison Square Garden audience, by that point in the fight, had been surprised by the unanimous decision for Frazier that followed.

The mural had frozen, in massive proportions, Joe Frazier's iconic career moment and most valued triumph. It was shot early in the 15th and final round of his 1971 bout with Muhammad Ali at "the world's most famous arena." Billed as "the Fight of the Century," it pitted two undefeated heavyweight champions against each other for the first time with the undisputed title on the line.

The Greatest came in as the challenger with a 31–0 record (25 by knockout). Smokin' Joe brought his WBC and WBA (World Boxing Association) titles to the contest, along with a 26–0 mark (23 by KO). For Frazier, it was also his chance to silence both the man who had taunted him unmercifully and the masses who openly called for his demise.

Anticipation for the fight could arguably be traced all the way back to 1967. That was when a dominant Ali, then a lithe, brash 25-year-old, had been sentenced to a five-year prison term and stripped of his championship belts. He had been barred from boxing for refusing induction into the armed forces as a result of the Vietnam War–era draft. The plight of the wildly popular, charismatic fighter immediately caught the attention of far more than just the dedicated boxing fans.

During his three-year exile from boxing and string of judicial appeals, Ali became a compelling presence within the antiwar, antiestablishment movement. He was also seen as an audacious Muslim spokesman for disenchanted people of color. By contrast, as Frazier rose to prominence, he was cast by Ali, then many others, as the conservative, pro-war brute—"the White Man's Champion"—who had regrettably usurped Ali's place as the star of the boxing world. Ali's legions of supporters yearned for the day he would return to set things straight.

Fight fever spiked in earnest when the Supreme Court supported Muhammad Ali's final appeal to overturn his conviction in 1971. With his boxing license restored, Ali shook off the rust against a couple of ranked but somewhat less talented opponents. Frazier had secured his championship belts earlier with knockouts of hard-hitting Buster Mathis and slick, light heavyweight champ Jimmy Ellis. Now most of America simply awaited Muhammad Ali's opportunity to finally razzle-dazzle the powerful but plodding Joe Frazier in the ring and take back the titles that were rightfully his.

The fight itself became an epic production. Both fighters were guaranteed a then-record purse of $2.5 million apiece. Madison Square Garden sold out far in advance, and millions of people around the world paid to watch the bout on closed-circuit broadcasts. Even A-list celebrities scrambled to secure the limited ringside tickets.

Frank Sinatra wangled himself a first-row seat to serve as a photographer for *Life* magazine. In fact, one of Sinatra's shots—Joe connecting with a left hook to the head as Ali hunched against the ropes—became the cover photo. Norman Mailer signed on to do the *Life* story on Ali, Frazier, and the fight. The article was aptly titled "Ego." And Hollywood star Burt Lancaster got close to the action by taking on the role of color commentator.

Early on, the fight went according to the fervent wishes of the majority of the crowd. Muhammad Ali controlled most of the first three rounds with a precision jab that raised angry bumps on Joe Frazier's face. However, Frazier finished the third round with a savage hook to Ali's jaw, shaking him to the core, and remained the aggressor after that. Frazier's hooks continued to pound Ali's body during the fourth round and eventually sapped his opponent's energy by the sixth.

Joe Frazier later connected with another vicious left hook just seconds into round 11. Ali dropped both of his gloves and a knee to the canvas. Yet the referee seemed to be responding to the pleas of the crowd when he wiped the former champ's gloves and refused to call the knockdown. Ali held on to Frazier as much as possible to survive the round.

After the early knockdown in round 15, Smokin' Joe closed the fight with a barrage of vicious blows to the body and head that would have put most fighters out for the count. Ali, to his credit, managed to stay on his feet to the bell. He got to take the announcement of his first professional loss standing up. Many in the crowd booed both Frazier and the decision. Still, given all that he had endured leading up to the Fight of the Century, the victory for Joe Frazier remained incredibly sweet for a long, long time.

———————

Once I stepped fully into the lair, I saw a now bloated Joe Frazier sitting on an exercise bike halfway down the left wall of the room. He wore a gray plastic sweatshirt and red rubberized shorts designed to produce prodigious amounts of sweat as he pedaled through his 10-mile workout. Glancing at Joe on the bike, and then across the room to the taut wrecking machine in the mural, I realized he had to be a good 30 or 40 pounds above his old fighting weight of 210.

It hurt to see how far Joe had fallen from his peak condition during that first Ali bout. He was still obviously strong, but too much weight made it hard to move quickly and change directions. Of course, at his age, dropping weight also took more work. He had a whole lot more conditioning to do before he could think about getting back in the ring for real.

In truth, I also felt guilty remembering how much I had once wanted Muhammad Ali to destroy Joe Frazier in that first fight at Madison Square Garden. Several years younger than Joe and somewhat older than Marvis, I had been one of those draft-age kids in 1971 who adored Ali for his grace in the ring and, even more so, for his fiery anti–Vietnam War rhetoric outside the ropes. Now, I was just starting to warm to Frazier's proud, plainspoken if somewhat brusque manner. I was surprised to find an often darkly funny or sentimental character behind the gruff public bravado.

Joe, cycling away, waved me over. He gave a shake of his head and then encouraged me to begin my questions. Still caught up in my thoughts about the mural, I immediately went off script. I hadn't intended to address Muhammad Ali's plans for a return to the ring until later on. I knew it would be a fraught conversation with Joe—one that hit close to home.

Ali had retired less than two years before in 1979. It was just a few months after eking out a win against a young, hard-hitting Leon Spinks for a piece of the heavyweight crown. He was now talking about fighting a supremely talented, in-his-prime Larry Holmes for the world heavyweight title. Like so many who followed boxing, I saw the potential for a debacle.

"Joe, do you think Ali will get hurt in this comeback?" I asked, initially expecting Joe's old animosity toward Muhammad Ali, and his knowledge of boxing's harsh realities, to rise to the surface.

"If he feels he wants to come back, he should do it," replied Joe, surprisingly coming to Ali's defense. "Nobody knows his true ability but him. People can sit around and guess all day long, say he's fat. But only he knows what he can do." Joe paused and casually glanced at his own belly.

I wondered if we were still just talking about Ali.

"Well, he is fat," I said, looking to push the issue.

"That's got nothing to do with it!" Joe snapped. "What guys haven't gained weight?" He again checked his stomach, and now we were definitely not focusing solely on Ali.

"Yeah, but he's getting old too," I said, taking a jab at Ali and, I guess, Joe. "That can't be good."

"He's 38 or 39," Joe fired back, as if that weren't old for a fighter. "I know some people say he hasn't fought a real fight since Manila, but it's not the fights [or age] that counts. It's the training. And if he's been in the gym working out, it should make a difference. He was together enough to go 15 rounds with Leon [Spinks]. He didn't just stand around and play with him. Ali had to really fight that fight."

I reminded Joe that was almost two years ago and a lot had changed. *Just like a lot had changed with Joe.*

At that moment, Marvis came in and quietly took a seat on the couch under the mural. I raised a hand in greeting and turned back to his dad.

It was time to cut to the chase. I asked Joe if Ali's plans were giving him thoughts of lacing his gloves up again too.

"If Ali made a comeback, it wouldn't make me think twice," insisted Joe, his voice getting a bit louder. "Not even one time. No. Enough is enough! I don't have any financial worries. Fighting and retirement have been good to me. I'm watching Marvis and the other young fighters grow, helping to run the business."

In one more attempt to push a comeback announcement, I asked Joe about all the time he spent working out in the gym.

Joe paused for a moment and then flashed a sly smile. "I'm just trying to be a good family man as usual."

This last remark completely broke the mood. Joe cracked up laughing, and Marvis began to laugh as well. I didn't know enough then to be in on the joke.

"Can Ali beat Holmes if he comes back?" I asked, not letting the reality check go. That abruptly killed the laughter.

"I don't think he can beat Holmes," confessed Joe, his bravado suddenly coming way down. "If Holmes is in shape, he wins easily."

Then Joe just as quickly tried to back off his surprising admission. He talked about how tricky Ali could be in the ring. He even suggested some big fights that an older, overweight Muhammad Ali should be able to win. He became more animated as he moved from one viable comeback victory for Ali to the next.

"There are plenty of guys around for Ali to fight now, and plenty of those guys that he can beat," said Joe, with a defiant shrug. "[John] Tate would be an easy fight for him. [It would be] the easiest he ever had. Scott LeDoux could hurt him, but Ali would still win."

Both of those predictions seemed open to argument. Yes, Ali had defeated LeDoux in a five-round exhibition match in December 1977. It was just months before losing his title in the first bout against Leon Spinks. But LeDoux had connected to Ali's chin early in the fight and had done some damage later on. What's more, that had been a bit younger, more in-shape Ali.

The "easy fight" for Ali against John Tate came across as one hell of a bigger stretch. Tate was the 25-year-old, undefeated WBA heavyweight champion at that time. If Tate were going to lose—which he actually did a couple of weeks later to an up-and-coming Mike Weaver—I didn't think it would be to a rounding-into-shape Ali, who was sneaking up on 40.

Yet, despite time and boxing sense, Joe seemed to be working hard to keep Ali's dreams alive. Maybe he was arguing to support his own dreams as well. It was all said like a man with visions of an Ali vs. Frazier IV fight dancing in his head. And that would have been the mother of all dream fights.

So, on that day, I decided to just listen to Joe Frazier's string of debatable winning scenarios for Muhammad Ali's comeback. I would like to think my silence served as a kind of stand-in for every boxing fan's prayer that another miracle fight could be in the offing. On a more practical level, it certainly became an important fallback strategy in dealing with Joe later on whenever things heated up. The best move with Joe was often to just keep my mouth shut and pick my spots.

––––––––––

Joe Frazier eventually got up off the exercise bike and turned his attention toward his son. He moved to the middle of a blood-red shag carpet in front of the couch, beckoning Marvis to rise and square off against him. Marvis quickly obeyed and took a spot two feet away with his arms dangling loosely at his sides.

Joe stared into a face that came across as his younger mirror image. Marvis's skin had the same dark brown hue but was much less marred or swollen. The kid also had an identical sprawling nose that covered a wispier mustache and thinner, chin-lining beard. There was the similarly close-cropped Afro behind a high forehead as well, except the hairline didn't recede above the temples to form a widow's peak. The same almond-shaped eyes stared back but with a softer glow.

The older Frazier, legs spread shoulder width apart, stood flat footed in his low, "shell" crouch. He began to bob slightly up and down and slipped visibly into his Smokin' Joe persona. His upper body looked massive in the gray plastic sweatshirt as he hunkered down for the sparring lesson.

Marvis, two inches taller at 6'1", chose instead to rise up on his toes just within reach. He had a broad, muscular back that tapered to a much narrower waist than his father could ever recall having. The teen wore a skin-tight white T-shirt under bright orange shorts that thinned to suspender-like straps. The outfit accentuated the graceful physique of a natural athlete. Marvis became completely still waiting for his dad to begin.

"Gotta plant ya feet when ya throwin' combinations," barked Joe, nudging his boy with a double left hook to the body and a solid push to the side of the head.

They wore unpadded workout gloves, but Marvis still skittered a few steps from the impact and shuffled his feet to catch his balance. An average man would have toppled to the ground.

"If I was in the corner, I'd have ya slippin' and slidin' and slamming those hooks in tight," said Joe, as he began to move in again.

Joe shifted his shoulders one way and then another. He fired off several multiple-blow variations—all purposely short of their target. Marvis reacted with a start to each flurry and ducked easily under a final high, sweeping right cross. His face stayed calm, but the eyes were now wide and keenly alert.

Joe's shoulders remained hunched as they feinted menacingly once again from side to side. He then moved directly ahead, in that Smokin' Joe crouch, to within an inch of his son.

"Stay right in front of your man *all* the time," urged Joe.

Bobbing up and down, he ordered Marvis to throw a jab and then cover his left ear.

Marvis stood tall and upright, the way his official trainer, George Benton, had taught him. He dutifully raised the unpadded gloves and poked out a half-speed jab. The second he recoiled to cover his left ear, Joe powerfully cuffed his son's glove.

After a more brisk jab from Marvis, Joe dropped his shoulder and rose up on a sharp angle to hook the right ear. Marvis displayed flash reflexes and danced back a step, anticipating the blow. The kid was instantly surprised by a hard slap to the arm and a jarring palm straight to the chest. It clearly could have been a damaging fist to the stomach or chin instead.

"You don't waste energy dancin' or backin' off from a dude like [Tony] Tubbs," said Joe, making his point without his usual camouflage smile. "Boxing these guys is good if the guy will stand there and box—you outpoint him. But [don't do it] with guys who run away and try to sneak a shot on you. You should have stayed close and nailed him whenever you could."

Joe was still fuming from Marvis's second fight with Muhammad Ali's prize protégé just a month earlier. He had been uncharacteristically muzzled for his son's fight with Tony Tubbs and blamed Benton for the loss. In the aftermath, a tug-of-war had emerged for control over his boy's fighting style.

Joe ended the minilesson with Marvis, then turned to me to continue making his point about that second Frazier-Tubbs bout.

"He didn't lose control of the fight," said Joe, looking over at his son. "He just did what the corner told him to do. That's what a good fighter does. They told him to box. If I was in the corner, I would have told him to go out there to slip and slide and punch."

"Did you like anything about Marvis's approach to the fight?" I asked.

"I liked the way he was throwing the left hooks—they were about a hair off target. But he can sharpen that up by being closer to the guy and timing him right. But I'd have sent him out straight from jump street because I know Tubbs was afraid. Tubbs knows that Marvis can punch and he wasn't going to stand in there with him."

George Benton wanted Marvis to take advantage of his height, grace, and natural quickness. He saw no advantage in having his boxer take punishment while grinding out wins. However, Joe saw a younger version of himself with surprising punching power for an amateur. He saw no reason for the corner to leave anything to chance.

Marvis Frazier had won his first fight against Tony Tubbs. It had taken place three months earlier on national television. The bout had been immediately billed as more than just a showdown between two top amateur heavyweights. It had been sold as both a preview of the next generation of Joe Frazier vs. Muhammad Ali and another round in their age-old battle.

Despite the Frazier vs. Ali theme, it didn't take the television crew long to pick up on the behind-the-scenes war of wills between George Benton and Joe. The NBC camera had shifted repeatedly between Marvis trying to follow Benton's instructions to use his reach and Joe at ringside bellowing for him to do the opposite. Marvis had kept throwing long-range jabs, dancing away, and then shooting a straight right hand before retreating again.

Joe, supposedly working as a color commentator, had been draped over the ring apron. He had started snorting out short-armed hooks and looked as if he were ready to climb under the ropes.

"Jam him," Joe had yelled, after having thrown aside his earphones. He had clearly given up on describing the action.

Joe's impassioned words had confused Marvis momentarily near the end. They had played on his son's compulsion to gain Joe's approval. However, Benton's message had ultimately gotten through and Marvis mostly kept to his corner's disciplined attack. Frazier, the 1979 National Golden Gloves and world junior champion, had come away with a unanimous decision that established him as the country's highest-ranked amateur heavyweight.

In the rematch just two months later, Tony Tubbs and Ali had gotten their revenge. Tubbs had taken a page from Ali's old fight plans to deal Marvis a crushing defeat. He countered Frazier's probing jabs with flurries of accurate taps punctuated by hasty retreats.

The quick in-and-out attacks frustrated Marvis and took him away from his corner's disciplined jab-and-move approach. He eventually jettisoned the official fight plan and let the Frazier instinct to swarm take over. Marvis unleashed awkward, lunging hooks coupled with a number of misguided uppercuts.

Marvis had ultimately inflicted the greater damage. Unfortunately, amateur contests are judged by frequency of contact rather than force of impact. The loss had stamped an indelible stain on Marvis Frazier's previously pure 44–0 record.

Joe believed that Marvis should have been in close, hammering tight hooks to the head and body from the first bell. He felt Tubbs never should have had the room to jab away and flee.

"George figured somewhere down the line I'd probably get Marvis excited [again] by calling shots he didn't want him to do," Joe said to me, the lingering resentment all too obvious. "So, I decided to pin my mouth because I'm not the chief trainer. I kept a damn hard promise to George. But I know with his ability, with his power and the little know-how he has, Marvis can go out there and slaughter cats right away."

————

Joe turned away from me and drifted back toward the stationary bike across the room. He seemed to be deciding on another round of cycling before changing for the real workout down in the gym. Marvis sat back down on the couch and waited for his dad to get ready. It was a good time for me to get *his* take on the loss to Tubbs.

"How do you cope with a stunning loss like that?" I asked. "It must hurt to lose your perfect record to someone you know you can beat?"

"Once more I put the fight in God's hands," said Marvis, already a lay deacon at his family's church. "Maybe the Lord wanted me to know just what my victims felt like. What it is to lose . . ."

"Mmm, mmm," grunted Joe from across the room, obviously leery about the direction the conversation was taking. "If Marv was allowed to talk to all these guys in the ring, he'd probably punch 'em silly. Then give 'em an Amen!"

Joe laughed loudly, and his son promptly joined in.

Marvis picked up on Joe's signal right away. He instantly turned back into "the chip" that his dad often insisted was not "too far from the old block." Marvis launched into an animated account of the taunting smile he had flashed to Tony Tubbs in the second round of their last fight.

"It was like Tubbs hitting me with his best shot," boasted Marvis, peering over at Joe from the sofa, "and me answering, 'Nah buddy, you ain't got nothing that can hurt me. And wait until you see what I put on you!'"

"Yep, yep, yep," said an excited Joe. He spread his legs apart like a chunky colossus, peeled off the plastic sweatshirt, and went into a taunting tale of his own.

"In all our fights me and Muhammad were always talking," said Joe with a broad grin. "He'd be sayin', 'I'm gonna kick your ass.' And I'd answer, 'Yeah, and I'm gonna wrap yours up as a goin' away present.'"

Joe's macho bravado, I assumed essential for any boxer, seemed to revolve around never admitting to being vulnerable, hurt, or weak. It showed up not just in conversations about boxing but in his approach to life. I wondered where that attitude originally came from.

"As one of the youngest in the family, I grew up around my dad," said Joe, obviously glad to talk about the hardscrabble life of sharecropper Rubin Frazier. "I learned to be a man when I was a boy. Where guys 12 and 13 were talking about going to school, I was talking about chasing the ladies. That happened because I was raised to work side by side with my dad."

According to Joe, in a later autobiography, Rubin's left hand had been lost, and part of the forearm amputated, due to shots fired by a drunk friend who saw his father as competition for a woman's affections. It happened a year before Joe was born. And Joe just assumed the role of his dad's left arm in the fields as soon as he was able.

"What was that like?" I asked.

"He used to let me go to parties with him and I used to boogie right along with him," said Joe, a smile lighting up his face. "[It was] to the point where it helped me to grow up and be a more secure man and to stand on my own in any situation. That's what I try to pass along to my own kids. Do what you want to do, be strong, and then stand up for it."

Joe climbed back on the bike and pedaled slowly at first. He seemed to be waiting for my next question.

"Is that *your* definition of what a true man should be?"

"A true man number one provides for his family and, second, does whatever is good for himself," said Joe. "He must be loyal to himself. If he can't be loyal to himself, then he can't be loyal to anyone else. A man stands up for what he believes in and runs the family and the business. The man must make the decisions in the family and be the leader if he wants to be a *man*."

"Does that mean a man doesn't compromise?" I asked, looking to stoke Joe's macho fire and clarify his southern farm boy philosophy.

"If he wants to be a partial man, then he can give a woman the final say," said Joe, in a deprecating tone. "You can talk things over with your lady, but the *man* should have the last word. That means this is what we're doing and there's no doubt about that."

With the women's movement heading into its third decade, I was curious to see how far out of step with the times this would go. Yeah, Joe was a bit old for the baby boomer cultural revolution, but this seemed to be from another century.

"How do you justify that authority for the man?" I asked, the challenge rising in my voice.

"Well, after all, they took a rib out of my side to make that lady,"—Joe laughed and cycled progressively quicker as the righteous spirit in him grew—"ain't no doubt about that! I'd have all my ribs if they didn't take one to make her. I might have been even stronger."

Years later I would wind up doing one of the last interviews with a founder of the modern women's movement, Betty Friedan. The author of the groundbreaking book *The Feminine Mystique* talked about how far society had come on gender equality. I couldn't help but smile and think back to Joe's comments up in the lair.

I wondered where Marvis stood on all this.

"Well, first of all I think a man must have faith," said Marvis, beginning on safe ground. "Secondly, he has to be the head of the family. I don't feel, however, that only the man has to make the decisions. There has to be a joint thing."

"Meaning what?" I prodded.

"If a man and woman make the commitment that they're going to strive together, I feel they should agree on things, work things out together," said Marvis, looking up to make eye contact with Joe churning away on the bike. "[There should] not be just one of them *loudly* voicing their opinion."

Joe glowered at Marvis and then me. He didn't like where I was taking things. I noticed that the man who always seemed notoriously thrown by Muhammad Ali's jibes could control the atmosphere in most rooms with a mere frown or grudging smile. Did he consciously try to bully people into doing what he wanted?

"I don't have to look angry for people to know this is what will happen now," said Joe, looking a bit annoyed. "It is very rare for me to get really angry. I try not to get angry, stay calm and natural. No, people don't misread me. No, no, no, no. Nah, I don't think there's any chance in the world that they could misunderstand that I said no from here." Joe pointed to his gut.

The ex–heavyweight champ fixed me with a stare.

"I don't fool people and I don't like them to fool me," said Joe, setting the ground rules. "I try to be strong, straightforward, honest—but at the same time a little shrewd hopefully."

Joe got up from the bike and walked to the wall refrigerator. He grabbed a quart bottle of beer and began chugging. I took the moment to absorb the message offered and forged on.

"Well, I know a good boxer doesn't show his emotions in the ring," I said, easing into my next point, "but what about out there with the public? Things must sometimes get a little nasty for someone who has had such high-profile fights. Do you need to keep your feelings inside?"

Joe thought about it for a moment and took another swig.

"Yeah, every man has to at times," he said, talking about hiding his emotions in public. "There are times I get hurt out there. You cover it up by maybe not saying nothing. [I use] a forced smile. Like to say, 'I'm hurt man, but I'm going to come back soon and retaliate.' I get people saying things that hurt me or bother me 24 hours a day walking on the street. I get it on the car phone, office telephone, and I get it by just going to the clubs."

"What kind of things do they say?" I asked, starting to empathize.

"People say things like 'Old Joe Frazier, what happened with George Foreman? What about Foreman?' And I answer, 'What about the brother?' I'll always try to answer people's questions whether it's a smart remark or just being nice. My answers usually match the attitude of their questions."

I started to sense the layer of pain lurking beneath the years of putting on a public face. That led me to ask if a true man ever let the painful emotions just come out.

"I don't think you're less of a man for crying," said Joe, taking me by surprise. "It's healthy for you. I cry if something goes wrong—I'll cry right out. But if I cry out of anger, look out! Somebody's in trouble. Crying shows a man has a heart and helps him let out his pressures. Just don't cry for nothing."

"What about all the terrible things Ali said about you before the big fights?" I asked Joe, remembering mocking comparisons to a gorilla, among other slurs. "It seemed a lot of the times you had to just take the public abuse."

Joe didn't answer right away. He seemed a bit thrown by the directness of my comments.

"Did you ever feel the urge to publicly complain about the way you were treated by Muhammad Ali, by the press?"

"I never complain about anything!" said Joe, agitated by the question. "If anything goes wrong, I'll come back here [the lair] and sit down with the door closed. I'll think about all the wrong ways I could react to the situation. That's how I handled all the bad things that have happened to me in the nearly 20 years in the public eye. I get all the wrong responses out of my system. Sometimes, of course, all you have is wrong choices. Often there is nothing right to do."

Joe stopped and put down the bottle of beer. He seemed ready to wrap it up.

"Yeah, but with the public, with the media, aren't you always forced to do something?" I asked, refusing to finish the session on a wishy-washy note. "Give me an example of a time when there are only wrong choices."

"Well, suppose I take this mic and knock it out of your hand," said Joe, shooting me a sardonic grin. He paused briefly. "No, that wouldn't be right."

He paused again, still grinning. "Well, what if I take the tape recorder and smash it up?" He stared at me, and I stayed silent. So did Marvis.

"No, that wouldn't be right either," Joe said. "Well, what if I hit this writer upside his jaw?" Joe asked, the smile clearly gone from his face.

There was a much longer pause. I was barely able to breathe.

"No, that definitely wouldn't be right," said Joe, in a husky voice.

I started to speak, and Joe raised a big palm to stop me.

"Or maybe I would say, 'I just don't want to talk about it,'" said Joe, his tone more exasperated. "That would probably be the best way to handle a writer who has said something to hurt my feelings."

With that, Joe peeled off the rubberized red shorts, turned his bare back to me, and headed for the shower.

I was left mumbling under my breath, "Good example, Joe."

2

Down with the Gym Rats

Twenty minutes later, after his shower, the boss returned wearing a blue Resorts International jacket over a tight T-shirt and a pair of navy slacks. He greeted me with a broad smile, as if nothing had happened, and took a seat next to Marvis on the couch under the mural. Thrown by how quickly his attitude had changed, I tried to apologize and confirm all was forgiven.

"Ain't nothing but a party!" said Joe, cutting me off in an exuberant voice with his palms out wide for emphasis. "Yep, yep, yep, yep."

The anger was obviously gone, and the smile seemed real enough. Yet it still took a moment for me to accept the transition. I later learned that this was Joe's signature catchphrase for rising above anything from a petty annoyance to a shattering disappointment. It represented a necessary resilience borne from years of dealing with a fickle profession and public. It was a character trait I would come to greatly admire.

The focus soon turned toward getting ready for the gym. The initial plan was for Joe to do a brief workout downstairs while Marvis continued to loosen up in the lair. Then Joe intended to guide his son through a much more rigorous routine. In preparation for Marvis's sparring session, Joe began greasing him up. I asked Joe to explain his usual workout and then his son's while he applied the petroleum jelly.

"I'm trying to work into shape by doing two sets of two minutes, two [minutes], two, and two—eight rounds," said Joe, carefully smoothing the grease over Marvis's cheeks and forehead to prevent unnecessary tears or swelling in the ring. "Rounds are the time I put in on the light bag, heavy bag, shadow-boxing and skipping rope. I haven't really worked out much in the gym for the past two months now. But I'll be stepping up and working out more with Marvis when I get back [from the road] in April."

"What about sparring?" I asked. "When you get in the ring with Marvis or some of these young guys, does it fire you up, revive the old fighting spirit?"

"Nah, nah, not worked up," said Joe, shaking his head. "I always keep my cool when it comes to working out, especially with the young fellas in the gym. I'm out there to help them, not to take 'em apart."

"Well, what if one of the bigger boys or Marvis here lands some solid punches?"

"Once in a while, I get hit with some shots I shouldn't get hit with," admitted Joe, rising up with a wry laugh and clenched fists. "Then I got to tighten up!"

Joe immediately crouched down and grunted out a pair of vicious hooks. He stayed low and hunched his shoulders for an extra few seconds to sell the effect.

"But seriously, if Marvis makes any mistake when I work with him—like we were doing before—I counter and take advantage of his mistake so he sees right away where he went wrong," said Joe, now pumping a couple of jabs. "He won't continue making that mistake and thinking he can get away with it. I *show* him he won't!"

"Is this preparation for possibly working as a full-time trainer down the line?" I asked, trying to set Joe up for my bigger question. "Maybe after the music career and a boxing comeback?"

Joe ignored the "comeback" remark and bit on the trainer issue instead. "I think I have the mind to be one of the best trainers in the world," he replied. "But I just don't have the amount of free time to handle it. I can show these guys what to do. The average trainer has been out of fighting too long to get in the ring and show exactly what he wants done."

The ex-champ talked about the tough training routine he and George Benton devised for Marvis. Joe said Marvis would begin with five minutes of bending and stretching up in the lair and then come down to the gym to shadowbox for five minutes and jump rope for 10. This would be followed by three rounds of sparring, with the last round running longer than usual. And he would be expected to work hard on the heavy bag and speed bag as well.

I thought about Marvis sparring in a gym that bore his father's name. "Hey Marvis, are the other boxers in the gym more out to get you because you're the boss's son?"

"Well, I guess they're naturally more out to get me because of my name and because I now have a reputation of my own." Marvis's voice was soft. "I have to go into the ring saying, 'If they're out to get me, I have to get them first.' But me and the guys in the gym get along."

"Yep, they get along," said Joe, with a loud laugh. He tapped Marvis on the chest.

"What do you mean?" I asked.

"Yeah, because they know he would kick their asses," Joe said in a hoarse voice. "A lot of guys figure Marvis is Joe Frazier's son and if we beat him, we'll get the big fights. At times, someone puts a kid out there who doesn't have the ability, but thinks he has Marvis's talent. My son is so powerful and knowledgeable for this stage of the game, I feel sorry for the other kid. I really do. Some of these guys are just in over their heads."

"So how does Marvis get the level of work he needs?"

"Marvis works with some of the really big boys in the gym here."

"You mean he's sparring with some of the pros?" I asked, knowing that was frowned upon in the amateur ranks.

"Not really," said Joe, with a little smirk. "We keep it clean. He fights the biggest, most experienced *amateurs* in the gym and more than holds his own."

Before I got the chance to press the point, Joe signaled we were through for now and started for the lair door. I fell in behind him. Marvis got up and began to bend and reach from the waist. He interspersed some long reaching jabs with stretching to loosen up his shoulders and arms.

Then the lair door opened, and we were met by a wall of human energy, a slew of pressing business concerns, and everyone looking to grab some time with the boss.

The charge was led by Ken Johnson, a fortyish, stocky white man shaped like a fireplug, in a three-piece suit. Johnson, Frazier's booking agent/road manager, grabbed Joe's arm and motioned for him to stay put until he got off the phone. He was hard at work putting together the upcoming southern tour for Joe's band. He had scratched the words "Chattanooga" and "Augusta" with question marks on a piece of paper. Then he blustered something undecipherable into the phone and hung up.

"Okay," said Johnson, leaning against Joe's oversized desk and pausing to steel his resolve. "They'll give you five thousand for the night."

Joe immediately got upset and started to pace. Johnson momentarily looked away.

"*Giving* me $5,000," Joe repeated, in a cross between sarcasm and disgust. "Might not be enough for a big white star, but they figure it's enough for a n----r."

Johnson threw his hands up and released a weary groan. "Please, don't start with that."

The two turned to go back into the lair to hash out the club arrangements as Marvis emerged to head down to the gym. Johnson stopped to inform Marvis and me that we were scheduled to meet up with the Smokin' Joe Frazier Revue during the tour down south. He said he'd tell us the specifics later once the bookings were set.

Marvis seemed pleased to be included, and I was ecstatic. I saw this as confirmation that Joe was truly over our confrontation and in this for the long haul. I also envisioned a chance to bond with Marvis. I hoped for some more revealing interviews with him, beyond Joe's influence, on the way there.

Marvis hurried down the stairs to the gym on the main floor, and I started to follow. Parked on the office couch was a short, wiry junior middleweight who suddenly rose to block my path. He put two fingers firmly against my chest and introduced himself as "Youngblood." It turned out his real name was Mike Williams.

The 23-year-old, an undefeated pro boxer with a 15–0–1 record, had been given his nickname years before by the beloved Philadelphia middleweight Bennie Briscoe. As a particularly vicious young fighter, Youngblood supposedly earned the alias by drawing rivers of blood from his opponents. His status in the gym suggested the story was probably true.

Williams was Marvis Frazier's longtime confidant and self-proclaimed protector. He often worked and traveled with Joe and seemed quite protective of him as well. At that moment, Blood was intent on sending me a pointed message.

"Marvis Frazier is too much of a gentleman for this business," Williams began, then mumbled something about "leeches" and jabbed a finger in my direction. "He doesn't want to hurt anybody's feelings."

Youngblood leaned into me with an air of menace. He had a wicked scar running through his eyebrow to the edge of the left eye, and other scars below the eye. My natural reaction was to back up.

"That is where I come in," he said, in a low, intense voice. "I'll do it! Especially if it means saving my friend from being in agony or getting some heartache. Damn right I'll hurt your feelings. And, if necessary, go upside your head."

After explaining the point of my interviews, Williams decided there were no heads in need of immediate hammering. He relaxed and offered me an appraisal of his friend's future as a boxer. He painted a picture of Marvis as a top heavyweight professional, a contender, in the not-so-distant future.

I interrupted to tell him that Marvis talked about winning Olympic gold, like Joe, but hadn't said anything about wanting to be a pro fighter. "That doesn't seem to be his vision of the future," I said.

"Marvis don't *want* to turn pro, but *he will*," confided Blood. "He don't need the money, but they're going to be talking millions. He will. He will."

Youngblood made it sound like Marvis was scheduled for fame and fortune whether he liked it or not. He went on to explain the facts of boxing life.

"In the beginning, boxing is fun for anyone," said Youngblood. "It was fun for me too in the beginning [at age 12]. Marv's probably a little tired of boxing, but he's *in* it. It's a job to him now. . . . It's a business."

Didn't Joe worry that his son could get seriously hurt as a pro?

"How is he going to get hurt?" asked Blood, noting Joe would protect Marvis without babying him. "If anything, Marvis is going to do the hurting. The only way you get hurt in boxing is when you're overmatched. On his level, nobody can beat him up. Even people one or two steps over him couldn't do him real damage. And Joe's not going to match him with somebody five steps above him—and just throw him to the dogs."

Yet, despite Joe watching out for his son, Youngblood suggested there were no shortcuts to the top. Marvis would have to pay his dues all the way up.

"This business is just like an exclusive club," he said. "You don't pay your dues you get kicked out. And in this club being kicked out hurts plenty. But sooner than people think, Marvis will be on the level of the big boys—top 10 guys."

Youngblood also warned that trainers—even concerned fathers like Joe—couldn't be too protective either. When there was a chance to win a tough but important fight, the trainer couldn't bypass it to try to save a young boxer's skin.

"Boxing is all a gamble," said Blood. "You got to take chances to make it. Marvis is being brought along right. He spars with all the best [pro] heavyweights. They come to the gym to fight him. Why? Because Marvis gives them good work. There is no other place in the country that gives you sparring like Joe's gym. Philadelphia fighters war in the gym and war in the fights. It's just in 'em."

The lair door slid open, and a haggard Ken Johnson came out looking like he had just gone 10 rounds with the boss. He went straight to the office desk to resume his phone calls. Joe, also appearing grim, walked past us heading for the stairs. Youngblood fell in next to him and asked about the trip. I lagged well behind to give them some space.

———————

It was four in the afternoon and the gym was crowded, hopping with energy. Within the ropes, two huge heavyweights, definitely pros, worked in close. Each body shot came with a loud sniff and thud as they jostled for the right leverage and opening. The big boys were surrounded by at least two dozen smaller amateurs and pros caught up in their own thoughts and exertions. And, behind the waist-high wooden gate, about 20 dollar-a-view spectators scanned the action and kept a lookout for Joe Frazier and his son.

Mixed in with the more experienced fighters were young kids and teens from the neighborhood. Joe welcomed them in the locker room after three o'clock when his schedule permitted. He usually just joked around, kept it light and friendly, and avoided bombarding them with boxing tips from the get-go. Most greeted him with a reverent "Hey, Smokin' Joe!"

The kids ranged in age from 10 to about 18 years old. They came in all shapes and sizes. Some still had skinny arms and legs—most were black, but white and Latino kids took part too. Joe brought them in to get their first taste of the game. He barred them from skipping class to come work out.

Most of these kids, and the older fighters as well, benefited from an informal mentoring system encouraged by the boss. Boxers at every level complemented the work of the trainers in the gym by offering casual advice on a regular basis to those less experienced. Both Joe and Marvis stopped several times that afternoon to pass along a boxing tip or correct a mistake in technique.

Joe was already poking at the speed bag in short bursts when I arrived. A few feet away, Marvis faced the long mirror, pumped one straight jab after another, and slowly eased into his shadowboxing round. They didn't speak or look at each other but soon got down to business with the same murderous scowl. The whole gym took notice, and many of the other boxers drifted in their direction.

As a rule, when Joe worked with Marvis he drew all the attention, people watched what they said, and everyone in the gym tried to pick up on his boxing instructions.

Joe eventually churned the speed bag into a steady, sustained blur that went on and on until brought to an end by a hard left-right combo. As Joe turned to his son, Marvis shifted into more of a crouch and gradually worked hooks and short uppercuts into the shadowboxing routine. His hands flowed nonstop for several minutes, from one combination to the next. He continually bobbed up and down, moved in and out, and taunted his mirror image with jerky shoulder feints. Marvis only let up when Joe yelled, "Stop!"

Joe waited a moment before slipping lightly padded gloves on his son's hands. He told him they would work on timing now. Joe then let the heavy bag swing free. He instructed Marvis to just wait and watch until he gave the order.

"Okay, two low lefts and go high with the right," barked Joe.

Marvis stalked the heavy bag with his eyes. He abruptly flashed a pair of line-drive lefts and connected up top with a thunderous right. The last shot echoed over the buzz in the gym. Joe seemed pleased, but he wanted to show Marvis how to get the same results without working so hard.

"Fool the son of a bitch," said Joe, easing between his son and the heavy bag. "Fake a low jab." Joe feinted with his shoulder while down in a squat. "Then go straight to the head with a hard right." Gloveless, the *clap!* of Joe's fist against the bag was startling.

Marvis did the combination Joe's way once. Then, on his father's com-mand, did it all more fluidly the second time. From here, the pace picked up. Joe called out one combination after another. Marvis instantly performed each one, down to the last suggested detail. The more he worked, the more he looked like Joe in the ring.

All went smoothly until Joe told Marvis to double up on his right hook. "Uh, uh!" he snapped, as he moved his son away. Joe attacked the heavy bag and accentuated every movement. He crouched lower than Marvis, his legs farther apart, and struck crisper with each hook. The yells were louder too, and each punch seemed more deadly, more final.

Joe's advice was obviously savvy but seemed to channel his own style rather than what George Benton preached to his son.

Nearby a husky 15-year-old stood entranced. He discreetly mimicked Joe Frazier's every move. I noticed his bandaged hands making small, mincing motions. Marvis was exactly that age when his dad arranged his first test rounds in the gym.

"I stepped into the ring with my cousin Russel," Marvis had said two months earlier in my first interview with the Fraziers. "First time I had the gloves on in the ring—we, like, sparred. Pop thought it would be a good idea. He wanted to test me out and see how I would react. He knew my cousin wouldn't hurt me."

I asked Marvis how it went.

"I looked pretty good," he said, flashing a broad grin. "It was a feeling I really enjoyed—something different. It was one-on-one. It was a little bit of macho and I was in there on my own, depending only on myself. My cousin Russel had been an amateur for two years, off and on, and he was 17. I wouldn't say I took him, but I caught him with a couple of nice shots."

Marvis said he was at a private school at the time, Wyncote Academy, that didn't have sports teams. Boxing became his main physical outlet. Yet when he transferred back to public school—where he had once excelled in basket-ball, football, and wrestling—he still opted to only pursue boxing.

"What was your dad's reaction to you choosing to stay with fighting?"

Marvis first made a vague analogy to Joe's attitude about his kids handling guns. Then he put it in more specific terms.

"His reaction was this is no plaything," said Marvis, the gravity showing on his face. "This was a serious game and you had to be dedicated. You have to be earnest because these guys are in the ring to take your head off. So, if this is what you want, you better be dead serious about it."

According to Marvis, Joe made it clear he better be damn good in the ring as well.

Joe signaled for his son to begin the speed bag round. Marvis instinctively got the bag up to a roll and picked up speed as he went along. His hands were fast, certainly faster than Joe's, and it all seemed so effortless. But after a minute or so, Joe stopped him. He wanted to talk about "head hunting."

Joe offered his son a lesson on how to follow through on a hook to the head without moving his feet.

"Make believe the speed bag is a man's face," said Joe, pushing the bag into motion. "You let him move, stalk him, set him up for the jab—then nail him with the left to the head."

Joe stepped in to demonstrate. "That ain't nothing but a man in front of you," he said, eyes fixed on the bag. "Watch him all the time." He suddenly struck the bag dead center with a left and it ricocheted loudly off the top board.

Now it was Marvis's turn to stalk the moving bag. "Keep watching," Joe said after a while. Marvis stayed still and poised to strike. Then Joe yelled, "Stop him!"

Marvis hammered the bag with a vicious left hook that sent it sailing across the gym. "Damn, he took his head off," muttered one of the kids standing next to me. Joe reconnected the bag, and Marvis whipped it back up to a blur once again. He finished off by slamming the bag two, three, four times side to side.

The whole time Joe and Marvis worked the speed bag, two of the younger boys did their own routine nearby to get their attention. One, about 13 and heavy with baby fat, leaned back comfortably against the wall. He acted as a human punching bag for a skinny, shorter 10-year-old who pounded double-barreled body shots at him nonstop. Every few seconds the smaller kid glanced over to see if Joe or Marvis were watching. The Fraziers never noticed.

Marvis transitioned to skipping rope, and Joe took a few steps back to observe. Suddenly, a slim, weaselly guy in shades, a long overcoat, and floppy hat sidled up to Joe and asked if he remembered him. Joe obviously didn't recognize the guy but knew just what to do.

"Don't know you, but maybe heard somebody mention you," Joe offered with a smile. The intruder relaxed into a long-winded story, and Joe patiently listened. The guy finally wrapped it up with a request for money. "No," responded Joe, the smile never leaving his lips.

Just as Marvis finished skipping rope, his sister Jacqueline breezed into the gym and through the wooden gate. She stopped to joke with some of the regulars and continuously flashed that Frazier smile. Jacqui stood 5'8" with a trim, athletic build. She wore a navy-blue cap, an iridescent blue shirt, and tight dungarees.

Jacqui was pretty and outgoing and reminded me right away of Joe. She commanded a room just like her dad. And, according to Joe, she had also embraced his always-ready-to-party attitude.

Jacqui, a freshman, was home on a two-week spring break from American University. She had stopped in to see Marvis and get some spending money from Joe. Within 10 minutes, she accomplished both missions, charmed all around her, and headed out the door.

As Jacqui left, Marvis was ready to move on to his sparring session. However, his scheduled partner was already in the ring with another fighter. It turned out that the other fighter had a match coming up a week or two before Marvis.

The unwritten rule of the gym stipulated that the use of the ring, or a sparring partner, went to the boxer with the greater need at the time. Neither Joe nor Marvis objected, despite their disappointment. I was surprised that neither even considered pulling rank.

Before heading back upstairs, Marvis stood with his arms dangling at his sides while Joe toweled him off. After wiping his son's arms and legs, Joe worked on his face and neck and looked intently at his eyes. The boss then called over Val Colbert, George Benton's assistant trainer.

I'm not sure exactly what Joe saw, but he obviously felt Marvis had been working too hard in his training sessions. "He's leaving it in the gym," fumed Joe. "You burn all the gas in his tanks, this boy will be running on empty. Overtraining is worse than not training at all."

————

Up in the outer office, I stood at the picture window looking out over the gym. Most of the younger kids had finished up, the heavyweight sparring match ended, and the dollar spectators began leaving after Joe headed up the stairs. Yet a number of the gym rats still plugged away on their boxing skills with no sign of winding down.

I was waiting for Joe and Marvis to finish their showers in the lair. They also had another meeting with Ken Johnson about the tour. Then I was supposed to get a few more minutes of questions in now that Marvis's sparring match had been canceled.

Marvis came out of the lair first. The kid looked more like a stylish young business executive than a prizefighter. He wore a natty, black-and-white-checked three-piece suit with a collarless black shirt. It made him seem cool, confident, and certainly more polished than the other fighters his age.

I joined him on the couch, and we just began to chat. I wondered why Joe hadn't stepped in to spar with him earlier. Did he ever get in the ring with his dad for real and just go at it?

"Well, when I first started out, we sparred together," said Marvis, choosing his words carefully. "But it was only for publicity, for newspaper photos. We never got into a thing where we both tried to get in there and put the other guy away."

"How come?"

Marvis laughed out loud. "Because *he's Joe Frazier*. You know what I mean. He'd probably knock my head clean off! I was just a baby [in the ring] then."

That was then, but what about now?

Marvis admitted that he hadn't seriously sparred with Joe for a couple of years. They apparently stopped because Marvis had become good enough to pose a threat.

"Now, if we got in the ring, he'd probably kill me because he'd consider me real competition," said Marvis. "Before I was a green kid, but now he knows I can fight. We'd be too conscious of each other's power to get in the ring together now."

Marvis also felt a real fight with Joe would be counterproductive. He wouldn't even be learning anything from the experience.

"Outside the ring, Pop will stand in front of me and show me moves or certain ways he wants me situated or a certain punch," Marvis said. "He never really showed me anything while throwing leather. We were too busy defending ourselves."

When Joe came in, I got up to give him my seat on the couch. We started to discuss the session downstairs, and I recalled his concern about Marvis "leaving it in the gym." Given Joe's old reputation for superhuman workouts, especially in preparation for his biggest fights, I wondered if overtraining was ever a problem for him too.

"Well, nobody outworked me back then," he said, hedging his answer.

Joe indicated that any problems with overtraining basically began—and ended—with his old mentor Yank Durham. He was the one who encouraged Joe to do marathon roadwork early on, and to spar more rounds, and do longer gym workouts than anyone else. Joe also credited Yank with recognizing when he was overtraining and making sure it didn't continue.

For instance, Yank realized prior to the first Ali fight that running in extreme heat sapped Joe's energy more than anything else. Like Ali, Joe had been training in Florida. Yank saw the problem with the heat and decamped for up north. Joe finished his training for the Fight of the Century in the cold of a Northeast winter.

Joe said Yank made a point of knowing how many miles an opponent put in during roadwork. He made sure Joe did more—sometimes several miles more—in rain, sleet, cold, whatever. Joe admitted he often opted to run even farther than Yank wanted him to do. He saw it as an extension of the work ethic learned from his father.

Yank and Joe were convinced that the extra roadwork helped build the stamina and endurance needed to prevail at the end of a tough round or in the later stages of a long fight. According to Joe, he ran harder than both Jimmy Ellis and Muhammad Ali before his first championship bouts with them. As a result, he remained stronger and fresher when those fights moved past the early rounds.

I wanted to get into other aspects of Joe's old training routines, but Ken Johnson called us into the inner office. The boss took a seat behind his desk. He was flanked by a brooding portrait and a chalky, plaster bust that both caught his look. We all listened intently as Johnson laid out the upcoming travel arrangements.

The band was currently on their way to North Philadelphia from Providence, Rhode Island, in two vehicles—the mobile home and the equipment truck. After the rendezvous at the gym, the full Smokin' Joe Frazier Revue was scheduled to be on the road and heading south by midnight. With Joe and Ken Johnson driving the boss's custom Cadillac "Big Red," the caravan planned to highball through one-night stands in Chattanooga and Memphis, Tennessee, and Macon, Georgia.

I broke in to ask Joe how they could keep up that schedule. Joe laughed and said their "cruising speed" would be between 90 and 100 miles per hour.

Marvis and I were told to join the tour in six days. We had plane tickets for Augusta, Georgia, on Sunday, March 16. Joe said Marvis could stay for only a couple of days. Then he had to return to the gym in Philadelphia to prepare for the AAU Boxing Tournament—the final obstacle before the Olympic Boxing Trials.

———————

Two days later, on March 12, Joe Frazier and his troupe were already well into their tour. I returned to the gym to ostensibly meet with Marvis about our upcoming journey down south. In truth, I was more interested in just hanging out with the guys in the gym without Joe monitoring my every move. I expected everyone to speak more freely when the boss was on the road.

I arrived at the gym early and stayed downstairs for a while. There were no spectators behind the waist-high gate, and fewer than a dozen boxers cruised through their workouts. The intense buzz from the other day was gone. One guy said things would pick up when Marvis and some of the pros got going later on.

Everything was calmer upstairs as well. The first person to greet me was LeGrant "Lee" Pressley. He was a big, rotund, teddy bear of a man who moved lethargically to the couch in the outer office. Pressley had known Joe since they were kids. Joe's uncle married Pressley's aunt, so they were sort of family.

Pressley started working for Joe right before the first Muhammad Ali fight. But he got promoted to "bucket boy" for the Rematch at Madison Square Garden and the Thrilla in Manila. According to Lee, he was the guy in the corner who handled the buckets with the water and the ice, and the one for the spit. And he took the job damn seriously.

"During the rounds of boxing you've got to protect the buckets [from sabotage]," he said. "And between rounds you have to have the buckets ready and in the ring. I used to also get Joe up for running every morning [sometimes as early as 3:00 a.m.]. I ran with him, sort of."

"What does that mean?"

Pressley gave an embarrassed, caught-me laugh. "He was running in the street and I was driving the Cadillac. I'd drive behind him. Joe liked music when he ran—so I'd have the window down and the music blasting. [Sounds ordinary] but I remember traveling with Joe and getting to shake hands with President [Gerald] Ford at the White House."

"How was it working with Joe in the days leading up to those fights?" I asked.

"Before a fight, Joe gets edgy and mean," said Lee, comparing him to a warrior gearing up for battle. "Lots of yelling and throwing himself around. And he can be pretty scary when he's acting mean."

Pressley noted that Joe saved a whole different level of mean for his sparring partners, especially before the Ali fights. Yet, away from training, Joe was both kind and generous.

"If he goes to the store to buy two suits, he'll buy you one," said Lee. "If he travels somewhere first class, so do you. If he hits the fancy nightclubs, so do you—like one big family."

Pressley said Joe still got really nervous before one of Marvis's fights. Marvis, on the other hand, got "calm and quiet."

Pressley then surprised me by boldly taking credit for Marvis becoming a boxer. He claimed it went back to the Thrilla in Manila.

"After one of Joe's workouts in Manila, I told Marvis [then barely 15] to punch one of the medicine balls as hard as he could," said Lee, getting on a roll. "He slammed the ball and I said, 'This kid's going to be champion someday.' Marvis lit up. Before this he had no thoughts of being a boxer. He always said he'd never put on a pair of gloves. So, in Manila, at the Ali fight, he decided to be a fighter."

LeGrant Pressley marveled at how quickly Marvis improved. Only three years later, the then 18-year-old was holding his own with Joe Frazier in the ring. In fact, Pressley reported, the father and son stopped sparring for real because Marvis did too well.

"The last time they sparred was two years ago," said Lee, repeating what Marvis had told me. "And Joe was not holding back."

Marvis, on the other hand, had to be encouraged by Joe and others in the gym to open up. He finally listened and delivered one hell of a surprise.

"Joe got hit by a right hand that picked him right up off the floor, just about," said Lee, bubbling with glee. "Joe said, 'Damn son, that hurt.' Hit him right in the eye."

Joe wound up with a big, swollen black eye. And he bragged about that black eye for a long time, recalled Pressley.

Pressley took off to get some food, and Marvis arrived about 15 minutes later. He sat for a moment before changing. George Benton was busy working with one of his professional fighters and wouldn't be ready for Marvis for a while.

I mentioned how relaxed everyone seemed with Joe on the road. I told Marvis that even he came across more at ease, his own person today—rather than specifically Joe Frazier's son. Did people naturally just expect him to be a version of Joe?

"Some do take the time to know me for myself, but I'm learning that strangers label me blindly," he said, pausing to think about his answer. "As a kid, it used to be a big thing with me. 'Why would people think of me this way when I'm totally different [than Joe Frazier]?' I would go out of my way to show people that Marvis Frazier was a good person—not just that he's Joe Frazier's son. Also, that I'm not Superman—I'm just like you."

Marvis noted that people just assumed he would have his father's commanding personality. They expected he would be an aggressive, take-charge guy.

"People expected me to be a carbon copy of my father—be like him in his forceful ways," he said. "A long time ago Pop sat me down and told me, 'Be yourself.' Now I'm working to be my own man—me—Marvis. I can't be, and won't be, Joe Frazier. I can't and won't do the things my father did."

I mentioned the conversation with Youngblood from the other day. I asked whether he might resist turning pro. Was there a chance he would not follow in his father's footsteps as everyone assumed?

Marvis said, for now, he saw the Olympics as the end of his boxing career. He talked about his desire to go to college. He worried, if he waited too long to go, that something might get in the way.

With that, Marvis went to change for his next boxing workout.

———

Down in the gym, Marvis spoke briefly with George Benton about goals for the afternoon training session. George went off to resume coaching his professional fighter, and Marvis got to work under the watchful eye of an assistant trainer. Right from the start the session seemed much more mellow than the one with his dad.

Marvis began by practicing a combination designed to set up an opponent for a hook to the head. First, he raised the trainer's head with an upward right to the chin that started from just above his waist. That opened things up for a tight hook to the head. They repeated the combo just once and moved on.

Marvis moved to the speed bag, whipped it up to a roll, and hit to the rhythm of the trainer's nonstop chatter. He broke in with a melodic *kush-kush* sound periodically when nailing a combination on cue. The gray-haired trainer never once looked at Marvis to see if the punches were done correctly, but he constantly nodded his approval. He said he knew Marvis had mastered the combos just by "the sweet music" the bag made when hit just right.

The training session got downright joyous after that. Marvis started to skip rope to the strains of "Get Up, Get Down, Get Funky, Get Loose" by Teddy Pendergrass. During the routine he regularly changed cadence, lapsed into a high-stepping skip, and eventually pumped his knees higher and higher while blistering the rope into a blur. Through it all his upper body seemed to sway just a bit to the sensual rhythm of the music, and his smile was infectious.

After shadowboxing for five minutes, Marvis stayed in front of the mirror for a series of calisthenics and complex bending exercises. He carefully studied the reflection of each movement he made while staying in sync to the music. It made me realize that narcissism and just plain feeling good about yourself can be a big part of training.

Before Marvis moved to the ring for his sparring session, we talked about what it felt like when you're in top form.

"You feel like a racehorse," he said. "When a racehorse knows it's ready it just can't stop moving. He's prancing and kicking before he gets to the starting gate. That's the way I feel when my body is up to par. I feel like I could kill King Kong, you know."

In the ring, fighters also look for different signs that things are clicking. "I know my fight is just right when my jab is almost knocking them off their feet," said Marvis, throwing a couple of sample lefts. "That's when I know I'm right and they're just meat."

"And when did Joe know he was in a groove?"

"Dad was right when the hook was getting in and hurting them," he said. "That was his power. He never had to develop a knockout right. When something is taking 'em out, you stick with it."

A couple of 12-year-olds from the neighborhood came over to get autographs. Marvis stopped to write them both a long, detailed message before signing. Then he chatted with them until it was time for his sparring session.

George Benton had arranged for Marvis to spar with one of his top professionals. Jimmy Young, a crafty veteran at 31, was ranked among the best heavyweights in the world. He had fought Muhammad Ali for the WBA and WBC crown in April 1976. The fight went the distance and ended in a highly disputed decision for Ali.

Less than a year later, Young defeated George Foreman in a 12-round thriller in Puerto Rico. That fight was tightly contested and action packed from beginning to end. Young knocked Foreman down in the final round and took the unanimous decision. *The Ring* magazine named the match its 1977 Fight of the Year. Foreman quit boxing for a decade after the devastating loss.

The abbreviated sparring session between Marvis and Young seemed brisk and workman-like but clearly lacking passion. Young was coming off a two-round TKO of Don Halpin in New Jersey just four days earlier. He scored well with sharp counterpunching, a trademark for him. Marvis stood straight up against his 6'2" opponent to effectively work his jab. To Marvis's credit, he avoided going into a protective shell, like other amateurs might have, when Young applied pressure.

After his workout, Marvis talked to me about meeting up for our flight to Augusta in four days. He then took off to the lair, I assumed, to shower and change. I stayed to talk with Jimmy Young and hoped to get an interview in with Benton. Young had nothing but high praise for Joe Frazier's son.

"I sparred with Marvis before my last two fights, right here [almost] every day," he said, still cooling down just outside the ring. "He was more competition than I really needed, to tell the truth. Yeah, he's real good. Matter of fact, I think he's better than the last two pros I fought."

One of those fights was a 10-round squeaker against the British champion John Lewis Gardner in London.

"I'm the first American who ever beat him, and only the second fighter to beat him in his whole career," said Young, referring to Gardner. "Marvis worked with me every day for that fight . . . and was *much better* than Gardner. He would have taken the British champion. So, he's a tremendous young prospect. I think he has the potential to move quickly into the top 10 and become the champ someday."

Just before my interview with George Benton in the outer office, he got paged to the phone and I followed. It was the boss calling from the road. Joe, as if all-seeing, apparently accused Benton of putting Marvis in the ring with guys who were too big or tough for him. Benton got furious and reminded Joe that he was the one who was sick and tired of Marvis sparring with amateur kids from the gym who couldn't give him a good fight.

"I gotcha on that one!" yelled Benton. "It was your idea to have him fight the better guys."

I backed away for a couple of minutes to give Benton some privacy. But when I returned to within earshot, he was still yelling into the phone.

3

Return to Black Roots

On Friday, March 14, two days before our flight to Augusta, Marvis woke me up at 9:30 a.m. with an urgent phone call. I had been working late the night before at my Manhattan apartment and tried to clear my head as my wife handed me the phone.

"I got to drop out of this trip," said Marvis in a soft, weary voice. "There's no way I can go. Pop says he doesn't want me flying."

When I asked why, Marvis gave me shocking news.

"The United States boxing team went down in a plane crash in Warsaw, Poland," he said. "And I was supposed to be on that plane. But Pop told me not to go." Joe, luckily, deemed the exhibition tournament as unnecessary for his son's progress.

Joe Frazier, mortally afraid of flying, went out of his way to drive to music gigs and other events whenever possible. He also tried to keep his family from taking airplanes when it was feasible. Now he had a tangible example to justify his fears.

Marvis said that after his dad had broken the news of the crash over the phone, Joe immediately pressed him on the dangers of flying. "Getting scared now yourself, aren't ya?" he had asked.

"I'm not scared," his son had replied.

Marvis, just starting to mourn his lost friends, said his father then reiterated one of his standard warnings. "Those planes will kill you."

According to Marvis, Joe often told a story about flying to a boxing match with George Foreman. Joe claimed their plane had been struck by lightning and they barely made it to their destination. Marvis said LeGrant Pressley told it differently. Lee described the incident as just loud thunder that shook the plane a little.

Later, I read a *New York Post* article about the 13 boxers and eight team staffers killed in the crash three miles from the runway at the Warsaw International Airport. The Polish jetliner carried 77 passengers and 10 crew members in all, and everyone was lost. Among the dead was a Philadelphia fighter, Lonnie Young, whom Marvis knew well. Besides Marvis's tale of why he skipped the trip, the article included a side story about Jimmy Clark, another top amateur heavyweight, who missed the flight. The headline for that piece read "Late for My Own Funeral."

————

Ken Johnson picked me up in Joe's Cadillac, Big Red, at the Augusta airport on Sunday evening, March 16. Instead of heading for our nearby hotel, he said we had a good 45-mile drive to get to an impromptu gig for the band. The show was at a remote, backwoods American Legion post on the outskirts of a small town called Thomson, Georgia. Johnson noted that all the regular clubs were closed on Sundays. So Joe had decided to perform "for his people"—a poor, black, agricultural crowd less than 150 miles from the farming community where he had grown up.

I surmised this would be Joe's ideal audience. But Johnson said Joe faced no color barriers when he performed.

"It's amazing," he said. "The whites are in awe of him. They flock to him for autographs. Joe is considered an international, interracial figure. His best audience is predominantly blue-collar whites. Then blue-collar blacks are second. But he fills up white clubs."

Johnson and I chatted steadily as we drove along. We seemed to hit it off right away. He told me about meeting Joe two years before while doing entertainment bookings for hotels. Joe called to ask about booking his show into a Philadelphia hotel and, out of curiosity, Ken decided to put him in for the weekend.

"I flew out to see the show and definitely felt the man had charisma onstage," said Ken, who told Joe everything worked for him but the band. "I told him straightforward what I thought and he respected that. We became friends and pooled our ideas—picked out a new band together. I was surprised by his knowledge of the music business, what should be done onstage."

This led to a discussion about Joe's business acumen. Ken described the boss's current ventures and implied there could be more due diligence and a central plan. He listed a limousine service in Philadelphia, plans for a meat-packing company to put out Smokin' Joe breakfast sausages, and a shelved chicken-and-ribs fast-food chain, Smokin' Joe's Corner. And, of course, there was the gym, Joe's aspiration to build a stable of top boxers and his various television commercials.

Johnson felt Joe Frazier's best hope for building a business empire rested with Marvis. He said the kid had a much better head for financial dealings than his father.

"I know Joe will give it all to Marvis," said Ken. "He will definitely make the whole operation grow. He's a very intelligent kid."

Ken told me he spent 40 weeks a year on the road with Joe, and most of the time they traveled with the caravan. The vehicles included Joe's big, comfortable 1975 Caddy with dark tinted windows, CB radio, telephone, and radar detector. A 28-foot mobile home, which carried the band, had a kitchen, dining table, and bathroom and slept 10. The equipment truck handled all else needed to put on the show. Ken said the mobile home often came from trade-offs Joe arranged when he did ads for local car dealerships.

The current tour was originally scheduled for six weeks and would cover thousands of miles, said Ken. It started in Chattanooga and Memphis, Macon and Augusta, Georgia. Then they were supposed to fly to Nebraska, but Joe had just canceled that. So it was on to Jacksonville, Florida; South Carolina; North Carolina; some jobs in Delaware; and Washington, D.C. It would wrap up in Atlantic City, New Jersey, at Resorts International, on May 15 for an engagement through July 15.

According to Ken, they flew only when it was mathematically impossible to drive to an essential business function. Then Joe could be really difficult. He often bailed on these appointments—even when they were important. But Ken said it was rare for Joe to play the star on the road. He recalled an incident on their first tour from Boston to California.

"A tire blew out on the mobile home and before I knew it Joe was out changing it," he said. "The musicians were sitting in the mobile home, and the sound man and roadie were just watching. I said, 'What the hell is going on here? This is backwards.' But Joe's that way. He's a regular guy."

I asked if Joe ever got really angry at one of the guys.

"He's never exploded," said Ken. "But he is really intense about covering your tracks—making sure your back [and his] is protected. He gets upset over a lack of organization."

Ken revealed that Joe sometimes chilled out on the road by playing a sermon by some preacher or other. "Joe is more the look-up-to-the-sky-and-gods kind of religious man. [He's] not much of the go-to-church type." Ken laughed. "Joe carries the church with him on tape."

Johnson suddenly slowed Big Red long enough to spot the closed grocery store that marked the place to turn. We made a right down a long, no-name gravel road enveloped by thick-woods darkness. After barreling along for a couple of miles, Ken decided we had gone too far. He backtracked twice before finally getting lucky.

We were saved by a naked bulb and a half-hidden sign reading "American Legion Post #576." It seemed like an ominous introduction to Joe's music career.

Ken and I entered a stark meeting room halfheartedly disguised as a nightclub. Red and blue crepe paper balls hung from the ceiling over a bare floor. Clusters of iron-legged tables, ringed by metal bridge chairs, filled the space. Part of the room boasted redwood walls with dim lighting. Yet other areas had institutional off-white walls with bright lights.

Directly opposite the entrance, about 60 feet away, stood a stage just large enough for the eight-piece, all-white Steppin' Out Band. The group blasted its funky, high-energy horn sound. The open area in front of the stage doubled as a dance floor and Joe's performance space, once the headliner came on. And, off to the side, was a makeshift bar that seemed to be a world of its own.

The crowd of about 75 black locals, pretty much all farmers, dotted a room that held 300. Most sat quietly at the tables and listened to the band, which overpowered attempts to chat. Just three couples took turns on the dance floor. About 20 men stood at the bar drinking mostly liquor, several straight from the bottle.

Ken took me back to see Joe in his "dressing room" before the main show. I found him in a bare, repurposed storage room with a few chairs thrown in. He sat in one chair while Youngblood tried to steam clean the boss's outfit for the performance on another. The room was embarrassingly cramped, and I felt like an intruder at first.

Joe and Youngblood were talking boxing, and I jumped in. I turned the focus to the current heavyweight champions and whether there should be a unification match. Joe recognized only Larry Holmes as the champ. He hated the idea of multiple heavyweight titles.

"I went through this two-champion thing in 1970, and I straightened that out between Ellis and myself," he said, holding up a big fist. "Too many guys are rushing in the last second and being given a title, and then being thrown in with other guys who really haven't earned a shot at a title. I don't consider these guys true champions."

Joe drew a comparison to the heavyweight division during his prime boxing years.

"Floyd Patterson, Ali, and myself, we went through the mill to get to the championship," he said. "And then we fought other guys like ourselves to keep it. Right now, nobody whatsoever has a shot at taking Holmes, except maybe [Mike] Weaver if he lands a lucky one."

Joe went back to preparing for his upcoming show. He talked about how hard it could be to get a performance just right. He tried to make a case for why entertaining was often more difficult than boxing. Both Youngblood and I had our doubts.

"You have a lot more people to deal with to succeed—the audience, eight musicians, a sound man, and when the sound's off it kills you," said Joe. "In the ring, it's just the three of us—me, myself, and I. In music, you're either good or bad. There's no in between."

I asked if he felt more appreciated by a down-home black audience, like the one tonight. Did he treat it differently than playing for, say, a wealthy white audience?

"I don't get any more up for them than any other club I work," said Joe, who fell back on his old work ethic. "Whether it's a low-income neighborhood, a classy club, 5,000 people in the audience, or just one lost soul in the place, I'm going to do my job. But it's nice to come back to the kind of people you began with. Let them know you haven't forgotten them. I want to show them money doesn't have to change or spoil people."

Joe noted, however, that these rural farmers were often uncomfortable about meeting him.

"A lot of these people get nervous when they see me and don't know what to say," said Joe, offering an example. "I was sitting in the car making a phone call this afternoon. A couple of these guys start with 'Hey, what's happenin' m' man? What it look like?' I played along to make them feel comfortable. I got all loud with them and gave them a chance to relate to me—as one of their people."

So, this applied to how he related to poorer black people?

"I don't mean only black people. I mean any people who don't know what it's like to reach the top. I've been to the mountaintop and want them to know a little bit of what it's like. And that I can reach back down to earth and relate to them."

Joe suddenly jumped up and started heading out the door. He wore a suit vest without a shirt underneath.

"In fact, I'm going out right now and do just that," he said. Youngblood and I followed him out to the bar.

Most of the men at the bar immediately looked up from their shots or lowered their liquor bottles. Several huddled around Joe and greeted him, while pawing at his shoulders or arms. They all wanted to make physical contact with the ex-champ at first, establish that he was real, and be able to say they had touched him. Joe patiently answered questions about his lifestyle and his fights with Muhammad Ali or George Foreman. He even offered a vague "We'll see" as to whether he planned to get back in the ring soon.

Some men claimed they lived close to where Joe grew up, and asked if he knew or remembered different people from back then. Joe never gave anyone an abrupt "No." He always made it sound like he just *might* know the person. He jived easily with all of them, signed autographs, and made it seem like old friends at a reunion. Yet a couple of the men had an edge to their voices when they spoke to the man who made it out, became famous. One older guy even asked for a "loan" from "the rich boxing champion."

Youngblood eventually gave Joe a time's-up nod, and we headed back to the dressing room. Joe sat down, took a deep breath, and began to get ready for the show. Suddenly, the door swung open and a slender, 5′6″ drunk of about 40 ambled into the room. The guy, dressed in denim with a cap pulled over his eyes, stood a few feet from Joe and swayed unsteadily.

"Ahyeahhh, how ya doin', Joe Frazier?" he crooned.

"How you all," replied Joe, turning in his seat.

"I want a contract with youuu," sang the drunk, reeling a step closer. "I want a piece of your ass. I think I can take ya. Give me a contract. Scared?"

Before the drunk finished his challenge, Youngblood sprang up and crossed the room. He coaxed the man back toward the door. "Now that's enough," said Blood, in a low, firm voice. "You got to be leaving now."

For the next 15 minutes or so, the drunk continued to shout through the closed door. When I left for a moment to check on the band's set, he offered to fight me too. Then he went back to challenging Joe.

"People know my personality," said Joe, nodding toward the voice outside. "They see that I talk to everybody. So, they come in all the time to push for more. If I was a cranky son of a bitch, they wouldn't bother me as much. Sometimes they have a tendency to over-relate."

I laughed and asked if anyone ever tried to whup the ex-champ during a performance.

"Nah, they'd have to be out of their Goddamn minds," said Joe, a tinge of weariness in his tone. "Some of these dudes are [crazy]. But I would never do nothin'. I'd keep performing and walk to the other side of the floor. Young-blood or Kenny would take them off the floor."

So, it wasn't his job to deal with every crazy fan?

"My job is to keep performing," he said. "I'm not a comedian or a preacher. If I deal with something like that, it will either be very funny or a funeral. If you enjoy my singing, sit down and listen. If you don't, the hell with you! Some people call me some bad names out there, but I don't care."

I asked what usually prompted the name calling. Joe thought for a moment and then sounded like he was remembering a specific incident.

"I said something about Clay, and they called me 'a dumb n----r.' I just laughed. A lot of people out there are still fighting those Clay fights. I tell them, 'I ain't ever coming back to prove any points from those fights.' Let them keep their doubts in their minds."

————

David Cherry, DC, took the floor first as Joe's warm-up act. The young James Brown clone, dressed all in white, had a fine voice and all the moves of the Godfather of Soul. He kicked off his act with an electric version of "Do You

Want to Party," and many in the crowd bolted to their feet. He left the audience more alive and focused on the show.

That's when the headliner came out wearing a black-sequined fighter's robe over a white shirt and two-piece, hot-pink jumpsuit. His opening song, "First Round Knockout," written just for him, allowed the ex-champ to sing about boxing, beating the odds, and winning in surprising fashion. While Joe sang the punchy tune, he pranced in circles in the open area below the stage, threw signature hooks, and celebrated victory. Huddled together just above him, the band belted out crisp notes and counted to 10 in unison when the final knockout came.

There was an intimacy to the setting that fit Joe's folksy approach and empowered members of the audience to say or do things they shouldn't. Heck, anytime somebody arrived or moved around during the show, they had to pass within a few feet of him. Joe also had a habit of speaking directly to people in the middle of songs, which they took as permission to talk back. The results were sometimes touching and poignant, other times not so good.

During the opening number Joe talked for a moment about rallying for wins against fighters he wasn't supposed to beat. A nearby customer took the opening.

"Are you coming back to fight Ali?" he shouted, loud enough for all to hear.

Joe interrupted the number to provide a testy reply. "I'm through beating on Clay," he announced.

The man got up to shout at Joe for his use of the name "Clay" and to challenge his dismissive attitude toward Muhammad Ali. Two other patrons yelled out hurtful remarks about Joe's career-ending loss to George Foreman. This emboldened a drunk to charge within a couple of feet of Joe, and Ken had to step in to ward him off. In response, some in the audience came to Joe's defense, shouting support. And the band got louder to cover the dustup.

During the next song, Joe again talked with the audience. He took time to make reference to his unique fighting style. He said he never tried to mix in other fighters' styles. He admitted to taking more blows with that straight-ahead approach, but bragged, "I gave out more than my share."

Some guy at ringside shouted out that he had lost money on Frazier's fights.

"You couldn't have lost too much money," Joe quipped. "I had 36 fights and lost only four."

Again, he heard more shouts about Ali and losing to Foreman. Through it all, Joe just smiled and offered his mantra for these kinds of situations. "Ain't nothing but a party," he said, before going back to the song. "Yep, yep, yep, yep."

Joe's earlier example of "people still fighting those Clay fights" suddenly seemed like more than just a nasty story. I now had a better feel for how those clashes with Ali had stayed with Joe all these years later. I saw firsthand signs of the way the Louisville Lip had managed to distance Joe from many of his own people.

Still the audience warmed up a bit after this, in part due to Joe Frazier's refusal to get angry. Applause for each song got gradually louder, but random jibes about Ali remained audible. One more intimate song, "Tonight's the Night," gave Joe a chance to sing directly to the "ladies" in the room. And he played it for all it was worth.

Earlier Joe had described his mind-set for performing that song. "Hey, we got to do it tonight," he'd said in a singsong, husky voice filled with desire. "You know I can relate to that. That's a get-in-touch-with-the-ladies song. I get all kinds of crazy ladies come running up on that number. It gets them going, but I can deal with it."

Joe had pointed out that no matter what the subject of a song, or the message implied, he tried to keep it energetic. "I'm a high-energy man," he told me, the smile spreading wide. "If I sing, 'Let's get undressed,' my style will suggest just *throwing* those clothes off!"

Joe, gauging the vibe in the room, decided to wrap up the show. He transitioned quickly from one up-tempo number to another. Suddenly, without warning, he motioned to cut the music.

"We sho' enough LOVE YOU!!" yelled Joe, speaking for the group. He then ran from the tight ring of tables, waving Vs for victory.

The whole time his "funky white boys" chanted "Smokin' Joe, Smokin' Joe, Smokin' Joe. . . ."

After the show, Joe held court in his little dressing room. He spoke almost exclusively to the two young women standing in front of him despite all the others present. I signaled to Joe's 22-year-old nephew, Stanley, to step outside. We headed back to the bar.

Stanley Frazier's mother, Rebecca, was Joe's slightly older sister. Stanley became a Frazier through coincidence when his mother happened to marry a man named David Frazier. He lived with 11 other family members on the historic South Carolina "plantation" Joe had bought for his mother Dolly right after the Fight of the Century.

"I help take care of the place for Joe," said Stanley. "We don't see Joe down there too often, but when he comes it's like a family reunion. And, when he's on the road, we try to see him whenever we can."

Joe had called his family a couple of nights ago. Stanley immediately headed out with his mother and aunt Julia for the over-100-mile trip. They managed to surprise Joe by making it to Augusta in time for the late performance at another club.

"He definitely plays to us when we're in the audience," said Stanley. "He wants to show the family that he can do it, especially me. Because I always tell him, 'You can't sing, you know you can't sing. Leave the singing to Jacqui.' Oh my God, *she* can sing. That's another Aretha Franklin."

Stanley went on to reminisce about the day "Uncle Billy," the family's name for Joseph William Frazier, purchased the plantation. He also explained how the family wound up coming along.

"Joe got the place and he went home and told his mama," said Stanley, recalling his uncle's exact words. "He said, 'Mama, I went and got a plantation for ya.' We were only about 25 miles away. But she didn't want to get away from her friends, relatives, everybody we knew in that area. So why not go along with her. The place is 366 acres."

Dolly had raised her enormous brood of kids in a shack built by her husband and the older children. It was in the poor, black Laurel Bay section of Beaufort. The Brewton Plantation, bought by her youngest surviving son in 1971, was located in Yemassee, another part of Beaufort County. The property dated back to the early 1700s and was owned by a number of prominent, southern white families over the years. According to SouthCarolinaPlantations.com, there were as many as 95 slaves kept on the property in 1834.

Joe reportedly purchased the plantation "sight unseen" and discovered it to be in particularly poor shape. According to the website, Joe invested a lot of money on the repairs and did a good deal of the work himself. He purposely broke tradition by not placing the plantation sign at the entrance. The heavyweight champ hung a pair of boxing gloves instead.

Stanley offered a description of the property and its current residents. He made it clear that Uncle Billy didn't necessarily save the best accommodations for himself.

"The big house has two bedrooms that can fit this whole club in each," he said. "And you can't say Joe has the master bedroom because the girls' room is just as big. My house has four bedrooms and the guest house has three. On the plantation is my mother and her kids, my aunt Julia and her kids. My grandmother and my oldest uncle live in the big house."

Despite the size and grandeur of the property, Stanley made it clear that he and the other Fraziers hadn't lost the family's age-old work ethic. This was a working plantation, and everyone preferred it that way.

"We raise cattle, hogs, chickens, goats, and I grow corn, grain for the cattle, and pickles for the Vlasic Pickle Company," said Stanley. "I also build houses on the side. Joe knows that I'll stick with the hard work all day long."

Farm life and hard labor were obviously major parts of Joe's early years in rural South Carolina as well. But he also had to deal with the special dangers of growing up in the final throes of the Jim Crow South. He was young, tough, assertive, and black. Not the safest of combinations back then before the civil rights movement and efforts to overcome hard-core segregation.

Ken Singleton grew up with Joe Frazier. In a *Beaufort Gazette* article published after Joe's death, he remembered the kid everyone called "Billy Boy" as a truly "bad dude" in a brawl. He said the young teen would fight with marines and locals in juke joints, usually with racist remarks as the cause. Yet he was generally kind to other kids at school. He prided himself on protecting the weaker kids from the bullies—of course, sometimes for a nominal fee.

An Associated Press piece, also on Beaufort's farewell to Joe, noted that Billy Boy was unfairly expelled from school in the ninth grade for brawling with a white student. The white boy had called his mother Dolly hateful names. In the Jim Crow South, black boys were not supposed to respond to white taunts.

In the long run, it was a combination of the racist environment, limited financial opportunities, and the underlying threat of retaliation from the white community that would convince Frazier he had no future in Beaufort.

Billy Boy had always worked hard with his father on the family's 10-acre farm. But the soil was poor and yielded a limited array of crops, a meager income. So Joe, like his mother and father, also had to put in long hours on the farms of prosperous white families to survive. Frazier often pointed to a particular incident on one of these local farms that finally forced him to make a move.

Young Joe had been working for a number of trouble-free years on the Bellamy family farm, according to his 1996 autobiography. Mac and Jim Bellamy treated him okay—"as okay as a black man was treated in those times." But the wages were poor—as for all other black workers—and Joe admittedly didn't expect much consideration from either man. One day a young black boy accidentally messed up a tractor, and Jim Bellamy supposedly whipped him with his belt right there in the fields. Joe went back to the packinghouse and told the other black workers about the beating.

Jim Bellamy was furious at Joe for running his mouth and threatened to whip him with his belt if he didn't get off his place. Joe let him know, in no uncertain terms, that he was *not* going to use that belt on him. That supposedly made Bellamy even more furious.

When Joe's mother heard about the incident, she made his options clear. "Son, if you can't get along with the white folks, then leave home because I don't want anything to happen to you."

In 1959, after months of working odd jobs to make traveling money, Billy Boy left Beaufort and headed north to New York. He planned to live with his older brother Tommy and his wife in Harlem. He was just 15, with no source of income, and had a pregnant girlfriend he planned to leave behind. Joe promised Florence to send for her, and the not-yet-born child, when he could.

That didn't happen until quite a bit later—when Joe had moved on to Philadelphia, the beginnings of a fascination with boxing, and a job at a kosher slaughterhouse.

———

The members of the Smokin' Joe Frazier Revue were staying at a rather drab Augusta motel. It certainly was not the kind of fancy hotel suitable for a sports celebrity. The entrance opened directly onto a four-lane highway about 15 feet away. The trucks and cars that whizzed by all day and night sounded as if they were passing right through the rooms. The billboard out front read: "Low Weekend Rates. Welcome Joe Frazier."

The Indian family who owned the place made sure that their honored guest and his manager had gotten rooms in the "redone" area. The band and roadies stayed in the less desirable "unretouched" rooms. The small pool offered water with a slight brackish color that discouraged jumping in. Neither Joe nor his employees complained about the accommodations. Nobody expected Resorts International–type digs for a mixed-race troupe in Augusta circa 1980.

It was late in the afternoon on Monday, March 17, when Joe finally emerged from his room. He was still with one of the women he had met at the American Legion post the night before. They had survived the day on fast food delivered by Youngblood. Joe stood for a while on a grass field near the motel watching me and some of the guys in the band throw around a football, then a Frisbee. As usual, Joe was friendly and relaxed but didn't join in on the sports activities.

Once the woman took off, I reminded Joe of our initial plan to do at least one formal interview a day while on the road. He nodded, and we settled in on the terrace of his room for a freewheeling conversation. Joe began by talking about how hard he had to work to fit into his tight outfits onstage.

"If I don't watch what I eat, do roadwork, and train in the gym, I'm going to get fat," he said, standing to show me how thin he supposedly looked. "I know, after doing two shows at night, I have to get out there and run my couple of miles. I psyche myself. Training ties the past to what I'm doing now."

I suggested the roadwork might also help to get him ready for a comeback sometime soon. He let that go and moved on to the difficulties of balancing his commitment to Marvis, the gym, performing with the band, and his other businesses. He saw the need to be more selective in the future about the gigs he took—and to make an effort to work closer at home. He implied how hard it was to make everyone happy.

That led to Youngblood's favorite topic—the leeches in the boxing world. He despised all those characters who tried to hang on to a champ's entourage without earning their keep. Joe laughed and said he knew that was common in show business too.

"I don't know about Frank [Sinatra] or Ali, but people around me have to work for their money," he said. "Everybody has a real job—no free rides. A lot of people depend on me for jobs. . . . I feel I owe them something. I have a responsibility to keep working and making money so they can keep making money."

What about all the people expecting a handout from the rich boxing champ?

"People who know my background, know I value money," said Joe, reminding me of the hard times as a kid in Beaufort. "When people put the pinch on me, I don't give them nothing but *tombstone*. You got to be dead to get one of those. No supporting the I-don't-work guys."

Joe quickly added that wasn't always the case. He said, when he was younger, he gave money to everyone who asked—even Muhammad Ali.

"I was trying to support the world," he said. "Now that I'm a senior citizen, I can handle the people trying to put the bite on me and separate them from the ones who really need some help."

It had been cloudy and drizzly most of the day. But just as we were finishing up the interview, the sun suddenly broke through. The sunshine, and Joe's cheery disposition, encouraged me to ask one final, really foolish question.

I wanted to know what it was like to be in the ring with a heavyweight champion. Joe looked around and saw that the rectangular terrace was only a little smaller than a standard boxing ring. He suddenly hunkered down into his Smokin' Joe crouch, bobbed up and down, and peered at me through his clenched fists. From two feet away his shoulders looked massive.

"Put up your fists," he ordered. "Throw some punches."

I was 5'10" and 180 pounds with a goofy, college boxing class for experience. I froze at first and then nervously flicked out an open-handed jab. Joe didn't move, but I backed up and attempted to dance away just the same. He then took two lightning-quick lateral steps while somehow moving forward to cut off the ring. I wound up in the corner of the terrace with a fist the size of my head winging toward my face.

Joe mercifully pulled back the punch at the last second—an inch from my nose. I know if that fist had landed at full force, it would have caused some serious damage.

———————

That evening the Smokin' Joe Frazier Revue began a midweek engagement at a nightclub in a notoriously rough, black section of Augusta. It boasted a multicolored façade with glass doors that made it look like the entrance to a psychedelic supermarket. We arrived in the midst of a torrential downpour.

Pasted to one door was a cluster of newspaper clippings on Joe's entertainment career. One in particular, from the October 23, 1979, edition of the *Nashville Banner*, caught my eye. It was titled "Smokin' Joe Lands Big Punch in Heavyweight Show Biz Act." At the top, there was a photo of Joe, in a white-studded boxing robe, singing joyously into a microphone. The article actually compared his sound onstage to Marvin Gaye and the lead singer of the Commodores.

In the piece, Kenny claimed Joe did about 200 dates a year. He said, "If I let him, he'd play somewhere every night."

Joe called music his "first love" and talked about the role it played in the early days in Beaufort. "I used to sing in the church with my mama and in the cotton fields with my daddy," he said.

A red sign nearby on the glass door, apparently in crayon, announced: "By Popular Demand Smokin' Joe—Monday thru Thursday Nites." The other door displayed posters of previous acts to have graced the club's stage. These were mostly gospel groups like Napoleon Brown and the Bell Jubilees, the Pilgrimaires, and Reverend Squeaky Morgan and the Harrison Gospel Singers.

Just inside there was a bar, jukebox, and a dance floor enclosed in iron railings. The football-field-long main room stretched out beyond that and offered the same kind of simple tables and metal bridge chairs found at the American Legion—except this room had an ample stage and seating for well over 500. Unfortunately, as the time for the 11:00 p.m. show neared, only about 25 patrons had braved the foul weather.

Joe, visibly upset at first by the turnout, threatened to cancel. After a meeting with the apologetic owner, he finally relented and prepared to go on. In fact, he eventually refused to take money for the performance in an essentially empty room. Joe often showed a touching sense of generosity in such situations.

Kenny, for his part, was furious. Yet he agreed to do one more night before blowing out the rest of the booking. It was his job to protect Joe's interests and look for something better.

At the last minute, a few more people arrived and Joe began to relax a bit. The late arrivals surprisingly included a very prominent local businessman. He was the only white paying customer in the place. This small-town mogul owned a formidable automobile sales company, and Joe was scheduled to appear at his main dealership that coming Wednesday. Ads for the engagement had been flooding the Augusta airwaves since the moment I landed.

The mogul wound up getting pretty drunk during the performance and began to draw more attention at times than the headliner. Joe took the whole thing in stride and even introduced the businessman from the audience.

"Without the next man, you couldn't make it to work," said Joe. "You couldn't even get to buy food."

The tipsy white mogul responded by standing and giving Joe a clenched-fist, black-power salute. He repeated the surprising gesture several more times. He also bickered later with some people in the audience he saw as rude to the ex-champ. The mogul only escaped retribution because Joe stepped in, took him to the dressing room, and later arranged for someone to drive him home.

Despite the heavy rain, Joe and Youngblood got ready to jog a couple of miles on the way back to the motel. Joe was wearing a sweatshirt, gray knit pants, and green patent leather shoes with high heels. He saw no problem in running in that kind of footwear.

Just as we were ready to leave, the singer James Brown walked in to visit his old friend Joe Frazier. Sure, why not? The day was already totally surreal. Brown agreed to meet Joe at his motel room later on.

Joe and Blood, as promised, still did the run. They methodically sloshed along in front of Big Red most of the way back. As they ran along, the band sped by in the equipment van and splashed both of them. The boys in the van yelled and screamed out the open windows. Joe shook his fist, managed a smile, and just kept running.

About an hour later, after Joe changed, I found myself in Frazier's modest motel room with a drink in my hand. I was—wait for it—talking music and boxing with the Godfather of Soul and Smokin' Joe. The two discussed what Joe needed to learn to produce his own records. Brown said he would gladly help Joe move up in the music business and even raised the prospect of doing a record together. He suggested Joe might be part of a tour called James Brown and Friends.

Joe kept pushing his friend for hands-on lessons in studio production, but Brown seemed more intent on talking boxing. He wanted to know, like everyone else, what Ali was going to do with his comeback. Joe shrugged and responded instead to Brown's request to get up and do a little sparring with him. The two squared off, poked out playfully at each other, and seemed as giddy as a couple of kids.

Frazier eventually got Brown to take an impromptu trip to his music studio out in the woods. In a matter of minutes, a small posse came together and piled into Big Red. The rustic music studio had platinum and gold records mounted all over. The singer started off giving Joe his production tutorial, but the conversation soon shifted to Brown's stories of his amateur boxing career from younger days. He obviously missed being in the ring. He even suggested that he and Joe should consider changing roles for a while.

"If Joe comes into music, maybe I'll go back and do some fighting," said Brown.

From there, the two discussed difficulties on the road, running businesses on the fly, and the roles of their sons in the family business. Then Brown wanted to know if Joe's white boys could jam like his black band.

Despite not getting to bed until well after 3:00 a.m. on Tuesday, Joe was up five hours later for a 9:00 a.m. interview at a remote radio station on the outskirts of Augusta. WRDW, owned by James Brown, stood in the middle of an open field down a very muddy dirt road. It had suddenly become the only black media organization on Joe's schedule.

We were greeted by the on-air interviewer Tara Haskins. She was a lithe, highly attractive black woman who seemed intent on asking Joe some serious questions despite his bantering and friendly flirting. She led off with wanting to know how the ex-champ got his Smokin' Joe handle.

"The name came from Yank Durham telling me to go out and smoke for a round," said Joe. He remembered getting so lathered up that he didn't have time to cool down between rounds. He said he'd still been smokin' when the next round began.

Haskins then asked Joe which boxers he idolized. Joe immediately offered Joe Louis, former welterweight champion Kid Gavilan, and Sugar Ray Robinson.

So far, so good. The question that got the interviewer in trouble had to do with how young men and women could get started in boxing.

"Women are not made to get in the ring," responded Joe, with a shake of the head. "Women shouldn't be fightin' or carrying no weapons. A woman belongs in the kitchen so she can give her man a kiss and make him some supper after a hard day's work. She should greet him with a sweet smile and say how glad she is that he's home."

Haskins made a face and openly cringed. She said, "We won't deal with that."

I cringed at first too. But then I caught the twinkle in Joe's eye. It made me wonder if we had been played. Don't forget that Joe's daughter Jacqui, like Ali's daughter, went on to become a very good professional boxer.

4

More Than the
White Man's Champion

By 2:00 p.m. Tuesday, March 18, Joe had finished up at James Brown's radio station. Now he now sat in Ken Johnson's motel room answering mundane questions from a local newspaperman. It was part of a kickoff to a swirl of commitments with the area's white community. Ken, ill from last night's road trip, was sitting up in his disheveled bed a couple of feet away.

Kenny listened, as best he could, to two businessmen making a pitch for Joe to take his act to an upscale club across town. They promised large audiences and a big TV campaign if he moved to the predominantly white venue. In the background, a television blared out a commercial featuring Joe and the local mogul from last night. They were hamming it up with phony punches and references to the fights with Ali, while hyping Wednesday's appearance at a car dealership.

One of the negotiators for the nightclub looked like a sandy-haired Ichabod Crane in an impeccable gray suit and mirrored sunglasses. He pushed his point relentlessly. Ken finally broke down and croaked out a promise for Joe to visit the club later that afternoon. We eventually all cleared out so Ken could pull himself together.

I tagged along for the drive across town. As we neared our destination, most of the homes became mansions. Some of these grand houses had tennis courts, and many had pools. The place itself was situated in a beautifully landscaped mall.

The posh club was also no more than a long tee shot and two-iron swing from the Augusta National Golf Course. That, of course, was the iconic home of the Masters—the most prestigious of all of golf's major tournaments. I visualized Joe taking the stage at the club in the Masters' traditional green sports jacket.

We were met inside by the 40-something proprietor. He had blond, slightly receding hair and a relaxed, friendly face and wore a partly open, casual shirt. He greeted us enthusiastically and made it apparent how thrilled he was to have Joe there. He leaned into Joe just a bit while making his pitch.

First, he gave us a little tour of the club. With his index finger, he pointed out the fenced-in mezzanine area in the back where the band would set up. It faced into a tiered dining area with plush seating. That, in turn, was flanked by a row of elaborate backgammon tables and an opulent, mirrored bar that ran the width of the room.

Off to the left, the owner indicated the large, formal dance floor. Beyond that, somewhat isolated, we found a quiet retreat furnished in expensive antiques, upholstered armchairs, and grand chandeliers. The room was decorated in muted yellows and grays with thick carpeting and subdued lighting. We were told this fit the somewhat older, more affluent part of their clientele.

The club held 600 patrons, and our host seemed convinced Joe's shows would sell out. He said he also owned another Augusta nightspot across town "exclusively for blacks." But he felt that Joe would go over much better in the white club. I started to ask why and decided not to interrupt.

Everything the guy said was on message. Yet, despite the warm, upbeat presentation, he referred to Joe as "boy" over and over again. After the first time, I instinctively braced myself for Joe's violent reaction. But it never came. Joe cheerfully agreed instead to do two shows tomorrow night at 9:30 p.m. and midnight.

"What the hell was that?" I blurted out as we exited the club. I couldn't help myself. I wondered out loud why Joe hadn't flattened the guy for repeatedly calling him boy.

Kenny seemed a bit perturbed as well but didn't say anything.

Joe calmly explained to me that this was normal for the South of 1980. That was just the way the club owner had been raised. Joe actually saw him as a good guy who didn't even realize he had been insulting.

I knew Joe was right. He had been raised in the South. He had a much better feel for true intentions down here than a New York native like me.

A moment later, Joe gave me a sly smile. He added one more point. If the same thing had happened in Philadelphia or New York, he would have knocked the guy out.

————

After leaving the club, we drove back to the motel. Joe and Kenny had booking arrangements to discuss, and I didn't hear an invitation to join them. I headed instead for a rambling interview with the Steppin' Out Band. We soon drifted into a conversation that picked up on the friendly relationship established yesterday afternoon.

All the guys in the band were around 24 years old, extremely talented, and college trained. Five of them had studied music at Berklee, and one had attended the University of Massachusetts Business School. Only David Cherry, the opening act, was older, at 30, and had a more informal entertainment background. He was already with Joe's entourage when the band signed on and had performed with several East Coast bands before that. The guys had readily incorporated DC into their group once they saw him onstage.

The band members said Joe had been performing professionally, on and off, since at least 1970, when he was already heavyweight champ. They acknowledged Joe had come a long way in his stagecraft. By way of example, John Desony, the bass player, referred to one of Joe's more painful early mistakes. Taking an awkward step on a Las Vegas stage, while still champ, Joe "fell off the stage and broke his leg." It was about a year before Joe's first fight with Ali.

John said they saw their main job as making the boss look continually more professional up there. It was not an uncommon mission for band members the world over.

"Hell, musicians are always in the position of making some front man look good—even a singer like Elvis Presley," said John. "Joe carries a share of the load. We just make it lighter and easier to take."

John then bemoaned the loss of the female backup singers and what they had brought to the show. "The group was better with Something Sweet," he said. "They covered Joe better—very talented, on a million-seller album.

Actually, the girls felt Joe's show was kind of a step down. For us, it's a step up. We've met Lou Rawls and many other stars through Joe."

Switching gears, John went into a litany of serious and somewhat amusing complaints about dealing with the boss. His key criticism centered around Joe's time spent with Marvis, the guys in the gym, and now his own training routines. Those absences had cost the band lucrative engagements and had impeded Joe's progress in show business.

"Joe has a lot of other commitments and is not with us to rehearse as much as he should," said John, who felt the ex-champ had the potential to be much better onstage. "Joe has the discipline from boxing to become a polished performer."

The musician said that boxing discipline made Joe a perfectionist at times, "a compulsive winner." Unfortunately, John only saw that discipline at work when Joe had the time to be fully engaged. "If something is not right, he'll ask one of us, 'How do I do this, does it sound good?' And he'll listen to us."

John also talked about Joe's fatherly attitude toward the band members while on the road. Although this could be funny at times, he thought the boss's heart was in the right place. He recalled Joe giving them lectures on a strong work ethic or even safe sex.

"Now if you're gonna go with 'em girls, make sure you use them rubbers," said John, mimicking Joe. "I don't want my boys getting sick now."

Rick Magnani, on sax, suddenly chimed in with a quirky complaint of his own. "I've been on the road with Joe for six weeks and he still doesn't know my name," he said. "He calls all the guys in the band by their instruments— Mr. Bass Man, Mr. Saxophone, Mr. Trumpet."

I laughed out loud and let out a sigh of relief. Ever since I had arrived in Augusta, Joe had been introducing me to people as "the White Writer." I had started to worry that it was a race thing—something I hadn't picked up on before. Now I knew it was only a memory thing that came from dealing with an ever-growing crowd of people in his orbit.

Steve Schwartz, the lead trumpet player, said he had a solution for Joe's forgetfulness. "He finally remembered my name after I won $50 off of him in blackjack."

Winners like Joe remembered losses all too well.

The interview finished up with a story about how physically tough Joe still seemed to be. Kenny and some of the band members had been hanging out in Joe's motel room on the road. Mike Leonardo, from the horn section, had heard that Joe used to work out with a medicine ball to toughen his gut. So he had been throwing a medicine ball into Joe's stomach as the ex-champ stood firm with his hands behind his back. Joe apparently psyched himself up and grinned through gritted teeth as the ball hit home.

Then Joe reclined on his back while Mike stood next to the bed. Mike brought the medicine ball above his head and slammed it down over and over again into Joe's stomach. Eventually, Mike was sweating and Joe was just turning casually from side to side. The demonstration had ended when Kenny got nervous.

"Hey, if he goes to the hospital, we'll be out of work," said Kenny, according to the guys.

———

The Tuesday night crowd at the club in the black neighborhood was even smaller than the night before. After about an hour, there were still only 12 people in the audience. Kenny was already regretting his decision to do one more night before canceling the rest of the engagement. He instructed the band to rapidly dismantle and pack the equipment after the first show. He didn't see a reason to do the second one.

Joe was clearly upset but instinctively fell back on his professional attitude. "This is my job," he said, before heading out onstage for another likely unpaid performance.

I felt for Joe as he looked out over the cavernous room with all those empty seats. Yet he just flashed his broad grin and ad-libbed a glib welcome.

"Ah yes, two's company, but three makes a crowd," he said, panning the tiny audience with an outstretched hand. "So, I'm gonna give this crowd everything I got."

Joe went on to keep his promise to the audience. Several band members told me later that Joe had performed technically one of his best sets of the tour that night. It seemed he was consciously trying to make up for the lack of customers by expanding his effort.

After each song, Joe got a smattering of applause from the small group. "Ain't nothing but a party," he kept shooting back. By the end, most of the audience had left and just four black women remained.

Joe closed his act with a farewell quip that finally let his anger show. "Well, Augusta, Georgia, you better look close at me now," he said, "because you ain't gonna see me here no more!"

By the time Joe emerged from his dressing room, the anger was gone. He even offered to reward the four women for their loyalty. Joe invited them to go across town to the posh white club for some late-night drinks.

What a difference in atmosphere! At 1:00 a.m. midweek, the upscale place was still hopping. More than half of the 600-seat venue was full, and the bar buzzed with loud chatter.

Although not scheduled to perform until the following night, Joe was instantly mobbed by adoring fans. He chatted easily with everyone and signed autographs for over an hour. One well-heeled person after another touted the ex-champ's accomplishments and took turns talking about how much he meant to them.

I noticed that some fans, in their enthusiasm, tended to treat Joe more like a racehorse than a boxer. They often gushed about how much money they had won betting on him. And, for some reason, they expected him to rejoice over their good fortune.

One well-dressed, gray-haired guy, about 50, offered Joe a story of a past triumph laced with some high praise. While he spoke, his wife pumped his hero's hand.

"Man, way back, that first Ali fight, nobody thought you would survive," he said, giving Joe a grave look. "But I bet on you and you made me *a lot* of money. You won that one—and I could swear you won it for me."

Joe laughed and shook his head in disbelief. "Yep, yep, yep," he replied, that big grin spreading across his face. "That's what I did it for."

The man went on to say how much he respected the ex-champ. He particularly appreciated the great job Joe did by facing down that damn Clay.

Several others in the crowd said they still considered Joe Frazier the champ. They didn't seem to like Ali very much and were glad to say so. And they referred to Joe more than once as "our" champion.

There it was out loud. These wealthy, white fans were basically calling Smokin' Joe "the White Man's Champion." They clearly meant it as a compliment that night, but it echoed the most damaging attack suffered by Joe Frazier in his career.

The White Man's Champion was Muhammad Ali's cruelest, most insidi-
ous racial slur aimed at his archrival back in the day. It instantly challenged
Frazier's integrity, history, and loyalty as a black man. And it had obviously
caught on better over the years than anyone thought possible.

————

In the run-up to the Fight of the Century, Ali had gone into high-volume
salesman mode. But it turned out he had been selling more than just tickets
to a boxing match. He had been pitching the image of Joe Frazier as the White
Man's Champion—the dumb black man duped into selling out his people to
the white establishment. By contrast, this allowed the Greatest to cast himself
as the Black Man's Champion and the defender of his race.

On March 2, 1971, an Associated Press article in the *Sarasota Herald-
Tribune* began by acknowledging that "Muhammad Ali once again called
Joe Frazier a white man's champion." This happened in a solo, national
telephone interview to promote the upcoming heavyweight title bout in
Madison Square Garden. Ali went out of his way to suggest Frazier was too
unsophisticated to handle the racial and political controversy the fight had
stirred up. In the end, he claimed this would undo his opponent both in and
outside the ring.

"I represent the masses," proclaimed Ali, clearly referring to all people of
color around the globe. "He's looked on in the eyes of the world as the American representative, as the white man's champion. This is too much pressure
for Joe Frazier. He can't cope with these outside pressures."

In an earlier interview before the fight, Ali had been even more direct in
his assault on his rival's politics. "Joe Frazier is an Uncle Tom," he had said,
according to an article in the *Guardian*. "He works for the enemy."

Ali later took that sentiment a huge step further. He suggested that almost
all black people supported him. What's more, he said any black person who
thought Joe could win was also an Uncle Tom. This certainly left little room
for any black fan to comfortably root for Joe.

New York Times writer Arthur Daley quickly zeroed in on how Ali's
rhetoric had hit home with the black community. One short paragraph in his
March 10, 1971, column on the outcome of the fight made it clear that Ali had
already alienated Joe from many of his own people.

Daley wrote: "'Whitey won again,' shouted one heartbroken watcher, angrily dismissing the Frazier victory as a prearranged coup by the Establishment. It matters not that Joe's skin is darker. Ali is their boy and he can do no wrong."

Muhammad Ali later admitted he had fabricated all these charges against Joe just to promote the fight. Yet the explanation had always rung hollow and never seemed to soothe the pain Ali caused. Now, in the last 48 hours, I had seen firsthand how fully those lies were embraced in both the black and white clubs around Augusta, Georgia—so close to where Joe grew up.

Joe Frazier's initial reaction to these attacks by Ali was one of shock and bewilderment. After all, the two had been friends early on. Joe was also one of the first boxing personalities to defend Ali after the 1967 ban. He worked for Ali's reinstatement and even came to his rescue when things got tight.

Frazier's friend Butch Lewis, quoted in a 1996 *Sports Illustrated* piece, confirmed that "on at least two occasions" Joe gave Ali money when he needed it. One time he handed Ali "$2,000 to pay an overdue bill at the City Squire Motor Inn in New York City."

That same *Sports Illustrated* article later captured just how betrayed Frazier felt back then by Ali's verbal assaults. He seemed particularly blindsided by the Uncle Tom references. Joe knew he had lived a more authentic, gritty, black childhood than Ali ever did growing up.

"He called me an Uncle Tom," said Joe, according to *SI*. "For a guy who did as much for him as I did, that was cruel. I grew up like a black man—he didn't. I cooked the liquor. I cut the wood. I worked the farm. I lived in the ghetto. Yes, I tommed. When he asked me to help him get a [boxing] license, I tommed for him. For him! He betrayed my friendship."

That betrayal became progressively more pronounced after Frazier won the Fight of the Century. Ali's remarks were ever more personal, graphic, and insulting as the rivalry intensified. By the lead-in to the Thrilla in Manilla, these comments were downright vicious and cut deeper and deeper.

Ali's attacks were usually masked with his famous charm, something funny. He set the tone for one press conference by whipping out a small rubber gorilla doll and introducing it as Joe Frazier. He then beat the gorilla doll unmercifully. This was accompanied by a not-so-funny little ditty.

"It's gonna be a chilla, and a killa, and a thrilla, when I fight the gorilla in Manila," he sang, according to a bleacherreport.com piece marking Ali's death. Ali was still punching away at the doll while he sang. Everyone laughed at the time. But as the words sunk in, some black people winced instead.

Other prefight jibes by Ali were impossible to ultimately laugh off or misconstrue. Yet they invariably began with some kind of humor as well.

"Joe Frazier should give his face to the Wildlife Fund," quipped Ali to a gathering of the press, reported the *Guardian*. "He's so ugly, blind men go the other way."

Again, everyone in the room laughed. It came off as a classic "he's so ugly" joke at first. Then it got really mean spirited and racist.

Ali, a black role model and voice for racial equality, suddenly spewed the worst kind of white supremacist slurs. He suggested his rival was an inferior kind of black man. He implied Joe's distinctive black features and dark skin color were an embarrassment. And he was doing it on the world's biggest stage.

"Ugly! Ugly! Ugly!" Ali shouted, without missing a beat. "He [Joe Frazier] not only looks bad, you can smell him in another country! What will the people of Manila think? That black brothers are animals. Ignorant. Stupid. Ugly and smelly."

At some point, after the fight in Manila, Joe summed up the damage done by Ali's remarks. He also sadly acknowledged the animosity some black people felt toward him.

"I know things would have been different for me if he [Ali] hadn't been around," admitted Joe, according to the *Guardian* piece. "I'd have gotten a lot more respect. I'd have had more appreciation from my own kind."

––––––––

On Wednesday morning, March 19, Joe was working on Big Red with Youngblood and his nephew Stanley when I showed up. The guys checked out the water in the radiator, the oil, battery, spark plugs, and just about everything else accessible without a hydraulic lift. Joe attributed his knowledge of cars to the time he had spent with his father. He said Rubin had seen it as part of the need to be as self-sufficient as possible on the farm.

After noon, we took off for the drive back to Thomson, Georgia. Joe was scheduled to do the big promotion event today for the local mogul's main car and truck dealership. After all the recent publicity, everyone expected an impressive turnout.

The mogul was just about my age and already owned quite a bit of this small town. His Thomson holdings included a wide variety of lucrative businesses besides his car dealerships. The town of 6,500 was relatively poor, with black residents accounting for around 70 percent of the population. Yet the mogul admitted to taking in many millions of dollars in the past year.

The way the mogul had likely made his fortune was not lost on Joe.

"[He] is a perfect example of how all blacks down south spend all the money, and the whites get rich from the blacks spending all their money," said Joe, with a certainty that came from experience. "All the whites make their money because the blacks [down south] like to dress nice, drive nice cars."

En route to the event, we passed one broken-down shack along the road after another. Joe stared intently out the window and seemed physically hurt by what he saw.

"He probably sold every one of these poor blacks a new car," said Joe, shaking his head.

Joe got quiet and just seemed to fume for a while after that. As we got closer to the dealership, he gave us an idea of what he had been thinking.

"[The dealer's] granddaddy might have been just the kind of man that would have strung me up to a tree not long ago," he said.

The mogul was there waiting for us when we arrived. He greeted Joe warmly and rushed him over to confer with the production team for the commercials. For the next half hour, a steady line of locals streamed onto the lot. By the time the team was ready to start shooting the ads, the crowd had reached about 200 and showed no sign of leveling off.

"I think Joe's loyalty to the fans exceeds their loyalty," said the mogul, despite the size of the turnout. "I would say there will be more whites to see Joe here today than blacks. Yet the blacks around here do look up to Joe as successful and a celebrity."

Joe's first commercial required him to drive a tan-and-brown truck a few feet and say a few lines. He inched forward, stopped, and instantly flubbed his first line. While Joe waited for the crew to do another take, a white man with slicked-back gray hair and a blue windbreaker sidled over to him.

"Why don't you go and take your championship back," he said to Joe. "Go on, now!"

"Oh no," Joe replied. "I'm a senior citizen now."

The guy just shook his head at Joe in disappointment, then settled for an autograph instead.

Joe went on to do nine more takes for that first commercial. He graciously laughed along with the mostly white crowd after each take. And he received a big ovation when he finally got it right.

At the end of that initial ad, the mogul was supposed to jab Joe with a solid right hand. But he wound up delivering a lame, awkward tap instead. Joe stopped the shoot, assumed a boxing stance, and started teaching the businessman how to throw a punch with authority. A good part of the crowd seemed bent on getting in on the lesson.

Between commercials, the champ posed with both a black and a white cop from a local police station.

For the second ad, Joe climbed behind the wheel of a T-top convertible. There was a beautiful young woman by his side. He eyed the woman, went over the lines, and got down to business.

"I'm sitting here in my Trans Am and it looks good, and it smells good, and it handles good," Joe said, flashing a broad smile for the camera and his passenger. "Just like a beautiful woman."

The production people beamed. Of course, that one Joe nailed right away.

From 5:00 p.m. to almost 7:00 p.m., Joe hunkered down at a big desk to sign autographs. The line of mostly white and black kids, with parents and grandparents in tow, came in the main entrance of the dealership, past the champ, and then snaked through the garage and out a side door. Many of the adults pushed their kids forward to get Joe's signature and then asked for another one of their own.

Smokin' Joe took the time to say a little something to everyone. As best as I could tell, he signed more than 300 autographs in the two-hour session.

Joe Ivory, a black farmer waiting patiently in line with his kids, wore a bowler hat, a frayed yellow sweater, and sneakers. I asked why he was willing to stand through suppertime just to meet the former fighter.

"Says he's a champ who cares about the people," replied the farmer, through splayed teeth. He didn't think he had to add anything to that.

About an hour into the autograph session, Joe halted the procession to greet an elderly black reverend he knew from his past. He also took time to slap five with a kid he recognized sneaking back for a second autograph.

After the promotion event, Kenny and I tagged along with Joe for a fancy, sit-down dinner in his honor at an exclusive country club nearby. The party included the mogul and his wife, a radio disc jockey and his girlfriend, a representative from a television station, and a local politician, among others. One glance around the table made it apparent that if Joe were not a celebrity he would have never gotten in the door.

The conversation started off amiably enough. We discussed Joe's boxing career, his fights with Ali, and even his fear of flying. Then a woman from Sparta, Georgia, who had tracked the champ to the country club, crashed the party and stayed at Joe's insistence. She was a black activist who quickly changed the subject to the state of race relations down south. This was going on while young black waiters in formal service attire hustled to fulfill the group's every demand.

The activist invited Joe to speak to a mostly black group in Sparta about more equitable living conditions for blacks in the South. She said Joe must tell black people to rally for a fairer share of the wealth. She demanded Joe push whites to give blacks better living conditions and a greater opportunity for land ownership.

"Shouldn't blacks live as well as the whites?" she asked.

Joe tried to converse quietly with the woman. Everyone else at the table either leaned in to listen or mumbled about their discomfort. Joe obviously wanted to keep things as light as possible without alienating the activist or anyone else. But, at the same time, he seemed reluctant to allow the woman to put words in his mouth.

Joe finally countered by saying that most people "just work for what they get" and don't expect to be given anything. He claimed that "us just sitting down and eating this fine meal in this club" with our prominent hosts "shows progress."

The woman began to object, and Joe calmly but firmly cut in. "People can't be forced," he said.

I found Joe's reaction disappointing at first, but several minutes later he took me and everyone in the room by surprise. Joe had obviously become annoyed by the way some of the white businessmen treated our waiters. He abruptly stood and took a large silver serving tray from one of the young men.

Joe instructed the waiter to sit in his seat at the head of the table. He took the waiter's place serving the group. Joe, not so playfully, warned the businessmen that they better treat him—and by implication the black waiters—with more respect.

There was stunned silence for a while. Joe might not have wanted to talk the talk of the black activist. But he certainly walked the walk of a proud, confident, caring black man. It seemed like the last thing a White Man's Champion would do.

5

Ali's Tap Dance
and Frazier's Flying Circus

We drove to the posh nightspot after the dinner party at the country club had ended. Joe wanted to have some time to prepare before the earlier show began. The sprawling venue was already filling up rapidly with a high-end crowd spending lots of money for dinner and at the bar. The band had just finished setting up in the fenced-in mezzanine area.

Joe found Dennis Peter, the keyboard player, and pulled him aside to go over some of the songs on their playlist. After a quick give-and-take, the boss seemed satisfied and headed to his dressing room. I stayed to speak with the piano man.

Dennis told me that he occasionally had one-on-one rehearsals with Joe. This was particularly necessary when there were plans to add a new number. For instance, they had recently been working on putting the song "Still" by the Commodores into the act. Joe first learned the lyrics from an original recording, and then he taped the two of them working on it.

According to Dennis, one of Joe's biggest problems onstage came from impatience. *Just like in the ring*, I thought, remembering some of his headlong charges against the much taller George Foreman.

Dennis said Joe had a compulsion to rush through songs—both new ones and old favorites. "If he has to wait a few beats without singing something, he gets nervous," he said.

The musician described how he tried to keep things light with Joe during their private sessions, especially when they went over a new song.

"I would have him count out loud 1-2-3-4 between certain lines to get the timing," he said, tapping along on a table. "It's like teaching a kid to play by rote. You have to be really definite, constant repetition."

Dennis said the boss seemed to be listening the first time they practiced, but sometimes it was hard to tell. At their next private rehearsal, Joe claimed he was ready to sing the song onstage. Yet as soon as Dennis criticized the performance, Joe began pacing back and forth.

"I thought he was upset initially," said Dennis. "But now [I see] he was working. Now, he was *really* trying. We worked for about an hour that day before the rest of the band came in. When he did that song with the band, and started to screw up that part again, he walked over to the piano. He looked at me and steadily pounded out the four-beat pause on the piano."

Dennis said it made him feel good to see Joe's effort, to know he listened to him. After all, a ballad like "Still" presented a much more difficult timing problem for singers than most other songs.

I left Dennis and went to see Joe in his dressing room. He had his tape recorder going, and he was playing around with various opening comments. Joe didn't seem to want an audience just yet. This reminded me of an exchange we had that first day up in the lair. Joe had been talking about his consistent desire for alone time.

"I take a lot of time by myself," Joe had said, referring to a need dating back to a childhood spent with an army of siblings. "I work [better] by myself. People I work with sometimes don't understand that. I got to travel by myself, go places alone."

Joe had noted that fans were always shocked to see him totally on his own in public.

"People see me in the street and say, 'Where's your crowd?' I'd say, 'Hey, you got the wrong guy. That's Ali. I never have a crowd.' I drive my car by myself, stay in a [hotel] room by myself."

Joe had said that yearning for solitude also applied to the moments in the dressing room getting ready to perform. The first thing he usually tackled was his opening speech. These remarks changed dramatically with the makeup of the audience and the town itself.

"Good evening ladies and gentlemen," Joe had begun, while pretending to talk into his tape recorder. "It's a pleasure to be in your hometown. The population of blacks is three and I'm proud to make it four. That's how I prepare—alone with my tape recorder. So, if I make mistakes getting ready, there is nobody there to sniggle about it."

———

By the time the show started, every seat and standing-room spot in the club was taken. The traffic at the bar ran 10 patrons deep, and people huddled shoulder to shoulder by the backgammon tables. DC immediately connected with the audience, and the band's horn section seemed to make the stage vibrate. Their warm-up received a loud, appreciative response.

After the band finished, the applause just kept going and built in anticipation of Joe Frazier's introduction. The crowd's enthusiasm skyrocketed when Joe finally came out. Shouts of "Hey champ!" and *"You're* the Greatest!" and "There he is!" filled the room. Joe kept his opening remarks brief before launching into his signature boxing anthem, "First Round Knockout."

The guys in the band had cued me in on how tonight's set was organized. Every song gave Joe the chance to play a role he relished. Each number also allowed the ex-champ to interact with the audience in a different way. It seemed natural for him to begin as the boxer pumping trademark hooks in Smokin' Joe fashion for his fans.

The song "So Glad You Could Make It" then permitted Joe to transition into the affable greeter-entertainer. He took several forays into the crowd to shake hands and accept adoring hugs. Each time he was mobbed.

In the past, according to band members, this ploy hadn't always worked as planned. One lady in Vermont made a show of refusing to shake hands. Another time a drunk just stood at the edge of the stage with his tongue out and refused to move. In both instances, Joe kept singing and smiling.

"My One Weakness," another original tune, found the ex-champ playing Sampson to a room full of Delilahs. The lyrics talked about how he was big and strong, but some girl remained his "one weakness." For emphasis, the band sang, "Ain't that the truth." Joe loved the vulnerable strongman role.

"Tonight's the Night (Gonna Be Alright)," by Rod Stewart, let Joe be the ladies' man. As he was singing to a woman in the audience, all the lights onstage inadvertently went out for a while. The crowd just applauded louder and louder as Joe persevered and sang right through the mini blackout.

"Shake Your Body to the Ground" had Joe in the role of cheerleader. He stomped his foot along with the piano and yelled, "Come on!" The crowd roared in response.

For "Amen," Joe transformed into the southern preacher. Here, he strutted around with the microphone stand and heavy base the way most performers do with just the hand mic. Three or four more songs, and special roles, rounded out his act.

But it was "My Way," one of supposedly 385 or so versions written by Paul Anka, that put Joe in his glory and stole the show. It gave Joe the chance to be the personal storyteller, talking directly to the audience about his punishing climb to the top—and the physical and emotional abuse that came with it. Joe also got to make the point of how *he was the one who always played fair*.

In truth, the room had begun to drift into a distracted buzz early in the song. Yet, as the message became more personal, the place quieted down. And by the last line, every person there was fixed on the headliner in the spotlight.

When Smokin' Joe wailed about taking the blows but "sho' enough doing it my wa-a-ay," the audience exploded. It was touching to finally see him get his standing ovation and rousing encore.

––––––

The club owner offered his critique of Joe's act after the show. He zeroed in on both the quality of the performance and the headliner's relationship to the crowd. For the most part, he couldn't have been happier about the way things had gone.

"I thought it was one great show," he said, taking in the excitement around him. "He's not the best singer. But the way he performs, the way he relates to the audience, makes them enjoy every minute of it. And his group is great. They loved it!"

This led to an assessment of why Joe did so well here but failed to fill the room at the black venue. The club owner saw it as a matter of location and the vibe Joe put out.

"The club Joe was playing is in a trouble-packed section of town," he began. "I don't think Muhammad Ali, Joe Frazier, or anybody else could draw there. I cater to upper-class blacks and whites in this club, and I own an all-black club on the other side of town. I booked Joe into the [mainly] white club because, personally, I don't consider Joe black."

"Oh *really*," I replied. "Explain that one to me."

"[Joe] appeals more to whites than he does to black people," he said. "I think white people like him better than black people do. It's his personality. He has a flare about him that white people like."

In fact, the club owner said he had experienced Joe's appeal to white people up close earlier in the day.

"I had breakfast with him this morning and he's really on the white people's level," he said. "He's on *our* level, you know. During the Ali-Frazier fights I personally was on Joe's side. And I think his popularity with whites in this area comes from those fights."

With some prompting, the club owner explained why local white people backed Frazier over Ali.

"I think people respected Ali as a fighter, but disagreed with his aggressive attitude," he admitted, harkening back to a time when Ali's Black Muslim brethren put out a lot of antiwhite rhetoric. "Joe was on an even keel with both races. People responded to that."

Right on cue, Joe sashayed out of his dressing room back into the heart of the club. He was still wearing the same black-sequined boxing robe. Several patrons ran over to grab hold of Joe and say how much they admired him. He had a kind word for each of them.

Yet, even here, among his most adoring audience, there were a pair of obligatory drunks in boxing poses attempting to take some swings at the ex–heavyweight champion. Joe just laughed and put up his outstretched hands in a defensive stance.

"You don't want to do that," he said, with just a hint of menace. "Do you now?"

The two shook their heads and eventually joined Joe's admirers.

The club owner pointed to the little scene with the drunks. He saw it as proof of Joe's irresistible appeal to white people down south.

From here, the conversation turned to how most whites in the area viewed the actual Ali-Frazier fights. The restauranteur claimed most white people he knew thought Joe could have won all three bouts. He was particularly adamant about how everyone believed Muhammad Ali had stolen the decision in the second one.

That claim about the wrong outcome to their second meeting resonated with me. Despite rooting for Ali back then, I had always had my doubts about the strength of his performance in the match.

Later, when I mentioned this to Joe, he heartily agreed. "I was robbed," he said.

Joe Frazier met Muhammad Ali in the fight they called "the Rematch" at Madison Square Garden on January 28, 1974. It was essentially a non-title bout, just Ali's North American Boxing Federation belt on the line, and supposedly the pair's least significant contest. After all, Ali's air of invincibility had been shattered in their first MSG match. And Frazier had recently lost his heavyweight championship to George Foreman in horrendous fashion.

As a result, experts came to the fight with questions about the current fitness of both combatants. They also had doubts about the prospects for either boxer to ever win another world title.

Yet from a broader perspective, the outcome in the Rematch became a crucial factor in determining the ultimate boxing legacy of both fighters. If Frazier had won that battle, there would have been *no need* for a rubber match a year later in Manila. Ali and Frazier might have met just those two times with Joe taking both battles. In addition, without the awful damage sustained in their third fight, Joe would have surely been in better shape for his second bout with George Foreman. He might not have lost the Foreman fight that initially ended his career.

So, it was reasonable to assume that a Joe Frazier win in the Rematch would have had a huge impact on the way boxing historians later treated him. He certainly would have been placed higher than his usual seventh or eighth ranking among the all-time great heavyweights. Conversely, Ali's stock among boxing experts would have fallen precipitously. He would have been denied his title shot against Foreman that followed this fight—the one that became the famous Rumble in the Jungle. And he would never have been given the chance to win the Thrilla in Manila.

In the end, a Smokin' Joe victory in Ali-Frazier II might well have cost Ali his mantle as the Greatest. Joe Frazier would now have been included in the discussion for that honor along with the undefeated Rocky Marciano, Joe Louis, and perhaps one or two others.

Muhammad Ali was awarded a unanimous decision in the Rematch based on what I called his "tap dance" approach. For most of the fight, he flicked out a flurry of gentle taps and then danced away or wrapped Frazier up in a bear hug to prevent retaliation. Joe clearly threw much harder punches and ultimately did more damage even though a number of blows missed their mark.

The two judges and referee apparently gave Ali the edge based on the sheer number of punches thrown over 12 rounds, regardless of their heft or effectiveness. Yet the volume of punches was meant to be the measuring stick for success in amateur boxing matches and *not the pros*. Professional fights were usually decided by the power punches that landed and the havoc they caused.

Joe, and others, suggested that Ali stole the win in the Rematch based on a combination of questionable factors. They felt he relied heavily on his celebrity appeal, constant complaints about not getting credit for the volume of punches thrown in the first fight with Frazier, and his infuriating jab-and-grab strategy. I, however, primarily attributed Ali's surprising unanimous victory to simple desperation.

It was desperation, felt by the boxing establishment, media, and sports fans worldwide that fueled the need for Ali to win this particular fight. A loss to Frazier might well have ended Ali's viability as a championship contender. That in turn would have jeopardized the continued popularity of boxing that Ali's return to the ring had initially promised.

Don't forget Muhammad Ali was the most recognizable sports figure on earth at the time. His fights attracted millions of more casual fans to boxing—the ones only interested in Ali. Neither the ticket-buying public nor the moneymen of boxing were ready to accept another Ali defeat. For all concerned, except maybe Joe, Ali had to win.

With all this at stake, it would seem only natural that the officials for the fight came in subconsciously rooting for an Ali victory.

Associated Press writer Will Grimsley homed in on that pervasive attitude—that initial desperation and eventual relief—with his January 29, 1974, report on the outcome of the Rematch. The headline read, "Ali's Back and So Is Boxing." In the article, he wrote that one thing was certain. Heavyweight boxing was "alive again." He also made it clear just who was responsible for bringing it back to life.

"It [boxing] is alive because Ali is back in full cry," said Grimsley.

The sentiment was obviously shared by the majority of boxing journalists working the fight. Most had readily jumped in to validate the Ali win. But I was sure there had to have been some trusted commentators back then capable of seeing through the mass desire for an Ali resurrection.

As a New York boy, my first inclination was to turn to the *New York Times*. It has always been my personal "newspaper of record." That meant checking out the original reporting and commentary of two of the most esteemed sportswriters of any time, Red Smith and his fellow Pulitzer Prize–winning colleague Dave Anderson. Both had been at ringside to cover the fight. And both had some very definite opinions on who deserved to win and why.

Red Smith wasted no time, in his "Sports of the Times" column on January 29, 1974, in challenging the validity of the Muhammad Ali unanimous decision. He began the piece by noting that many in the sold-out crowd sitting closer to the action disagreed with the officials, and they might have included Ali's own trainer. Smith observed that Angelo Dundee desperately communicated his take on the fight to his backpedaling fighter in the final round.

"You gotta stop him to win!" Dundee yelled at Ali.

Smith obviously saw the scoring for the fight going into the last round in much the same way. He also agreed with Joe Frazier's assessment that Ali's power just "wasn't there." In essence, he thought it looked like Ali was throwing a lot of scoring shots to the fans way up in the cheap seats. But, at ringside, Smith said he clearly saw most of them as just ineffective love taps.

Red Smith said his scorecard showed seven rounds for Frazier and five rounds for Ali in the end. He defended his take on the outcome with a basic question for every fight fan and boxing official.

"Do aggressiveness and heavy hitting cancel out several light shots when the shooter is running away?" Smith asked.

Dave Anderson filed a straightforward report on the Rematch the day after the fight. There were no judgments made in the piece about the decision. But that all changed in *his* "Sports of the Times" column on January 30, 1974.

"Joe Frazier thought he won," wrote Anderson. "So did this ringside seat's scorecard, which had him ahead 6 rounds to 5 with one even. Perhaps the referee and the two judges, in their unanimity, were influenced subconsciously by Ali's persistent dispute with the 1971 verdict. . . . Perhaps he had the referee and judges more aware of the number of punches, rather than their effect, than they usually are."

Both Smith and Anderson saw it as a close fight, but both clearly saw it for Joe Frazier. The officials scoring the fight had seen it as relatively close as well. Even so, they were unanimous and unyielding in their support for Ali. I decided it was time to see for myself if Joe had actually been robbed—in this fight and, perhaps, in discerning his rightful place in boxing history.

Like most American boxing fans, I had originally watched Ali-Frazier II on the *ABC Wide World of Sports* broadcast. Back then, I was absorbed in the action but didn't bother to keep careful track of who won which rounds. I was now determined to go back and rectify that. Luckily, all these years later, I found a video of the entire program posted on YouTube, complete with commentary from the inimitable Howard Cosell.

I had interviewed Cosell in the late seventies for an article on *Monday Night Football*. I recalled that he got stuck on one point and just would not stop talking about it. I literally couldn't get a question in edgewise as his diatribe went on and on. He was knowledgeable, but his voice left room for little else.

So, this time around, I decided to basically tune Cosell out. It allowed me to more fully weigh the action in each round exactly as I saw it with a minimum of outside influence. I stopped after each round to see where my scorecard deviated from the findings of the fight officials. It was eye opening to see how wrong they appeared to be at times in their assessments.

The tone for the Rematch was actually set five days before the opening bell. Frazier had joined Ali in ABC's New York studio to go over film from their first bout, with Cosell serving as referee. While viewing the 11th round, Ali had called Frazier "ignorant." That had set Joe off, and the two eventually wound up in a bear hug, rolling on the studio floor. The animosity, at least on Joe's part, was real. And Ali continued to employ that wrestling approach throughout the real fight to come.

The scoring for the fight followed a "per-round system"—with a supplemental point system in place in the case of a tie based on the round scores. This allowed an official to give a fighter an extra point for winning a particularly lopsided round.

Judge Tony Castellano wound up giving Muhammad Ali the greatest margin of victory. He scored the fight seven rounds for Ali, four for Frazier, and one even. Judge Jack Gordon had it slightly closer at 7–5–0 in favor of Ali.

And the young referee Tony Perez barely gave Ali the edge at six rounds to five with one even.

All three officials gave the first two rounds to Ali, and I did too. But it was based more on Joe's typical lack of activity early on, as a slow starter, than any damage done by Ali. Yet certain patterns for the fight were set in those rounds.

Frazier continually pursued Ali across the ring. Ali backed away while trying to unload light combos with nothing meaningful landing. Joe occasionally connected with a lunging left or solid body punch and moved in for more. Ali responded by wrapping up Joe's left arm, smothering any additional threat, while pressing down on his neck with the other hand to sap his energy.

In the final moments of the first round, Ali caught Joe coming in with a right lead and quick combo that looked impressive but carried little power. Yet it was enough to excite the heavily pro-Ali crowd. It also seemed just enough for me to award Ali this mostly feeling-out round.

The second round followed a somewhat similar script. Frazier connected early with a light hook to the face while chasing Ali across the ring. Ali stood his ground momentarily to throw some long jabs at a bobbing and weaving Frazier before dancing away. Midway through the round, Joe scored with a solid left hook to the belly, his most effective punch in the first fight, and Ali once again grabbed his opponent's arm and neck. Joe, as always, played the aggressor but still seemed too stingy with his punches.

Still, with under a minute left, the round looked pretty much even. Joe then got caught with a good right to the head while charging in and staggered back a bit. Ali, pursuing for the first time in the fight, missed badly with a couple of follow-up punches before finally connecting with one more light shot. Referee Tony Perez suddenly ended the round early at this point, and both fighters went to their corners. The referee, quickly realizing his mistake, had them come back for 10 more uneventful seconds.

After the bout, many Ali supporters touted this as their fighter's best round. They insinuated Joe was in trouble and survived only because of the referee's error. Some even suggested there were grounds for awarding Ali an extra point. None of that was true.

Yes, Ali caught Joe with one fairly effective punch that caused him to stumble. But, despite all the ballyhoo, Joe was never seriously hurt or in any kind of trouble.

Both the referee and judge Jack Gordon gave round three to Frazier, but Tony Castellano somehow saw it as Ali's. It made me wonder just what Castellano had been watching. Joe dominated the round from the start. He charged out right away and landed a hard right-and-left-hook combination to the body. Ali responded with a soft combo of his own and a whole lot of holding.

Midway through the round, Frazier caught Ali with a strong left to the jaw that snapped his head back, and he did the same moments later. Joe also worked well to the body and clearly did some damage. He missed with a sweeping hook to the head as time ran down but then grazed Ali with a lunging hook. Ali's only answer was some powerless taps while in retreat.

Will Grimsley, in his AP article, bent over backward to give Ali the edge where possible. But even he had to acknowledge Joe's prowess in the third round. "It was a round he won," wrote Grimsley, "twice jarring Ali's head back with vicious left hooks and pounding telling blows into Muhammad's mid-section."

Round three had put Joe Frazier back in the fight. Yet it was the heavily disputed rounds four, five, and six, and a couple near the end, that essentially decided the match for all three officials and me. They were the difference between a comfortable but competitive win as opposed to a crushing defeat. And I was determined to assess them in an honest, neutral light.

Rounds seven and eight were awarded to Frazier by all three officials. Rounds nine and 11 were universally given to Ali. I saw no glaring reasons to challenge those unanimous views. So, I approached the five most disputed rounds with Ali leading 4–3–0 on my card.

Round four was seen as "even" by Castellano and the referee. Judge Gordon felt compelled to give it to Ali. I was two-thirds through the round and ready to call it even as well. Ali came out fast throwing some light left-right combos that Joe caught on his gloves. Ali moved a lot in the round, danced more than usual, and impressed the crowd. But Joe also landed some heavy body shots that forced Ali to go back to his holding strategy.

With under a minute left, Joe pursued Ali to the corner and bobbed under a lazy hook to rise up with a solid left hook of his own to the face and a short, hard right to the body. Both punches landed and did some damage. Ali danced away from Joe and held a lot from there on. In the final seconds, Joe struck with a few more body shots in close, and Ali landed a very light jab to the face that got an undeserved rise from the MSG crowd.

Joe scored with more forceful punches in the round and, especially, down the stretch. Joe was clearly the aggressor again in this round. No doubt Joe won the round in that last minute. My scorecard now read 4–4–0. I had the fight dead even at this point.

Joe charged out and immediately backed Ali across the ring to begin round five. He scored with a solid right to Ali's ribs and a stinging left to the face. Ali started to back away again and, when he stopped to throw a flurry of taps, Joe connected with another left hook to the face. Ali was now in full retreat with Joe in pursuit.

For the first time, some in the crowd sensed Ali might be in trouble, and Frazier supporters took heart. They yelled, "C'mon Joe," and "He can't run forever." Ali seemed desperate in the way he held on to Joe at times.

Midway through the round, Ali stopped to stand his ground and throw long jabs that missed badly. Frazier ducked under one and popped a right hook to the body. Ali backed into the corner again and attempted some light jabs that missed. With a minute to go in the round, Joe landed another straight right to the face, and Ali spent most of the final seconds in one desperate clinch after another.

By the end of the round, even Cosell bemoaned Ali's lack of movement and all the time he spent against the ropes. Judge Gordon and the referee surprisingly gave the round to Ali. Castellano had it for Frazier. I scored it easily for Frazier and now had Smokin' Joe ahead five rounds to four.

In round six, two of the three officials—Judge Castellano and the referee—again went for Ali with Gordon giving Frazier the nod. I saw the pros and cons for each fighter in this round. Ali connected with an early jab to the face and some taps up high as Frazier moved in to land strong body shots. Ali's jabs were easier to see and drew a buzz from the crowd. But Joe's less flashy body punches put Ali back into the grab-and-hold mode and did a bit more damage. Joe seemed to be motioning that Ali's punches lacked power at this point.

Later in the round, Frazier backed Ali into the corner and flashed a light combination to the face. Ali held on and tried to follow with several gentle flurries that caught only air. With time running down, Joe connected twice again to Ali's face; the response was more holding.

Frazier's punches to the face and body were stronger, more effective in the round. Yet Ali stepped up his activity level despite the continued holding. Even though I thought Joe earned a slight edge, I scored the round as even. Frazier now led 5-4-1 with only two rounds left to analyze.

Two of the three fight officials had given both round 10 and 12 to Frazier. My only question was how *anyone* could justify giving either round to Ali.

Frazier began the 10th by backing Ali into the ropes and scoring with a short left hook to the chin. He then chased Ali to the opposite corner and threw a lunging right squarely to the chin followed by a light combination to the face. Many in the crowd roared for Joe. Ali simply reverted to holding again and again.

Ali now had blood coming from a cut on the cheek under the right eye. Frazier, sensing an opening, threw another lunging hook at a retreating Ali that grazed his face. When Ali tried to clinch, Joe pummeled his ribs with short, stinging hooks. Ali's decision to once again tie his opponent up drew boos from the audience. Later, after viewing a tape of the fight, Joe's trainer Eddie Futch said he counted well over 100 times that Ali initiated a clinch without having points deducted.

Ali danced and jabbed away in the last seconds of the round, but nothing landed. When he grabbed Frazier to prevent a punishing response, boos started up again. Joe ended his dominant 10th round with a sold left hook to Ali's face. I now had Joe up 6-4-1.

In the final round, both fighters came out throwing multipunch combinations. Ali's lighter shots were caught by Frazier's arms. Frazier connected with a couple of short hooks but missed dramatically with some wild lefts and rights. Joe later pursued Ali to the ropes and shook him with a hard hook to the face. Joe, showing some desperation of his own, seemed to be going for the knockout.

The more Frazier pressed the action in the round, the more Ali backed off and held. Frazier occasionally pushed through and connected with light shots to the body and face, but the attacks usually ended in another Ali armlock. At one point, Ali was allowed to hold for more than 20 seconds before Frazier managed to break free. Ali seemed to be resting in these clinches and looked exhausted near the end.

Frazier, energized but frustrated, stayed the aggressor down the stretch. He backed Ali in the corner and once again caught his chin with a lunging right. After more holding from Ali, Frazier scored with body shots and a left to the head.

In the final moments of the fight, Frazier blocked an Ali hook and countered with a straight left to the face. He then bounced Ali's head back with a right to the chin. Ali, appropriately enough, finished off the contest by locking up Frazier until the bell sounded.

Joe Frazier's demeanor while waiting for the decision was clear. He thought he had won. My 7–4–1 scorecard supported Joe's confidence at the time. It also lent credence to his later claims of being robbed.

My analysis of the match made me wonder what might have happened if the fight plans had been reversed. Could Joe have won on the officials' scorecards by using Ali's tap-run-and-hold technique? The answer was certainly no—it wouldn't have made a difference. Heck, barring a knockout or a number of knockdowns, it seemed the officials meant for Ali to win this career-saving match no matter what.

From my perspective, the boxing record books may merit revisiting. At the very least, there may be some grounds for putting an asterisk next to Joe Frazier's ranking on the hierarchy of greatest heavyweights. And they might want to place another asterisk next to Muhammad Ali's place on the top of the list.

————

Just before the second show at the posh club, Ken Johnson came by to remind me that I should be ready to head to the airport later that night. He had told me yesterday that Anheuser-Busch, the maker of Natural Light beer, had notified them about an important Thursday meeting in New York at noon. It had to do with Joe's series of high-profile television commercials that included other sports legends like Mickey Mantle and Walt Frazier, among others. And, given the time constraints, it was obvious that the three of us would have to fly there.

Joe's first reaction was to try to find a way to drive to New York on time while still honoring that night's commitment to the club. He had even made a frantic request that a high-ranking state trooper arrange a police escort after the show to Georgia's northern border. He had hoped to then drive 100 miles per hour straight through to a Washington, D.C., Metroliner bound for New York. That plan had failed from the start.

"I wouldn't even do that for the president," the state trooper had replied.

After the second performance, Joe was still in denial about the impending flight. He certainly wasn't happy about being snatched from the afterglow of the show to prepare for the New York trip. He eventually went back to the motel but later escaped for a while by promising to buy candy for the whole crew.

By 2:00 a.m., despite loud objections, Kenny finally convinced the boss that this trip was happening. Joe, now deflated, agreed to take the 4:37 a.m. shuttle flight to Atlanta before flying on to New York. That meant two takeoffs and two landings for Joe to survive.

Joe began to openly talk about his fear and decided he had to get seriously drunk. He figured the alcohol might knock him out and allow him to fall asleep on the plane before taking to the air. It didn't quite work out that way.

When we piled into Big Red for the ride to the airport, Joe's bulk took up most of the backseat. Kenny, tucked behind the wheel, told me to climb into the back next to Joe. He said my job was to keep the reeling fighter calm.

Joe was wearing a three-piece suit without a shirt and had his suede fedora with a feather nearby. As we approached the airport, Joe's anxiety level visibly climbed and he began to rock back and forth. I tried to give him as much room as possible.

"You're not going to get me on that plane, White Writer!" Joe suddenly yelled as he pinned me to the rear passenger-side door with a beefy forearm.

I told him that was okay with me. And that he shouldn't worry.

"You're not getting me on that plane!" he repeated.

Kenny finally pulled over and came back to calm Joe. He convinced him to sit back and finish the ride. Joe meant no harm, and I doubt he even knew what he was doing. But Joe's fears and mine at that moment were certainly real.

At the nearly deserted airport, Joe stood glassy eyed against a wall with the plumed fedora now atop his head. "God didn't intend us to fly," he muttered.

Joe had earlier told me that his fear was based on his need to be in control. When Joe was driving, he took control of maintaining and steering the car. With planes, he had to trust someone else to do those things correctly. He was not comfortable with giving someone else that power over him.

Kenny bought two seats up front in the small plane and one a bit farther back. At boarding time, Ken and I each rested a hand on one of Joe's arms and half coaxed, half begged him to get on board. Ken agreed to sit with Joe, and I retreated to the other seat.

The early morning plane was just about empty. Yet, strangely enough, the two men sitting behind me turned out to be the famous singing duo Sam and Dave. This was the same pair of soul singers who recorded huge crossover hits like "Soul Man," "Hold On, I'm Comin'," and "I Thank You" during their prime.

The singers seemed to know Joe and were amused but sympathetic to his plight. Halfway through the short flight, Kenny came back and said he needed a break from Joe's agitated state and sharp elbows. He sent me to temporarily take his place. Half-kidding, I asked Sam and Dave if they would calm Joe with a song. They laughed and declined.

Sam Moore and Dave Prater broke up the act the next year. According to an April 13, 1988, *New York Times* obituary, Prater was later killed behind the wheel of a car that veered off Interstate 75 near Sycamore, Georgia, and struck a tree. He was 50 and likely visiting his mother who lived in Ocilla, Georgia.

Somehow, we eventually got Joe to Atlanta safe and sound. Kenny continued to mellow him out prior to the second flight to New York. Joe seemed somewhat braver and calmer as he boarded.

Joe Frazier and his road manager flew in a proper first-class section on that plane. I thankfully wound up in coach.

6

Lessons on Beating a Bear

On March 28, about a week after returning from Augusta, I was back in Joe's North Philadelphia gym. The boss and Kenny were down south again with the tour. With Joe gone, his son seemed particularly relaxed, enjoying the heightened attention from those around him. He also looked locked in on his big amateur fights coming up and worked comfortably with trainer George Benton to get ready.

In two weeks, Marvis had the Regional Semi-Finals of the 1980 AAU Heavyweight Championship. The Regional Finals were scheduled for the week after that. One key goal for this year was for Marvis to win the National AAU title and the recognition as the United States amateur heavyweight champ that went with it. After that, it was supposed to be on to the Olympic Trials in June, glory at the Moscow Games, and—by Joe's account—the debut of a rewarding professional career thereafter.

Exactly a week before, however, Marvis's dream of winning gold in the up-coming Olympics had been all but shattered. It had suddenly become highly unlikely that he would ever get to team up with Joe as the first father and son Olympic heavyweight boxing champions. He should have been devastated. I had expected to find a despondent kid with no desire to train. That clearly was not the case.

President Jimmy Carter had officially informed an elite group of American athletes and coaches on March 21 that the United States planned to boycott the 1980 Summer Olympics in Moscow. The announcement was prompted by the Soviet Union's refusal to adhere to Carter's February 20 deadline to withdraw its troops from Afghanistan. The Russians had invaded Afghanistan in December 1979 to supposedly support the country's pro-Soviet government against threats from Islamic fighters. Carter saw the invasion as more of a "stepping stone to [Soviet] control over [Afghanistan's] oil supplies."

In his speech, Carter had admitted that he wasn't sure what other countries would do about the boycott. He even acknowledged the possibility that some athletes from the United States might try to make an end run around the boycott by competing under a neutral Olympic flag. The president argued against that strategy given the resolve of the U.S. government and the nation. He pointed out that Congress had "voted overwhelmingly, almost unanimously" to approve the Olympic boycott, reflecting the will of the American people.

Marvis's first reaction was a qualified optimism—at least when he talked to me. He reminded me there were still almost four months until the start of the Summer Olympics on July 19. That left plenty of time for the president and his advisors to find a political solution or to show their displeasure in another way. If that failed, he talked about how he might stay amateur for four more years and compete in the 1984 Olympics in Los Angeles. And, of course, he had the option of succumbing to pressure from Benton and his father to turn professional.

I had already been dealing with a slew of heartbreaking phone calls from Olympic hopefuls all week. The calls were a by-product of a widely circulated Summer Olympics cover story I wrote for the Sunday magazine *Family Weekly* in June 1979. The article, predicting the fortunes of the top American athletes set to compete in Moscow, had appeared in over 360 newspapers nationwide. The athletes I had befriended either wanted to bemoan the loss of years of work and sacrifice or ask me about the chances of a reversal by Carter. Most didn't have a pile of family money or a promising pro career to fall back on.

George Benton, embracing his fighter's optimism, had already stepped up the intensity of Marvis's workouts in preparation for the AAU and Olympic Trial fights. Despite Joe's protests, the trainer insisted Marvis spar more often with up-and-coming pro heavyweights. Benton believed that if Marvis could hold his own against these more dangerous fighters, amateur opponents would have less of a chance to do damage. He also realized Marvis might be battling exclusively with pro fighters sooner than they had originally expected.

Marvis was initially scheduled to spar with Michael Dokes that day. The 6'3", 220-pound fighter was widely considered a heavyweight champion in the making. He was currently 17–0 as a professional with an impressive win over Jimmy Young. He also had a promising televised exhibition bout against Muhammad Ali that opened a lot of promoters' eyes. Dokes was trained by Benton and had been in the ring with Marvis several times in the previous weeks.

Unfortunately, Dokes had to leave early. That left Marvis matched up with Dwight Triplett. He was another pro prospect signed to a management contract by Joe Frazier. Triplett came into the ring that day at 180 but usually fought as a 175-pound light heavyweight. His record showed only 35 amateur fights, but he had already posted a draw and a victory in two pro contests.

What the record didn't show was the kind of toughness Triplett brought to the ring after spending time in jail. He was on a work-release program under Benton's supervision. George worried that Marvis might feel the need to match Dwight's jailhouse aggression. He didn't want Marvis to charge straight forward like his dad when challenged.

Benton began by reminding his fighter to box, to use his left hand more effectively, and to make Dwight miss on his jabs.

"He knows how to fight and rip," said Benton, looking over to Marvis. "But now I want to see him get back to boxing. He gets into too many fights and he forgets about defense. He knows how to do everything, but now he has to learn how to stay cool."

I didn't see the problem with fighting and ripping. It seemed to me the whole idea of boxing was to mix it up and get into some nose-to-nose fights— especially when you could hit as hard as Marvis.

"He gets reckless, [gets] hit unnecessarily," said Benton. "Sometimes [that] makes an easy fight tough. In the amateurs, you got to get your hands going. You don't have to knock guys out—just outpoint them."

Benton noted that a lot of the kids in the amateur ranks made the same kind of mistake. He said they "constantly throw hard" and think "offense is their defense." He felt Marvis was too good a fighter to waste his energy on that approach.

"I want Marvis to be more polished, a pro-looking boxer," said Benton.

Before the sparring match began, Marvis confirmed that he had heard George clearly and he would work on his jab.

I followed up by asking what exactly he wanted to do with the jab today.

Marvis looked at me wide eyed, like I was stupid or crazy. "Hit him with it!" he said, pointing to Dwight.

Then he laughed loudly and nudged my shoulder in jest.

————

George Benton stood next to me at ringside as the sparring match began and provided a running commentary throughout the three rounds. In the first round, he purposely emphasized some of the things that made Marvis such a promising prospect.

For starters, Benton alerted me to the kid's prowess as a counterpuncher—even against an opponent with a two-inch height advantage and three-inch greater reach. On cue, Marvis went into a shell to draw Dwight's off-balance lead jab. Then he connected with a clean counterpunch followed by a leap inside to do more damage.

"The other man is taller, so Marvis [always] stays just within his own [punching] range," said Benton. "So, he can counter [while] he slips and slides and catches punches. Marvis probes with his jab and makes his opening [to move inside]—like a surgeon."

I wondered why George had his fighter moving straight in on the counterattack all the time. Wouldn't some side-to-side action have made him more unpredictable, dangerous?

Benton shook his head and offered me a boxing lesson.

"Marvis only moves side to side when it is necessary," the trainer said. "When a man is firing right at you, you stand directly in front of him and duck, dodge, catch, and slip punches. You only move side to side when your man is in a shell and you're trying to open him up."

Benton turned to face me and slipped into a tight boxing stance.

"Move to one side, hit!" he said, throwing a strong left jab and sliding laterally. "Other [side], hit! Marvis has more thrust in his jabs because he plants in front of his man."

Later in the round, Marvis led with a low jab that brought Dwight's hands down and opened up room for a straight right to the nose. He continued to pop in and out effectively with what Benton called his "direct technique." But, as time ran down, a couple of looping hooks invited a particularly heavy exchange. And Marvis got hit with some jolting shots to the body.

Between rounds, Benton told his fighter to keep his elbows closer in, and then turned to me to explain.

"[Keeping the elbows in] gives more power—tighter punches," said George, leaning toward me. "Also tightens up his defense of his body. Head down, left arm pulled in closer to protect the stomach."

Benton had Marvis working up and down in the second round. "First body, then head," he yelled, and the kid complied with crisp jabs to the midsection and neck.

Marvis, on demand, also mixed in a series of fakes with his jabs. Benton wanted to throw Dwight off balance and make him nervous.

"Can't see where or when the jab is coming," said George, about the effect of the fakes. "Makes Dwight edgy, miss, start overdefending. Then underdefending to compensate for the fakes."

In the final round, Marvis was backed into his corner trading punches with a suddenly more aggressive opponent. He instinctively covered up in a "rock-a-baby" crouch behind high hands and elbows. George nodded his approval. And he gave a giddy laugh when Marvis finally exploded, bobbing and weaving, out of the corner with a sustained left-right flurry.

Benton opted for the third round to run long. He liked the way Marvis had stepped in close to throw shorter, harder shots near the end. His fighter grunted with each blow. The kid kept the barrage of hooks and uppercuts coming until time was called.

"That's finishing strong!" said George.

———

Benton's reaction made me wonder why Marvis didn't whale away like this to close every fight. Hell, I mused, why not finish off most key rounds with both fists flying?

"You can make an easy fight the hardest fight in the world," said Benton, warning me against a one-style-fits-all approach. "You can get one of those little, strong *bearish* guys—like Joe Frazier. And it doesn't make any sense to get in there and grind with him if you don't have to. And Marvis doesn't have to grind with anybody. He's got the height and he can box."

Benton said "the bears"—Joe in particular—always wanted bigger, leaner fighters, like Ali or Marvis, to stand in close with them and mix it up. He noted that the guys with the bear physique—"a short body; short, thick arms; and stumpy legs"—had to be on top of their opponent to win. Marvis, on the other hand, had the option to use his speed and range to move, counterpunch, go in tight when openings appeared, and then get safely away.

George abruptly turned to Marvis and offered him a little ditty on the dangers of standing toe to toe with bearish guys like his dad.

"He who fights and stands his ground might not last another round," he sang.

I laughed—Marvis didn't.

Benton credited Joe Frazier's ability to work his compact, bearish body inside against taller, quicker boxers like Ali as the key to his greatness. Once inside the taller fighter's jab, Joe usually landed devastating hooks to the body. George said these body shots sapped the life out his opponent and inevitably brought the guard down. This, of course, allowed Joe to reach the bigger man's head.

The trainer smiled at the thought. He marveled at how Joe had managed to make his bearish features an asset rather than a terrible liability.

According to Benton, George Foreman had been the only boxer to totally frustrate Joe Frazier and keep him at bay. Benton saw Foreman's first bout with Frazier as a veritable master class in how to beat a bear in the ring. It had taken place in Kingston, Jamaica, on January 22, 1973, and came to be known as "the Sunshine Showdown." It had matched the undefeated heavyweight champion Frazier (29–0) against the unbeaten, number one WBA and WBC contender. Foreman had won his first 37 fights, and 34 had been by knockouts.

Foreman, listed as 6'3", was four inches taller than Frazier and had a much longer reach. But Joe had just proven he could overcome those impediments with a convincing win against Muhammad Ali in the Fight of the Century. It had been Foreman's superior strength and punching power that made him the true bear killer that day. Joe had never faced a taller, longer-limbed opponent who could both outmuscle him and hit harder.

As usual, Joe Frazier's fight plan had called for him to get inside and smash the body. Foreman had used his strength from the outset to keep Frazier pinned outside. That had left Joe just inside his opponent's jabbing range but forced to lunge to make contact of his own. This had allowed Foreman to stay back and pick his shots. The onslaught began less than two minutes into the fight.

Foreman had initially jolted Frazier with a flurry of punches that culminated with a right uppercut, a stunning knockdown, and a mandatory eight-count. Foreman immediately continued his attack and soon put Joe down again with another uppercut. As Joe got to his feet, Foreman landed a combination that put him down for the third time. When the bell rang, Joe had somehow managed to survive the round on sheer guts and willpower.

The Foreman formula for beating a bear had called for constant pressure, no breathing room. Not surprisingly, Foreman began the second round by charging in with an overhand right that put Joe down. The champ reached his feet, but Foreman quickly pounced and leveled him again. The final knockdown had come moments later after another stunning right hand connected. The referee had finally stopped the slaughter at 1:35 of the second round.

Foreman had knocked Frazier down three times in a span of 35 seconds in the first round. Big George had sent Joe to the canvas six times during a four-minute period in the fight.

Foreman had made the point of his boxing lesson crystal clear in Jamaica. When a bear failed to penetrate a taller, stronger fighter's defense, the only way to go was down. That lesson had cost Joe Frazier the heavyweight title he had won from Ali and his undefeated record.

———

After the sparring match, Dwight walked over to compliment his opponent. "I don't know what you're doing, but boy did you look sharp, much better today," he said. Dwight particularly liked the way Marvis had ducked smartly under a roundhouse in the second round to deliver two quick hooks.

During the chat with Dwight, Marvis was toweled off by an old fighter turned trainer named Mickey Grandinetti. Mickey, who boxed in the 1930s and '40s, claimed to have fought more than 200 amateur matches with only two losses. He said he had never lost in his relatively short time as a pro.

Grandinetti talked about how he had watched a lot of the great ones early in their careers. He considered Marvis one of the best amateur heavyweights he had ever seen. He singled out one of Marvis's recent workouts against Michael Dokes as proof of his potential.

"Marvis looked good with Dokes, holding his own all the time," said Mickey, watching Marvis go off to skip rope. "With some seasoning, he could give Dokes a fight. Marvis is the best amateur in the world."

The old boxing man then compared Marvis to Joe at a similar time in his amateur years.

"I think he's much better than his dad [at that time]," said Mickey, noting the kid's polish and toughness. "There's nothing to stop him from being the heavyweight champ. In a year and a half, he could be fighting for the title. [He's] too overanxious now, but he got the guns, can take the punch."

As we spoke, I noticed that Grandinetti's forehead and eyebrows seemed particularly puffy all these years later. It reminded me of the way the middleweight champion Gene Fullmer had looked near the end of an especially brutal career. I wondered if it had been the physical punishment that had prompted Grandinetti to exit the ring prematurely.

"Nah," said Mickey, claiming it wasn't the punches that had hurt the most. He blamed the lack of money for pushing him out of the game. "My biggest purse was $500. In boxing, timing is everything. And it was just the wrong time for boxing."

Grandinetti credited the first Ali-Frazier fight for dramatically raising the purses for heavyweight title bouts—and eventually for all of pro boxing. He recalled that the Fight of the Century drew a huge international audience via closed-circuit venues. That, in turn, had changed the way big fights in all weight classes got promoted.

In Mickey's view, the economics of boxing had historically broken down to two clearly defined eras. There was the pre–Ali vs. Frazier period and then the years after their first fight. And it was much better financially for those boxers who came after Frazier's initial clash with Ali.

————

The workout ended, and Marvis headed for the showers. This allowed me to sit down with George Benton for our first in-depth interview. He began by talking about his 21-year career as a savvy middleweight who had fought most of the really good boxers in his weight class from 1949 to 1970. Remarkably, as the number one contender for many years, he had beaten three world champions without ever getting an official championship fight of his own.

Benton blamed the emphasis on nepotism over talent back in the day. The rampant racism in deciding who got a title shot didn't help either. For example, after he had topped Joey Giardello back in 1962, Benton appeared in line to fight Dick Tiger for the championship. But Giardello's manager, Lou Duva, finagled the title match for his white fighter instead.

"Yeah, I screwed George out of his shot," admitted Duva in a 1992 article about Benton titled "The Master" in *Sports Illustrated.* "He didn't even know about it until I told him many years later."

George might not have known about *all* the behind-the-scenes efforts to screw him over during his career. But he certainly knew the score and who called the shots.

"At the time, there was a lot of politics involved," said the ex-fighter, who had been in the ring with the likes of Bennie Briscoe, Jimmy Ellis, and Rubin "Hurricane" Carter. "Either you were in or not. Used to be that certain people decided who got shots and who didn't. It depended on who your manager, trainer was then."

Benton admitted things still weren't perfect. However, he saw the boxing game as moving in the right direction. The Ali-Frazier matches had again played a major part in that improvement. The trainer saw how their rivalry made things better for every professional boxer—and especially for fighters of color.

"Today there's more money, exposure, and awareness," said George. "Fighters have more respect for themselves—and their lawyers get them more respect. Boxing used to be the kind of sport where it was glamorous for a businessman to be at ringside, but not managing a boxer. A racehorse, football or baseball team was a different story."

George Benton had been forced to hang up his gloves in 1970, not too long before Ali first came back to fight Frazier. But, unlike Mickey Grandinetti, the decision had nothing to do with tiny paychecks or even missed title bouts. George had been shot in the back by a man who had a dispute with members of his family. After years of failed operations, the bullet had remained imbedded just inches from his spinal column. And it was still there.

The ex-fighter had first learned the ins and outs of being a trainer by studying with some of the best in the business. In fact, he had been in Joe Frazier's corner for the Thrilla in Manila as the assistant trainer under Eddie Futch. In the years after that, he had trained great fighters like Leon Spinks and eventually Meldrick Taylor, Pernell Whitaker, and Evander Holyfield. His ingenious tactics had soon earned him the nickname "the Professor."

Benton currently saw himself as a "free-agent trainer." He spent a lot of time working for Joe and with Marvis. But he also attended to a growing stable of top professional fighters—several of whom were ranked or likely to be in contention for a title at some point soon. Yet Marvis held a special place in the trainer's heart.

"In the beginning, I treated Marvis just like any other kid," said Benton, remembering what it had been like to teach Joe Frazier's son how to box. "Being a Philadelphia kid, he knew his boxing and had plenty of competition. All over the world the Philadelphia boxers are put on a pedestal. But watching Marvis grow was like easing into big money."

I gave him a quizzical look.

"One day you have a hundred dollars," George said. "Then a week later another hundred, then a week later another hundred, then another. You don't suddenly get rich. You grow into big-time money without making any startling jumps. You don't get excited about Marvis because his growth is so steady and a bit at a time. But it adds up. He can go all the way."

I expected Benton to compare Marvis in some way to his dad. But he likened Marvis's demeanor to Joe's boyhood hero instead—both outside and in the ring.

"Marvis's mannerisms are similar to Joe Louis," said George. "[He's] warm, level, easygoing—not flamboyant. When boxing, like Joe Louis, he's all business, strong, keeps his eye on ya, stalks ya, never smiles. Looks like he's ready to break you in half. But Marvis moves better than Louis."

The trainer admitted to often hitting heads with Joe about how the kid should fight. He implied that Papa Frazier treated his son like a version of himself. Joe always wanted him to adopt his bearlike style. Benton said that meant pressing Marvis to "stay stationary in front of the man" and move straight in to "overpower the guy" just like Joe would.

George then smiled and confessed to a system he had worked out with Marvis. It was meant to prevent the kid from succumbing to the pressure to swarm opponents when his dad looked on. The trainer told his fighter to nod his head in the ring at whatever Joe said. But he was to only follow instructions that came from the corner.

"Appeasement," said George. "Keep [the] boss and old man happy."

I wondered how much it would actually hurt for Marvis to listen to his dad, to try to please him. After all, Joe *was* the heavyweight champ.

"This is a touchy conversation," confessed George. "The one fight Marvis lost was because he was fighting the way his father wanted—not the way I told him it should be fought. He was hooking and swarming when he should have been moving and jabbing."

I recollected that Joe had seen Benton as responsible for that loss to Tony Tubbs when we first talked up in the lair. Now I was a whole lot less sure who should get the blame.

Benton said that despite the boss's success in the ring, he really didn't have much finesse or flexibility in his attack. Now he wanted his son to take on the same plodding approach. The trainer said this showed that Joe Frazier was not equipped to instruct Marvis on how to take the next big steps up to the professional ranks.

"All Joe knew was to come straight forward," said George, down in a crouch and moving in my direction. "Joe Frazier was a tank coming right at you. All you could tell your fighter was to get in shape because this guy is attacking."

"Oh yeah," I said. "What would you tell your fighter about preparing for Marvis?"

"I'd tell my fighter to watch Marvis because he, and his punches, come from all angles," replied George. "Marvis has to box these guys and hurt them before he swarms in on them. Marvis is deceptive. He doesn't punch as hard as his father now. But as he thickens, and gets older, he might hit as hard as Joe."

Benton explained his startling projection about the kid's future punching power.

"He should be 212 [turning pro] and Joe only weighed 190 for his first fight," said George. "When I first got Marvis he was only 165 pounds at 15. He'll eventually be 210 or 212 but look 225."

Benton paused seemingly lost in thought. Finally, he acknowledged that above all else Marvis had to become "a thinking boxer." He wanted him to be able to adjust on the fly to whatever his opponent threw at him. And he implied that the kid would never become that thinking fighter under his dad's tutelage.

The interview moved on to Marvis's choices after the Olympic Trials if the American boycott continued. I repeated Marvis's desire to go to college and stay amateur until the 1984 Games rather than turn professional. The push to go pro had become more urgent in the Frazier camp in the last week. I just assumed the impetus for the move was coming from Joe.

I told Benton that I had been against Marvis turning pro from the start. I said I couldn't understand why the son of a famous millionaire, with brains and a good heart, would risk his health against hungry pro fighters. I admitted that Joe had gotten annoyed whenever I broached the subject with Marvis. It turned out the trainer didn't love my view of things either.

"Honest to God, it would be the biggest mistake in the world for Marvis to hang around for 1984," said George, the passion rising in his voice. "The longer you stay in the amateurs the worse you get. You can only get so good in the amateurs. Only going three rounds, having to fight straight up, can only punch a certain way, all that bowing and scraping to the judges."

George Benton took a breath and summed up what he feared most about Marvis's plan to wait for the next Olympics. He worried that Marvis would become one of those great young fighters who spent their best years in the amateurs fighting inferior competition.

"Plenty of fighters have left *it* in the amateurs," he warned.

––––––––––

As the interview with Benton wound down, Marvis returned from the lair. He was dressed for a trip down south with his family. He said everyone wanted to get away a little early for the Easter holidays. We agreed to cram in one of our quick chats before he took off.

The conversation rambled from Joe's financial support of the extended family to the way employees reacted to Marvis as the boss when Joe wasn't around. It then took a surprising turn to the kid's apparent desire to marry young like his dad. In the end, it lighted on issues of race and the constant pressure of being Joe Frazier's son.

Marvis remembered first growing up in a "tough, black neighborhood" not far from North Philadelphia that he categorized economically as "lower middle class." He lived there from age four until he turned 10. After that, he moved to the mostly white, more affluent White Marsh community. He talked freely about the challenges both environments offered.

"I have found that all people, blacks, whites, greens, and yellows, are going to say dumb or mean or ignorant things," said Marvis. "You have to be mature and ignore it. You handle ignorance with maturity."

Surprisingly, Marvis remembered being picked on more in the poorer black area.

"I used to have my lunch money taken away from me in school," said Marvis with an embarrassed shrug. "And all the kids wanted to beat me up or fight with me to see if I was tough like my father. I was always being chased home from school."

Marvis paused, and a smile spread across his face as he relived the victory. "I finally got a white German shepherd, and he went to town on those guys."

"So, you never were a fighter as a kid in the black neighborhood?" I asked.

"No, but I was good runner," replied Marvis, grinning at the memory.

Marvis saw the move to the upscale community more like a tenuous transition at first rather than an escape. He had no idea how the white people of White Marsh would react to him.

"I thought I'd be fighting there too," said Marvis. "But they treated me like some kind of hero. It was like 'Wow, you're really *his* son.' It was a combination of the black kids being a bit jealous of what we had and I was older when I went to the white neighborhood."

After almost a decade in White Marsh, Marvis now claimed to have a clearer perspective on how the relocation had impacted his upbringing.

"The move there was a big bonus for me educationally, and as far as getting a well-rounded knowledge of people," he said, referring to the advantages of attending a top private school. "It gave me a chance to accept who I am and to be at ease with white people who might have been foreign to me otherwise. I can be friends with anybody now."

Marvis said he was unsure about Joe's comfort level living in White Marsh. His dad just wasn't around enough for him to get a reading.

"Dad's a goer," he said. "He's not comfortable unless he's on the move. All his life he's been running, doing something."

Marvis never seemed to embrace that wanderlust. He mused about finding his own path. This got me back to what Benton said about staying too long in the amateurs—to what Marvis saw for himself after the Olympic Trials.

"If I can do anything next year, I would go to school for business," said Marvis. "The money, and businesses, my father has waiting for me is like blood money. I am looking forward to getting out on my own rather than being dependent [on dad]. Mom says, 'It's your life—do what *you* want to do.' I can still see myself marrying young, but it has to be to the right person. Somebody who can deal with being married to a businessman—or a fighter."

We finished up and Marvis turned to head for the exit. But before he could leave, someone pointed out a pile of flyers next to the ring. They featured a photo of Lonnie Young. He was a local American-team boxer who had died recently in the plane crash in Poland.

The flyers announced Young's upcoming funeral arrangements. This prompted a discussion with other fighters nearby about the official services for the boxing team at Andrews Air Force Base. Marvis turned solemn and promised to meet them all there.

Before he left for his trip down south, Marvis noted that there were worse things to deal with in life and sports than an Olympic boycott.

7

In the Shadow of Champions

Exactly two weeks later, on April 11, I returned to Joe Frazier's gym to meet
Marvis. He was my ride to the Pennsylvania National Guard Armory for the
AAU Eastern Regional Semi-Finals. Marvis was running a bit late and Joe had
remained on the road with the band. Trainer George Benton had taken off
as well to revitalize the career of a recently slumping Jimmy Young. That left
Yank Durham's old business associate, Morty Holtzer, to greet me upstairs
in the outer office.

Holtzer had been with Joe pretty much every step of the way since the
beginning of his amateur career in 1962. Now he said Joe had him penciled
in to handle the business aspects of Marvis's career whenever the kid turned
professional. Morty believed Marvis had all the intangibles for an easier
transition to the pro ranks than Joe. After all, he saw Marvis as much more
worldly and polished than his dad at a comparable age.

"Joe couldn't shake his dirt-poor upbringing," said Morty, recalling those
early years. "You'd walk into his bathroom on the road and there'd be socks
and underwear hanging out to dry. That's how he initially spent his leisure
time. In the beginning, before a fight, Joe would go back to his room at 9 p.m.
and read the Bible while everybody else partied."

Holtzer credited Joe Frazier's relationship with Yank Durham for ultimately widening the boxer's view of the world. He also saw the trainer as the
true key to Frazier's fighting success. He said they were closer than any fighter

and trainer he had ever seen. And, unlike Marvis, Morty suggested Joe needed that all-consuming relationship with his trainer to move forward.

"I think they were *closer* than father and son," said Morty, without denigrating the relationship of Joe and Marvis. "Anything Yank told Joe to do, he would do. Yank always had Joe do things his way. He brought Joe the championship."

My only impressions of Yank Durham up to now had come from photos. I knew he was a husky black man with a pleasant smile. And, of course, he had a great reputation as a trainer. But how did Morty remember him?

Morty thought for a moment and then stood with his hands stretched high over his head.

"He was a *big* man, over six feet tall and over 200 pounds," he said. "Yank was a welder for the Pennsylvania Railroad. Hell, he sparred with Joe Louis. The three of us [Yank, Joe, and Morty] were like brothers."

"You and Joe must really miss him," I said.

"We all loved each other," said Morty. "White, black—don't mean nothing. At Yank's funeral, Joe and I held each other at the grave. When they put Yank down, we both cried."

Holtzer went on to talk about the traditions Yank Durham had created. He felt those traditions had gone a long way toward shaping Joe's attitude toward boxing, and adult life in general.

"After every fight Joe fought as a pro, we had a party," said Morty. "That was the [Yank] thing—*big* parties! [Joe] didn't drink much, but he got the taste of busting loose after a fight."

Morty paused for a moment before continuing. "After Yank died, Joe didn't look like the same fighter. [He] lost something."

Holtzer said the after-fight party was one of Yank's traditions that stayed strong following his death. He thought Joe saw it as a kind of salute to his old mentor. He used events from the aftermath of the Thrilla in Manila to show how passionate Joe was about honoring that tradition.

"In Manila, Joe's eyes swelled shut [in the final rounds]," said Morty. "Joe didn't cut, he swelled. That's why Ed Futch stopped the fight."

According to Morty, Joe ignored the pleas of those around him to recuperate in his hotel room or a hospital after the fight. Instead, he insisted on attending an official celebration at the palace of President Marcos. Joe went with a heavy dose of medicine in his eyes, accompanied by Marvis, Florence,

Morty, and the rest. He even made a point of trying to sound upbeat when he ran into Muhammad Ali at the event.

When they left the palace, Joe was supposed to go back to bed at the hotel. But he found out about a big party in his honor at the penthouse of the Hyatt Regency. Then, despite all reason, he decided to attend that party as well.

"We said he couldn't go," said Morty. "His eyes were swelled shut—he couldn't see. But there were about a thousand people up there and Joe wouldn't let them down. They were all in his corner."

Here the order of events got a bit sketchy. But Holtzer was on a roll, and his description of Joe's desire to party punched through. So I just went with his flow.

"Joe said, 'Help me get dressed or I'll go the way I am,'" said Morty, suggesting the fighter had no longer been dressed to party. "We helped him get the tuxedo on. His hands were sore, [his] ribs and whole body ached. He promised me in the elevator that he would just get up there and sit quietly in the corner. [He would] let us bring people over to him."

"How did that go?" I asked.

"As soon as we walked in, he tore his arm away from me," said Morty. "He said, 'All right sucker, I'm dancing!' And he grabbed Flo and started dancing. And he was in agony all over. And then he got up and sang [for the crowd]."

Morty recalled finally getting Joe to sit down, but it took some time and effort. "[Sportswriter] Dick Schaap said, 'You better get him to sit down or he'll pass out.' But Joe seemed happy. He said, 'Nobody is going to party without me.'"

———

Marvis finally arrived a few minutes later. He refused to admit to being late. He claimed to be just following his typical fight-day routine.

The kid said he purposely slept late on fight days. He relaxed, watched television, and never thought about the upcoming fight. The day before the match he also stuck to a really short workout routine. It was all about staying calm and conserving his energy for what he had to do.

Marvis was dressed in his blue USA team warm-up suit with the red, white, and blue stripes. It had an AAU patch on the front and "USA" emblazoned on the back. He had been given the outfit as a member of the boxing team that competed in Tokyo.

The warm-up suit went well with the sky-blue, 1976 Caddy Seville Marvis used to drive us to the National Guard Armory. He told me the car had been a present from his father for his 16th birthday. When we pulled in front of the armory, a group of young guardsmen ogled the Caddy. It stood out in sharp contrast to the military trucks, khaki Jeeps, and more modest cars owned by the other amateur boxers. Marvis seemed accustomed to standing out at a relatively low-profile boxing event like this.

In the armory, we walked down a beige corridor leading to a large, stark room where the prefight check-in took place. Marvis was flanked by Val Colbert, George Benton's assistant trainer, and a stone-faced family bodyguard named Ed Harrell. If Marvis was upset by Joe's absence or Benton's other commitment, he initially didn't show it.

Marvis nonchalantly mentioned that Benton was at the Playboy Club in New Jersey training Jimmy Young for a recently rescheduled fight with contender Gerry Cooney. What's more, his father had been home only once in the past two weeks, for a quick pit stop.

I asked if Joe had called to give some advice about this must-win fight tonight.

"I haven't heard from dad in a few days," said Marvis with a dismissive shrug. "I'm not sure exactly *where* he is."

The check-in space also served as the tournament business office and a holding pen/changing room for the 40 or so muscular street kids and their handlers. In truth, it was just a converted classroom, complete with chalkboards, encased in cinderblock walls and lit by harsh fluorescent lights. The room filled up quickly with twitchy competitors, noise, and a whirl of activity soon after we arrived.

Most of the fighters ran to queue up for weigh-ins and physicals and to officially get their draw for the evening. Others playfully baited each other or moved around the room snapping towels and fooling around. Many of the media-starved boxers could be heard bragging loudly to each other about obscure wins or explaining away troubling defeats. Their graying trainers, who usually handled several fighters in attendance, played would-be promoter to anyone who could remotely do any good. This included a young writer desperate to just fade into the woodwork.

Marvis, the only boxer with a dedicated team of handlers, remained the calm in the storm. He silently weighed in at 200 pounds and awaited his turn for a cursory physical examination. The doctor, who knew Marvis's name before he gave it, quickly checked his blood pressure, heart, lungs, peripheral vision, and depth perception. He nodded his approval as he moved along.

The doctor also had to ask each fighter if he had won or lost his last bout. Marvis was the only one I heard confess to a loss. The doctor smiled in recognition.

"I knew that," said the doctor. He looked up and admitted to having seen the Tubbs fight on television.

After all the preliminaries, Marvis retreated to the far corner of the room, yawned, and slipped on a pair of mirrored sunglasses to deflect the glare of the lights. Harrell, one of Joe's long-trusted "Grey Wolves" and a former Philadelphia police officer, set up two chairs for his charge. Marvis sat down on one and propped his feet up on the other as the ex-cop folded a towel behind his head. Colbert and Harrell took a chair on either side of Marvis to insulate him.

It was six o'clock and still two hours away from the first fight on the agenda. Marvis hoped to sleep away the hours until his night-capping contest—the 19th bout on the card. That fight had been scheduled for around 11:00 p.m., which meant hopefully being ignored for five hours. Unfortunately, in this very public lair, Marvis Frazier was the man.

Several boxers elbowed each other and gave you-know-who-that-is nods, as Marvis crossed his arms, stretched his legs, and worked to shut them out. Some inched toward his stronghold, offered short-armed waves, and did silly things to get his attention. And every 10 minutes or so one mustered the nerve to reach out and nudge the slumbering number-one heavyweight amateur in the country to shake his hand.

Every time Marv gave a sign of recognition, the other fighter lit up with pride. About 80 percent of the young fighters in the room were black, and Marvis knew they identified with him, looked up to him. He seemed painfully aware of his status but fought to maintain his prefight routine. So the king of the amateurs kept the exchanges low key, cordial, and short.

It took a visit from a scrawny, little kid to break through Marvis's defenses. The boy woke the heavyweight with a hug and wished him luck. Marv startled at first then broke into a broad smile. The two chatted away like old friends for several minutes.

"That nine-year-old is fantastic," he said, acknowledging me for the first time in more than an hour. "He does the Ali shuffle, zinging the left hand, [throws] combinations."

I took the opportunity to ask Marvis directly if Joe's absence annoyed him. Did he resent his dad opting for the road over being there with him at the arena?

"No, not at all," he insisted, shoving the sunglasses above his forehead. "I have my job and my dad has a job to do."

His recital smacked of Joe's regular rhetoric, and I took it as such. "If his job permits him to be at my job, that's good," Marvis said. "But, if he can't, I understand."

Marvis considered my next question about the crowded holding room. Did they jam 40 fighters together in a big bullpen at the National AAU and Golden Gloves Tournaments?

"In the [National] Golden Gloves, we started out in a room with 167 cots," said Marvis, eying the comparably empty holding room here. "Next round there are 100, then 50, until only 24 cots [remain]. If you're still lying there, you made it to the Final."

En route to his 1979 National Golden Gloves Championship, Marvis had beaten both Tim Witherspoon and James "Bonecrusher" Smith in the Pennsylvania Tournament. Both were destined to become champions as professionals. He had also beaten highly regarded Jimmy Clark in the Eastern Regionals.

Our conversation was suddenly interrupted by one of the other boxers. He offered Marvis a shot of honey, pure energy. Marvis opened his mouth and accepted a squirt from a squeeze bottle. With that, he yawned widely, slipped the sunglasses over his eyes, and went back to looking for those elusive few moments of sleep.

At eight o'clock, it was finally fight time. As the bouts began, patrons jostled and outflanked each other to grab one of the chairs around the spotlighted ring. Florence Frazier opted to move farther back in the anonymous shadows of the bleachers.

Joe's wife was surrounded by two of her four daughters and some friends. The short, prim woman caressed the recently adopted four-year-old Skeeter, who fidgeted in her arms. When Florence talked, she was firm and explicit about her feelings.

"No, I'm not thrilled that Marvis is fighting," she said, fixing me with an intense stare. "I'm usually fine until Marvis gets into the ring. Then, I get jittery, nervous, shaking, and everything else. I watch every move in the ring. I don't think I miss anything."

Florence bristled at the notion that she and Marvis were too easygoing. I suggested that they tended to give in to Joe's demands—whether or not it was something they liked.

"Marvis is like I am, a Smith," said Florence, alluding to her maiden name. "We are shy, responsible people, who are just as determined as the Fraziers. They are two personalities that naturally collide." Florence's tone warned me that too much of her was invested in Marvis for her to just be bumped aside. "Whatever each sets out to do, they do!"

In the ring, a slicing right dropped a battered lightweight. The spectators roared with approval. Florence fell silent. Conversely, a quiet lull in the violence perked her up.

Marvis's mother started to outline an optimistic plan that put her son in college and outside the ring for quite some time. She seemed to seize on the boycott and the odds against the Olympics working out.

"His personality has remained about the same since he started to box," said Florence, talking about her son as a good, fun-loving person. "But it has drawn him away from other things. I would like him to spend four years in school, get a better education. Get into the business end of the gym and help Joe with different businesses he has."

I raised the possibility of an imminent professional fighting career bumping college aside.

"We don't talk that much boxing in *my* house!" Florence's voice took a particularly sharp tone. "I don't know how much pressure is on Marvis to turn pro."

One combative issue she elected not to avoid was her husband's absence.

"I think he [Marvis] resents Joe being on the road so much," Florence said, not bothering to mask her own resentment. "But he's the type of young man that doesn't say what he feels. He respects Joe so he holds back telling Joe what he would like him to do. I know he would want Joe to be around for the fight tonight, but he would never say it."

Florence suggested that Joe had made a conscious decision not to attend this fight. And Marvis saw it as part of a familiar pattern.

"[Marvis] feels that Joe is always out doing what *he wants to do*," said Florence, showing a rare spark of anger. "I think deep down Marvis is hurt by Joe not being here or spending more time with him."

Later, I felt compelled to report Flo's views about how she saw the next four years to Marvis. Against Joe's specific orders, I once again pushed my agenda about Marvis opting for college over a professional boxing career. This was overstepping my role as a reporter. But I found myself more and more concerned about the kid's future and safety—and talking to his mom didn't help.

At eleven o'clock, Marvis rose and removed his USA warm-up suit. He slipped on the knee-length, Philadelphia-style, black velour trunks with the "MF" monogram his mother had crocheted over the thigh. Only four of the biggest amateur gladiators now awaited their turn in the arena.

Marvis crooned a spiritual learned in the church choir while Val Colbert bandaged his hands. He then shook out his arms and circled while shooting a few jabs and skipping over an imaginary rope. Colbert reminded Marvis of Benton's classic boxer fake-and-jab-jab-jab strategy. It was meant to offset Joe's put-down-the-head-and-charge teachings. Both relied on the "matador and bull" analogy, but in Benton's scenario Marvis was holding the cape.

Marvis and I talked about the images that went through his head prior to a fight like this. Did he visualize his famous dad throwing vicious hooks or combinations like back in the gym?

"No way," Marvis replied, reacting as if I were crazy. "I *only* image me. Hell, I'm the one going in there. He gets in the imaging only when *he's* fighting."

Marvis then got up and rifled off a barrage of straight, hard jabs into Val's open hands. The impact reverberated across the room. He danced a bit more and repeated the onslaught with some shifty jukes thrown in.

None of this was lost on Marvis's sullen challenger, Johnny Lee Pitts, sitting on the other side of the holding room. Pitts, "The Greatest" emblazoned on his white robe, had lost a decision to Frazier just six months earlier. In the spirit of his namesake, Muhammad Ali, he had bragged moments ago of a weight, strength, and know-how advantage over Marvis. He also claimed that the decision in that previous fight should have gone his way.

But, as the match drew near, the bravado evaporated. There was an air of impending doom instead.

"I felt I should have stopped him," said Marvis, reflecting on his last run-in with the 24-year-old, 210-pound Pitts. "He was afraid of me. Scared to death. He got hit hard the first round, then ran the next two."

The assistant director of this AAU event had seen the Frazier-Pitts fight in Cherry Hill, New Jersey. He said it was a good fight, but Marvis won all the way.

"He can give Marvis a little trouble," the official surmised. "Last time Pitts tried to swarm, but I think he'll run today."

I got the impression that beating up on Ali wannabes had become fairly commonplace for Joe Frazier's son. He certainly didn't react much to the irony of going into the ring with someone sporting "The Greatest" on his robe.

Johnny Pitts ultimately walked into the arena without ceremony—just his solo handler by his side.

Marvis, however, followed in the midst of a full, traditional procession. Morty and another of Marvis's trainers, Sam Hickman, had come back to see their fighter just before showtime and got recruited into the group. Ed Harrell went out ahead to clear the way.

Marvis, resting his gloves on Val's shoulders, fell in behind Morty and Sam, and I gladly brought up the rear. We snaked, conga line–style, through the long corridor leading to the arena curtain. The group seemed charged with purpose and ceremony, and I could see Marvis loved it. We all somberly put our heads down and shuffled out toward the noise.

The fight went exactly according to the Benton script. The Greatest was dazed in the first round, was pummeled in the second, and cowered in the third. Florence Frazier prayed before the action, twitched during the exchanges, and cheered the decision.

———

One week later, on April 18, Joe Frazier was in Philadelphia for his son's AAU Regional Finals bout. He had come back the day before. The question was just how much back Joe really seemed to be.

At 7:15 p.m., Marvis and his crew were encamped against the same far wall of the holding pen as the previous week. Marvis and Val reclined sleepily while Ed Harrell and some boxers from the gym settled in nearby to watch typical fighter fare, *The Newlywed Game*, on a portable television. Joe was nowhere in sight. In fact, he had been just out of reach all day.

Before Marvis was able to nod off, I asked had he spoken with his dad about last week's fight or the upcoming bout?

"Nah, we didn't talk about the fights or his trip," said Marvis, with a what-can-you-do shrug. "Dad ate breakfast with me in mostly silence and said, 'I'll see you later on.' That was it."

The kid shook his head and laughed. "That was it! He split!"

It turned out Marvis had been home relaxing during the day. He had been sticking to his fight-day routine. His dad had used most of that time to do a serious workout in the gym. I interpreted the session as perhaps another indication that Joe had a comeback on his mind.

Marvis said he had stopped by the gym at 5:00 p.m. to pick up his mouth-piece. But he and Joe had still not talked. He had instead met up with his entourage for the drive to the armory.

Although George Benton had been back to work with Marvis during the week, he was not at the arena that evening to greet his fighter. The trainer was once again on the road with Jimmy Young. Marvis gave no indication of being put out by Benton's disappearing act.

"He's been back all week and he's been working with me on my jab," said Marvis. "He feels the AAU fights are a good place to practice my outside fight—to work safely on my boxing ability. I felt I was a little sloppy last week. I intend to use my jab more tonight."

Marvis claimed that Joe, whenever he showed up, would not influence his fight plan in Benton's absence.

"Val's my trainer tonight," he said, glancing over at Colbert. "So, tonight I follow his instructions—not my dad's or George's from yesterday. I don't think Pop would put his nose in it. George and Val are the ones who work with me every day. And Pop's not there enough to know exactly what I *can or can't do*."

I didn't offer a comment, but I was definitely taken aback. It was the first time I had heard Marvis so clearly minimize Joe's input—especially due to his time away from the gym.

Joe Frazier, resplendent in his beige three-piece suit, open brown shirt, and feathered suede hat, finally made an appearance close to nine o'clock.

He straddled the outermost chair in the Frazier corner of the room without greeting his son. But he sure as hell greeted everyone else. In fact, Joe's arrival generated an instant, all-consuming excitement in the room. And shifted all attention away from Marvis.

Right away a local reporter knelt at the ex-champ's feet. Before the journalist was able to ask a question, Joe decided to conduct some business. He introduced his business partner George Figueroa. The man mumbled about some plans in the works for a chicken-and-ribs franchise called Smokin' Joe's Corner.

The reporter feigned interest for a moment and then got down to business. He wanted to know about comebacks. What about Ali's comeback? What about Joe's comeback? When would the two rivals meet?

Joe smiled, gave vague nonanswers, and kept breaking away to interact with the crowd forming around him. Half-dressed finalists waiting for their fights mixed with young fans vying for autographs. At one point, Joe brandished a huge fist at a little kid shoving a piece of paper in his face.

"Hey, you back again," Joe mugged, gradually softening his threatening glare. "This is your third autograph. You sellin' 'em?"

Everyone laughed—even Marvis.

––––––––––

The excitement in the armory soared when word got out that Joe Frazier was in the house. It later climbed yet another notch when current heavyweight champion Larry Holmes also entered the building. Holmes's younger brother Mark, one of Marvis's close friends, was a finalist in the 156-pound class.

This prompted the local reporter to return to the holding pen to ask more questions about Muhammad Ali's chances against Larry Holmes in his planned comeback. Joe surprisingly painted a picture of Ali getting stronger and Holmes "worse" in recent months.

"Ali has a good shot at him." Joe now said, contradicting what he told me up in the lair in March. Joe later claimed Holmes "doesn't have a takeout shot."

That seemed like real news to the fight people in the room. After all, Holmes was undefeated as a professional at the time. He had won 25 of his 34 fights by knockouts. That included KOs or TKOs in his six straight title defenses since taking the WBC crown from Ken Norton in June 1978.

Joe hung around for a few more minutes and then took off. He didn't say anything directly to his son before departing.

I wondered what Joe's friend Larry Holmes would think of his fight assessment. But I decided not to ask when the reigning champ dropped into the holding pen a bit later to wish Marvis luck. However, I did ask how far he thought Marvis might be from a pro title shot.

"I saw Marvis fight Tubbs in Atlantic City," said Holmes, looking over at his friend's son. "He's a good prospect because he's very aggressive. Joe's bringing him along just right. I think he's going to be up there."

"Can you predict when?" I asked.

"I would say Marvis is about two years away from the top 10 [pro heavyweights]."

"Do you see a title fight against Marvis in your future?" I asked, softening the question with a smile.

"I don't think I'll be stepping into the ring with him someday because I won't be around that long," said Larry, in an attempt to be diplomatic. "I'm gonna take the money and run. I don't want to worry about a Marvis Frazier in two years."

Once the night's fights got under way, Holmes made one more appearance in the dressing room. It was right after his brother lost his match. The champ's presence caused a commotion and allowed Mark time to gather himself. Marvis also moved in next to his friend to console him.

After Larry Holmes left and his friend Mark seemed good, Marvis slipped the hood of his white terry cloth robe over his head. He then faded back against the white wall and practically disappeared. He again came across as calm and aloof. For the moment, he was out of the shadow of the two champions.

––––––––

Joe didn't return to the holding pen until after the 15th fight at about 11:30 p.m. He held the hand of little Skeeter, who wore a Superman shirt. Joe did some play sparring with the boy and pretended to be rocked by a slapping right hand. Skeeter ran to his big brother afterward. Joe soon retrieved Skeeter and headed out again without talking to Marvis.

A while later, Joe agreed to present a trophy to the light heavyweight winner at the center of the ring. He received a standing ovation from everyone in the crowd, except his wife. Florence Frazier had apparently picked up on the strained vibe between her husband and oldest child. She sat passively in her seat, clearly unimpressed with Joe's behavior tonight.

At just after midnight, Joe finally stopped in to talk to Marvis. It was minutes before his son had to go out for the final fight on the card. Joe's advice sounded colorful but somewhat superficial. He basically warned Marvis about not taking his opponent too lightly.

"Even if you're in there with your mother, you go out there and crucify her." Joe balled his fist. "The name of the game is *fight!* Eighteen years I fought and the worst injuries usually came in the gym, not the ring—when you're just fooling around, playing with some kid."

Joe paused and waited for a response from his son. After a prolonged silence, he continued.

"See what he does, stay on top of him," said Joe, pressing his point. "Don't waste punches."

Marvis didn't say anything, and Joe abruptly left to talk to someone out in the corridor. Marvis shook his head and started dancing, pumping his arms, jumping up and down. Little Skeeter came in and wanted his brother to pick him up, but Marvis just smiled while he continued to work up a lather and threw a couple of mock jabs. He put on his headgear, and his friends from the gym crowded around him, pumping him up. Joe grabbed Skeeter and drifted to the outer reaches of the room before leaving to sign more autographs.

Val, in his final instructions, reminded Marvis how disappointing his jab had been the week before. He said if the jab had been more effective, Marvis would have knocked that guy out. He urged his fighter to stick the jab over and over again tonight.

"Joe yells instructions from the audience, but it doesn't matter because Marvis can't hear what he's saying," Val said in a confidential tone. "He's concentrating on what I told him and his opponent. Every fighter has a key. Between rounds I try to tell Marvis what I think the key is to the guy he's fighting."

Marvis's opponent in the heavyweight finals was a relatively inexperienced 20-year-old named Ricardo Peterson. He came in at 198 pounds and had the ability to stick and move. He also had showed some real power in previous fights, but not against the likes of a Marvis Frazier.

"I have psyched myself up to believe he's just flesh and bone," said Peterson, when I asked if he was afraid. "He's a man and I'm a man, you know." There was a definite quiver in his voice.

The trainer for Peterson began his prefight remarks in an even more hesitant fashion.

"We can't run anywhere," he said. "We can't hide. Everything should be easier after this."

The trainer's words turned out to be prophetic. There was no place for his overmatched fighter to hide. And, in case Peterson tried to block out what was coming, the announcer introduced Marvis as "the number one amateur heavyweight in the country."

Marvis started by faithfully channeling his trainer's instructions with several measured jabs that gradually grew sharper and more stinging—first to the stomach and then the chest. He kept bending low to work the body. He soon mixed in a couple of hard hooks to go with the now jackhammer jabs that landed in spurts. There was no brawling, but Peterson was clearly hurt, tottering, and defenseless at the end of the first round.

Joe, positioned two rows behind Marvis's corner and a good 50 feet from Florence's reproach, sensed a knockout in the making as the second round began. He whipped off his hat and screamed, "Cut off the ring! Cut off the ring!" His son responded by suddenly abandoning his game plan. Three heavy rights allowed Marvis to swarm in, unloading double-barreled hooks.

When the fight was stopped, Marvis looked immediately for Joe's reaction. The boss nodded abruptly and got up to join the family. Skeeter shot past Joe into the ring and wrapped his arms around his brother's leg.

Val Colbert shook his head and didn't seem all that pleased. For better or worse, Joe was back. He was here for the glory bouts that lay just ahead.

———

After the fight, Joe, Flo, Marvis, and friends headed for a North Philadelphia nightclub to celebrate. Larry Holmes joined the group later on, but his brother Mark and Marvis bailed to find their own fun. Marvis also had a girlfriend he wanted to see.

Marvis dropped the older crowd off in a limousine and stayed in the car as it sped off. So much for sharing a long-awaited triumph with Joe.

The band members at the club had a history with Joe Frazier. They had performed with him a while back. The band leader greeted Joe's arrival with a musical salute and introduced him to the crowd as the "once and always heavyweight champ." Joe received a prolonged, standing ovation. It was as if the Philadelphia boxer had never retired.

The band leader invited Joe up to sing. He surprisingly demurred and chose to sit and chat with the club's manager instead. A while later, before the festivities got into full swing, Joe and Larry Holmes slipped away to a mostly empty bar area. I decided to go along with them.

Joe soon ambushed his old friend and former sparring partner with a big request. He asked Larry not to retire without giving Marvis a shot at the heavyweight title. Holmes didn't answer right away and seemed openly uncomfortable.

Larry said he would never want to hurt Marvis. He reminded Joe about how long he knew his son. But Joe replied that Marvis's safety was his concern. Larry had to just promise to give his son the title shot.

Holmes pointed out that once a fighter stepped into the ring, he had to protect himself. He said nothing was more dangerous than holding back in a fight. He warned Joe that if he ever fought Marvis, he would have to do everything necessary to win. Larry worried that would include having to hurt Marvis really bad.

The conversation ended with Joe apparently unwilling to take no for an answer.

8

Bumpy Roads
to Olympic Glory

In early May, Marvis Frazier flew with trainer Sam Hickman and other regional winners to the National AAU Boxing Tournament in Las Vegas. George Benton was still concentrating on his professional fighters. He felt confident that his top amateur heavyweight would prevail without him.

Joe Frazier, holding fast to his new resolve "to be there" for his son, drove cross-country to witness the milestone event. His sacrifice was immediately rewarded. Marvis began the run to the national amateur title with two, quick, brutal first-round knockouts.

On Saturday, May 10, 1980, Marvis met the highly touted Chris McDonald in the Finals of the heavyweight division. The husky, 6'1" New England fighter weighed in at about 210 pounds and had a reputation as a hard, natural hitter. He had just recently turned 17 years old, but boxing commentators were already pushing him as the next Great White Hope for a future World Heavyweight Championship.

Before the fight, Joe reportedly urged his son to stay focused, patient, and on top of his opponent from the start. It reminded me of what Joe had told me the first day we met. He had lectured me about the differences in strategy needed for winning a professional main event as opposed to a big amateur bout like this.

"In the pros you can pace yourself over 10 rounds," Joe said at the time. "In the amateurs you got nine minutes to get the job done. But you have to remember it only takes one good punch to give you victory. You must take your time and put together your punches. Some of these kids get foolish and throw wild, crazy punches."

I had asked Joe if he was more disciplined than Marvis as an amateur. He had laughed at that one.

"I've seen Marvis take his time, measure a guy and bang, bang! Put him away with two shots," Joe had said, pounding his fist into his open palm. "A lot of kids, including me when I was just starting out, would come out wildly swinging without a true feeling for the tempo of the sport. Marv, he's got all the ability and experience he would need to pick apart anybody he has to face."

With Joe in the audience, Marvis stayed true to his dad's words and methodically picked McDonald apart. In fact, he totally ignored the prefight hype and went into slaughter mode from the opening bell. Marvis spent three butcher-shop rounds viciously chopping away at the White Hope and his future aspirations. After each round, he eagerly looked at Joe for emphasis and approval.

Marvis took a lopsided three-round decision from McDonald to capture the 1980 National AAU Heavyweight Championship. The day clearly belonged to him and his father. For Marvis, it was a confirmation of his number one amateur ranking and vindication for that single loss to Tony Tubbs people still referenced. For Joe, it represented a national title to further smooth his son's lucrative transition to what should be big paydays ahead.

This was especially important now to Joe because the American boycott of the 1980 Moscow Olympics still had not been reversed. What's more, the Muhammad Ali Amateur Sports Club had already become the first such group to officially support the boycott. Its track athletes and boxers, like Tony Tubbs, had agreed to follow Ali's wishes. None of them would compete in any event that included Soviet Union competitors. The pressure for Marvis and Joe to conform to this policy was enormous.

At the end of their Las Vegas stay, Marvis opted to ride shotgun with his dad all the way back to Philadelphia rather than fly home. It was a show of family solidarity that turned out to be short lived.

On the phone with me after returning to Philly, Marvis still talked about winning a meaningful Olympic trial. But he also said he saw college and staying amateur until the 1984 Olympics as an alternative if the boycott held. Joe only talked about the plans to take his son pro.

———

Joe Frazier's own amateur boxing career rivaled his son's in titles and accomplishments. However, those glory days didn't start until Yank Durham and associates had made some dramatic changes to their young prospect's conditioning, mechanics, and fighting style. In fact, Morty Holtzer admitted to being downright disappointed with his first look at Joe.

"Yank called me to Philadelphia to see a fighter in the 23rd precinct gym," said Holtzer, smiling at his recollection of the 18-year-old. "Joe looked like a big barrel of you-know-what. I never thought he had the talent to be a fighter. But he had determination."

Frazier had first come to the Police Athletic League (PAL) gym weighing a blubbery 230 pounds. His original idea had been to maybe lose some weight and get in shape. There had initially been no talk of a boxing career of any kind.

The manager of the gym was a tough, retired policeman named Duke Dugent. He immediately pushed Frazier to give boxing a try and, fairly soon, threw him in the ring with one of the biggest guys around. Joe had mentioned more than once how that big guy kicked his backside.

The beating was a rude awakening for young Billy Boy, who had whupped all rivals in his South Carolina farmland community. It graphically showed him how much he had to learn about the art of boxing. Yet, instead of dampening Joe's desire to fight, the thrashing fired up his competitive spirit. He committed, on the spot, to doing whatever it would take to win in the ring.

Yank Durham was working part-time, mostly nights, as a trainer at the PAL gym in 1962. During the day, he had his job as a welder for the railroad. Durham noticed after a while that Joe's boxing technique kept improving. The big hitter on the heavy bag had also started to spar with the other heavyweights at the gym. And he had soon run out of big boys to pound on.

Yank's solution to Joe's competition problem was to pit him against some of the lighter boxers. He convinced the lumbering heavyweight to tie his powerful left hand down by his side. This guaranteed that Joe wouldn't be putting the smaller guys in the hospital. It also forced Joe to move more smoothly, and with more agility, when chasing these faster fighters around.

Yank, after a while, finally decided to commit to managing and training Joe. They relied on a simple handshake to seal the deal. This was when Joe's conditioning routines jumped up to yet another level, recalled Holtzer.

"We told him to run at 5 a.m. every morning," said Morty, during our original chat at the gym. "Yank and I would go drinking at night and park in front of Joe's house. He would be out there at a quarter to five, ready to go. He did it religiously."

According to Holtzer, Yank soon recognized the killer power in his young boxer's left hook. He knew few boxers at that level could defend themselves against it. That was especially true when those hooks came in bunches.

Holtzer described how Yank worked diligently to get Joe to fire flurries of left and right hooks nonstop. The expectation was that any amateur the kid met would soon cave under the pressure. The trainer figured these inexperienced boxers couldn't mount much of an attack if they were busy fending off sledgehammer hooks to save their lives.

Of course, all that sustained punching took superior stamina. That explained why Yank emphasized conditioning above all else. It allowed his novice to be successful while still perfecting his basic boxing skills.

Some of the more exotic early training methods developed by Joe Frazier and Yank drew quite a bit of attention. Two, in particular, became immortalized in the Oscar-winning movie *Rocky* in 1976. In the film, a Philadelphia club fighter, just like Frazier back in the day, worked at a slaughterhouse, again just like Joe. The title character also copied Joe by taking his training runs to the streets of the city.

Frazier talked about his workouts at the slaughterhouse, and the connection to Sylvester Stallone's movie, in a 2008 interview with the *Guardian*. The comments were later included in a 2011 piece for the *Hollywood Reporter* as well.

"I was the drain man," said Joe. "My job was to make sure the blood went down the drain. But sometimes, early in the morning, I'd go down the long rail of meat and work on my punching. That's how Stallone got the idea for Rocky—just like he used the story about me training by running up the steps of the museum in Philly."

Although he was given a cameo role in the film, Frazier resented not earning anything for his contribution to Rocky's backstory. He made his feelings about that clear in the same interview.

"He never paid me for none of my past," said Joe. "I only got paid for a walk-on part. *Rocky* is a sad story for me."

Ironically, the same sports publicist who initially introduced me to Joe Frazier in 1980 had also arranged for me to attend the New York City press premiere of *Rocky II* the year before. After the movie, my wife and I wound up chatting with Stallone and costar Carl Weathers over cocktails at a Manhattan steakhouse. Stallone made mention of Frazier in the course of a story. And Weathers talked about how his character Apollo Creed owed a lot to Muhammad Ali.

Joe Frazier fought regularly as an amateur from 1962 to 1964. Yank Durham booked his still raw boxer into all kinds of funky venues, anywhere the competition helped to hone his skills and move him forward. Frazier fully embraced Yank's plan and began to build his reputation as a heavy hitter.

Florence remembered those early fighting days somewhat less fondly than Joe. She said Marvis got treated like royalty compared to Joe and the other amateurs back then.

"We would go to Allentown, Pennsylvania, and rural places in New Jersey for state fairs," said Florence, when we had spoken at her son's AAU Eastern Regional Semi-Finals. "You know, rings set up outside, barns and stalls of food and animals all around."

I asked what else stood out for her from those fairground fights.

"At the time, Joe would get a hot dog and Coke to hold him for the day," she said. "Now Sam Hickman takes the kids and gets them complete dinners. All Joe's teammates would work full-time jobs and have to get time [off] from work, and have to be up early the next day to work. When Joe started, he was at a sheet metal place. Then he got the better job out at the meatpacking company."

Joe had been forced to stay closer to home for tournaments than Marvis did as an amateur. He had more limited financial resources for travel. Even so, Joe won the 1962, 1963, and 1964 Middle Atlantic Golden Gloves Heavyweight Championships. His three-year amateur record, prior to the 1964 Olympic Trials, was typically listed as a dominant 38–1. Record keeping in the amateur ranks had been known to get a bit sketchy in those years.

Young Joe's sole "official" loss came at the hands of jumbo Buster Mathis. The heavyweight from Grand Rapids, Michigan, stood 6'3" and tipped the scales at about 300 pounds. The "Fat Boy," as Joe sometimes called him, had a loose, somewhat flabby physique. As a result, Joe and others made the understandable mistake of underestimating his speed and mobility.

On this occasion Mathis surprised Frazier with his quick hands, graceful moves, and nonstop activity. He just kept jabbing away. Joe reportedly did more damage with his heavy hands, but Mathis beat him on points.

Some sources ascribed another "unconfirmed" amateur loss to Frazier in 1963. It supposedly took place at the National AAU Tournament in a three-round bout with Tony "Irish" Doyle. He was a tough 6'4" fighter from Utah who eventually lost to Vic Brown in the Finals that year. Doyle wound up winning six Golden Gloves and AAU titles while posting a record of 51–5 as an amateur.

Joe never admitted to the amateur loss to the Irishman during our conversations. But he certainly relished his second-round dismantling of Doyle as a professional. In part, that was due to the memorable time and place Smokin' Joe had chosen to exact his revenge.

Frazier's pro fight against Doyle topped the card at the first ever boxing event at the newly opened Philadelphia Spectrum. This was to be the city's premier fight venue—its answer to New York's Madison Square Garden. The headliner on this night had to be a top Philly fighter and one of the biggest draws in boxing.

It was October 17, 1967, and Muhammad Ali had recently been stripped of his heavyweight title for refusing military service. Joe, already aiming to fill that void, came in as the number-one contender. The victory over Doyle left him still undefeated at 18–0 and moving toward an inevitable championship shot.

According to a *Philadelphia Daily News* piece the day after the fight, Frazier landed a crushing left hook early in round two and Doyle "came apart like a shattered mirror." Reporter Tom Cushman went on to describe how Doyle managed to pull himself together and get up from the first knockdown of his career. But Joe immediately unloaded a barrage of punches that sent his opponent falling down into the arms of referee Zach Clayton, who stopped the fight.

In October 2007, an ESPN.com piece came out to commemorate the 40th anniversary of that first big bout at the Spectrum. The writer asked Joe how he would characterize Tony Doyle as a fighter. The cutting reply showed there was no expiration date on a Joe Frazier grudge.

"He was tall. He was tough," Joe had said, in mock reverence to Doyle and the fight he put up as a pro. "But not *that* tough."

The article also reported that Frazier had given an explanation for the quick knockout in an interview right after the fight. He had sweetly begun by acknowledging that Doyle's wife had recently given birth to twins.

"I figured, let's get him home to see them," quipped Joe.

––––––––––

Joe Frazier's Golden Gloves success got him invited to the 1964 U.S. Olympics Boxing Trials at the New York World's Fair from May 18 to May 20. He began by scoring a third-round knockout over a game Wyce Westbrook and followed that up with a second-round TKO against Clay Hodges a day later. Buster Mathis advanced by relying on his fast hands and footwork to take a pair of convincing decisions.

The Finals were billed as a rematch between the power puncher and the nimble giant. The 20-year-old Frazier was seeking a knockout to avenge his one official loss. By contrast, the 21-year-old Mathis hoped to jab, jab, jab his way to a decision. In the end, it was the big man's trickery, of all things, that made the difference.

The trick Buster pulled would have been hysterically funny if Joe didn't find the whole thing so painful at the time. Mathis started the fight by pulling the waistband of his boxing trunks way up to just below his jiggling chest. Frazier, who usually did his damage by hooking to the body, came across like he was throwing low blows rather than legal midsection shots.

In the second round, the referee finally penalized Frazier a whopping two points for supposedly hitting below the belt. Joe still seemed to have a slight edge in the match when the final bell rung. But that two-point deduction turned out to be too much to overcome in a short three-round contest.

Buster Mathis was designated to go to the Tokyo Olympics to compete in the heavyweight division for the United States. Frazier was forced to return to Philadelphia in defeat. Joe recalled being disgusted by the way he had lost to Mathis and seriously considered quitting boxing. He also had been worried about making enough money to take care of a growing family. By now, Marvis had been joined at home by two younger sisters.

Frazier's boxing future was saved by an offer from the Olympic boxing team that he originally had no desire to take. The coaches wanted Joe to serve as a combo sparring partner and alternate for Mathis. Joe initially refused, claiming he didn't want to lose his job at the slaughterhouse for such a meaningless role. However, Yank Durham convinced Joe to take the offer after the people at the slaughterhouse promised to give him back his job when he returned.

"In 1964, I lost to [Buster] Mathis here and I went as an alternate," Joe had told me when we first met, the bitterness still in his voice. "Number one, I thought I was more of just a guinea pig at first to get Mathis in shape. [Then] they passed the word down to me that if I came down to a light heavy, I could represent the United States as a light heavyweight. That was a bunch of garbage! Somebody had legitimately won the right to represent us in that class."

Joe went off to train side by side with Buster Mathis for the Olympics at the Hamilton Air Force Base near San Francisco. While he was gone Florence did her best to keep money coming in, but things got tight. According to Joe, the financial difficulties at home were constantly on his mind while he prepared with the team.

Joe worked extremely hard, especially for an alternate, during the training camp. But he thought Mathis appeared somewhat distracted and homesick. At times, he said the big guy seemed to be just coasting through those pre-Olympic workouts.

On September 18, 1964, Frazier's hard work strangely managed to pay off in the midst of defeat. Conversely, Mathis's nonchalant ways caught up to him despite a victory. The two met in an exhibition match set up for the military bigwigs as the training camp activities wound down.

Frazier started off hooking with power as usual, while Mathis piled up points with the jab like he always did. During those routine exchanges Buster busted the knuckle of his right middle finger against the top of Joe's head. Somehow, he held on to win the decision.

The knuckle didn't heal in time, and Buster took off to his beloved Grand Rapids home. Joe gladly replaced him as the United States' heavyweight boxer in Tokyo. At our first interview, Joe confessed that the Olympics still stood out as one of the best times of his life. And that didn't even take into account his time in the ring.

"The Games, as I remember, were really exciting and educational," said Joe, while Marvis had listened in. "We tried to communicate with the different athletes from the other countries. Sometimes you got across and sometimes you didn't. But the best thing was that everybody in that Olympic Village knew how to party. They didn't worry about language, nationality, or color. These athletes all could boogie!"

"And you boogied with the best of them, I bet."

Joe had nodded emphatically and laughed. Then he had looked over to his son.

"I really enjoyed the Olympics," Joe had said. "That's why I want Marvis to go. But I hope a lot of things can be straightened out. We have to iron out our differences with the Soviet Union over Afghanistan and Iran. If they are still having problems over there, I'm not sending my son."

I had told Joe they might call off the boycott even if everything didn't get completely straightened out. What would he do then?

"Marvis ain't going if things are the least bit shaky or dangerous there," Joe had shot back. "If necessary, I think we should have our own Olympics right here in America and take care of our kids right. Instead of going over to Moscow and risking something happening to them like the killings in Germany in 1972 [of the Israeli athletes]. That left me with some bad remembrances. . . . He might go over there and I might not be seein' him anymore. I'm not going to have that!"

———

Joe Frazier's boxing experience at the Tokyo Olympics began with a couple of dominant performances. He won his first fights in well under two minutes. On October 15 the referee stopped Frazier's destruction of Uganda's George Oywello, one of the few heavyweights his size, in 1:35 of round one. A few days later, the Philly fighter ended his bout against Australia's 6'5" Athol McQueen in just 40 seconds.

Frazier had barely broken a sweat, except for his nights out partying, and he was already into the medal rounds. In the Semi-Finals of the heavyweight division he faced off with the burly, 6'2" Russian Vadim Yemelyanov. Joe worked over his Soviet opponent in the first round and knocked him down twice early in the second.

As Frazier continued to pummel Yemelyanov's body and head, he suddenly felt a searing pain in his left hand that bolted right up through the arm. Joe had somehow managed to break his thumb. Yet the Russians didn't seem to notice.

Frazier's adrenaline was pumping so hard, he never backed off, and for a while, the pain remained muted. Unaware of their advantage, the Russians decided to throw in the towel seconds later. Joe had survived to win the fight in 1:49 of round two. And he now became the only boxer from the United States with a shot at a gold medal.

"Out of 10 American boxers, I was the only guy who made it to the Finals," Joe told me, in that same dual interview with Marvis. "I got the nickname the Lone Boxer—not the Lone Ranger. Everybody was concentrating on me. If I had lost that would have been a defeat for the whole American boxing team."

Frazier, one fight away from the gold medal, kept the injury to himself. He was afraid to lose his shot at Olympic glory and the big money it promised. Two days later, on October 23, he boxed the 6'4" German Hans Huber for three rounds. He miraculously eked out a 3–2 decision.

Smokin' Joe rarely used his notorious left hook. Instead he kept Huber off him with one right lead after another. He virtually won the biggest fight of his life to date with one hand behind his back.

"I dislocated my left thumb before the finals," Joe told me, vastly understating the damage at the time. "And I had a lot of bone chips in there. I fought the Final with a dislocated thumb. When I got back [to Philadelphia] they had to operate and take the chips out—pin it back."

Joe Frazier ended his amateur career by winning the 1964 Olympic boxing heavyweight gold medal. He did it despite a loss in the United States Boxing Trials and a left thumb broken in several places. His feat seemed to far outshine Floyd Patterson's 1952 Olympic win as a middleweight. And it even came across as a greater victory than Cassius Clay's light heavyweight gold in 1960.

For that moment, Joe Frazier's life really was nothin' but a party.

———

In Joe's mind, the amateur party was scheduled to end for his son—one way or another—after the June 1980 U.S. Olympic Boxing Trials in Atlanta, Georgia. The American boycott loomed as an irreversible certainty. Even the strategy of competing under a neutral flag, supported by an international coalition of boycotting nations, wound up blocked by President Jimmy Carter. He threatened to revoke the passport of any United States athlete trying it.

Savvy observers, like sports columnist Phil Pepe of the *New York Daily News*, didn't see why they even bothered to hold Olympic Trials. In a June 15 piece, he had dubbed the American boxing squad as the "Olympic team to nowhere." What did any young fighter hope to gain by even showing up to compete?

"These Trials are all there is," Marvis had told Pepe. "There is nothing else to look forward to. This is our Olympics."

Marvis bemoaned the missed opportunity but made his priorities clear as well.

"I am an American first and an athlete second," he had said. "The decision not to go is an arrow in the heart of all athletes, but I stand behind the President 100 percent."

The Trials began, appropriately enough, on Father's Day. Papa Frazier celebrated by priming his son for the Quarter Finals the next day. George Benton was unable to be there, and Joe offered plenty of advice to fill the void.

On June 16 Marvis went up against a truly big, bad man. Mitch Green, the four-time New York Daily News Golden Gloves champion, was a former gang leader. He stood 6'5" and owned an "official" record of 64–6, with 51 knockouts, as an amateur. In truth, according to a bio later posted on BoxRec.com, he had fought an amazing 180 or so fights before going professional.

Marvis gave away several inches in height and reach to his older, vastly more experienced opponent. He really had no choice but to follow Joe's suggestion to get inside and swarm Green with a barrage of punches. That strategy worked well for the first two rounds. In the third, Green fought back with some vicious combinations and dominated the round until Marvis finished with a final flurry.

Frazier barely outpointed Mitch Green to move on to the Semi-Finals of the Olympic Trials. That narrow victory seemed even more impressive several years later as the brawler quickly climbed the pro rankings. Green was 16–1, and a top 10 contender, when he finally hit the wall against an undefeated Mike Tyson in May 1986. Yet, even against Tyson, Green managed to go the distance before losing. He was only the second guy to do that in Tyson's first 21 fights.

In the Semi-Finals three days later, Marvis drew 22-year-old Army Specialist 4 James Broad. The 6'4" world military champion weighed in at 215 pounds and seemed tailor-made for a beating. He offered just the right mixture of plodding style and inexperience to guarantee an easy win.

Joe, again at ringside, saw no reason to play it coy. The swarming approach had worked with the likes of Mitch Green, and this guy didn't seem to be in the same league. What's more, George Benton was AWOL once more. Everything screamed attack, attack, attack. The confidence in the Frazier camp rightly soared before the bell for round one.

The fight began and ended so quickly, so strangely, that spectators found it hard to believe. Marvis started out with a testing jab to the arm and two lefts to his opponent's shoulder. As the aggressor, he then ducked low to charge Broad's midsection. The soldier boy, up on his toes and fading back, caught Marvis with a short, off-balance right to the chin.

It was the only punch Broad threw. At 21 seconds of the first round, Marvis Frazier, the National AAU heavyweight champion, fell forward and crumbled to the canvas. He remained lying there, with his head cradled in his arms, for nearly three minutes. He never moved as he was counted out and for a long time after that.

"He jammed my head down and pinched a nerve," Marvis told me days later in a joint phone conversation with Joe from their gym. "It paralyzed me from the neck down. It felt like the pin-needles when your foot falls asleep or when you bang your funny bone. I couldn't get up."

Joe, in his best ain't-nothing-but-a-party style, made light of the physical damage and the mind-boggling loss.

"I had something like that plenty of times in the gym," he said, then laughed. "I just say to Marvis in the dressing room, 'Go out and boogie' and that's what he did."

Marvis acknowledged that he never imagined finishing his amateur career in this fashion. He came across as embarrassed by the way he lost—and by the fighter who had beaten him.

My response was to shift the focus away from that disastrous last bout. I dwelled on his final amateur record of 56–2 and all the championships he had won. I advised him to look at the body of work he had put together and what that said about him.

That seemed to work for a while, but Marvis still talked wistfully about fighting in the Olympics. He sounded like he might not be ready to leave the hunt for Olympic gold. It reminded me of something he said the first day we met.

"Right now, the Olympics are the ultimate in boxing for me," he had said, comparing the allure of staying for another Olympics as opposed to turning pro. "If I win the Olympics, I'll be the heavyweight champion of the world because I'll be fighting people from all the different countries—Russians, Cubans, Austrians, etc. Somebody who turns pro without fighting in an Olympics really never gets a chance to fight internationally. He'll never fight the great Russians or Cubans as a pro. So, the Olympics are the ultimate—you can't get any higher."

The current conversation continued with Marvis musing about his tentative future plans. He said maybe he would try LaSalle College business courses. He said he could always wait for the 1984 Olympics.

Joe seemed to have heard enough. He jumped in to end that kind of talk right away. He indicated he already had his sights set on revenge. And that revenge had to take place in the professional ranks.

"Can't think of nothing until we get James Broad out of our hair," said Joe, knowing that Broad, like Tubbs and other top amateurs, was turning pro. "Anytime you want me, I'll be right here in the gym. [I'll be] working out with Marvis and the boys."

And that was the end of that conversation. Score one big win for Smokin' Joe Frazier and one convincing loss for Florence and the Smiths.

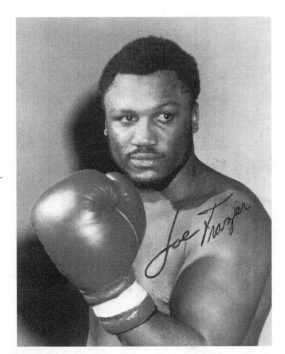

An autographed photo of Joe holding up his lethal left hand. *Courtesy of Joe Frazier press packet/Glenn Lewis*

Joe takes a defensive stance in the gym. *Courtesy of Joe Frazier press packet/Glenn Lewis*

Manager Yancey "Yank" Durham stands next to his young protégé Joe Frazier. *Courtesy of Joe Frazier press packet/Glenn Lewis*

Joe Frazier onstage putting in the work behind the mic. *Courtesy of Joe Frazier press packet/Glenn Lewis*

Smokin' Joe unloads that classic left hook while working the heavy bag at his gym. *Courtesy of Joe Frazier press packet/Glenn Lewis*

Joe ends his roadwork in front of the newly purchased Brewton Plantation in Yemassee, South Carolina. *Courtesy of Joe Frazier press packet/Glenn Lewis*

Joe Frazier stands over a dazed Muhammad Ali in the final round of "the Fight of the Century." *Courtesy of Joe Frazier press packet/Glenn Lewis*

A dapper Joe Frazier flashing his championship rings and big left hand circa 1980s. *Photofest*

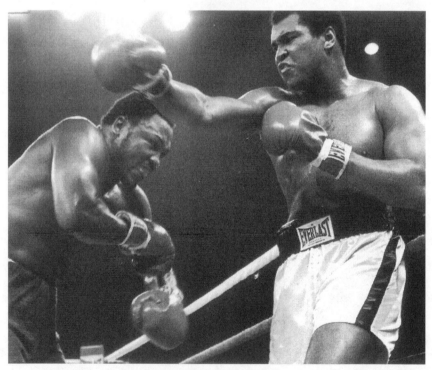

Joe crouches low to move in under Ali's right in the seventh round of the Thrilla in Manila, October 1, 1975. *Photofest*

Joe Frazier skips rope in training for 1971 Fight of the Century. *Photofest*

Marvis and Joe Frazier speaking to the press after Marvis's pro debut victory against Roger Troupe at MSG in September 1980. *Courtesy of Getty Images/The Ring magazine, Editorial ID: 158704947.*

Joe Frazier and son Marvis in their North Philadelphia gym one year before Joe's fatal illness. *Photofest*

9

The Fraziers Go Pro

After the post–Olympic Trials interview in June, I lost contact with Joe Frazier and his son over the summer. It was late August when I received the phone call inviting me to Marvis's professional boxing debut. The fight was set to take place at the Felt Forum in Madison Square Garden on September 12, 1980. Although glad to hear from the Fraziers, I remained conflicted over Marvis's decision to turn pro.

Still, there were some genuine perks to covering the fight at the Felt Forum. I knew the Garden public relations people well from past reporting gigs there. In addition, Gil Clancy, the MSG matchmaker for the event, had consented to sit next to me at ringside. I envisioned picking his brain on the nuances of the fight from beginning to end.

Before the Friday boxing card kicked off, I roamed the area closest to the ring. I soon spotted Florence Frazier and her family settling into their seats. She greeted me warmly and gave me a look-at-where-we-are expression. I empathized with her but decided to only talk about the impending fight in positive terms. I knew she didn't handle the violence well. And I had no desire to add to her anxiety.

My visit to the dressing room later on was not as well thought out or diplomatic. As a result, it didn't last very long.

I once again chose to remind Marvis that he didn't have to risk injury in the pro ranks. In truth, I don't think he was paying much attention to me. He was rightly focused on the more pressing task that lay ahead. But his dad, as usual, heard every word.

Joe, in a flat, controlled voice, told me this was not the time to mess with his son's concentration. He said it could get him hurt. He strongly suggested I leave the room to find my seat in the arena.

As I walked from the dressing room, I was furious with myself. Not Joe. I knew he had done the right thing. What's more, I'd committed one of the cardinal sins for a reporter. I had gotten thrown out of the venue where my story was unfolding.

All my time with the Fraziers had likely made me too invested in their welfare. I was foolishly trying to interfere with the arc of my assigned story. I had mistakenly stopped being the fly on the wall and opted instead to buzz in the ear of one of my protagonists. I muttered recriminations to myself as I went off to find my front-row seat next to Clancy.

Gil Clancy was one of the most respected trainers and commentators in boxing. He had trained some of the greatest champions of all time—including heavyweights like George Foreman, Muhammad Ali, and Joe Frazier, among others. Late in his career, he came out of retirement in the 1990s to help train Oscar De La Hoya. Under Clancy's tutelage, De La Hoya rose to truly legendary status. He wound up winning titles in six different weight classes that ranged from super flyweight (115 pounds) to middleweight (160 pounds).

Earlier on, Clancy had been the sole trainer for Emile Griffith, who won both the Welterweight and Middleweight World Championships. Clancy was also in the corner for Griffith's infamous March 1962 welterweight title bout against Benny "Kid" Paret. Griffith wound up virtually killing Paret in the ring. And, as a kid, I was part of the television audience that had watched the live broadcast.

Griffith had initially taken the title from Paret and then lost it back to him. The rubber match at MSG had included a clash at the weigh-in and two fighters who seemed to truly hate each other. Sometime during the 12th round, Griffith backed Paret into the corner and went to work.

Griffith pinned his opponent and started punching. He connected once, twice, then several more times to Paret's head, and the Cuban fighter stopped throwing back or defending himself. Griffith wound up delivering a prolonged barrage of unanswered blows to Paret's head that just went on and on. The referee eventually put an end to the fight, and Paret fell motionless at his feet.

It was later revealed that Paret had blood clots in his brain by the time he hit the canvas. He was essentially brain dead while lying in the ring. He officially passed away 10 days after the fight.

According to an April 2011 *New York Times* article following Clancy's death, the trainer had discussed the Griffith-Paret fight with Dave Anderson for his book *In the Corner*. In that interview, Clancy admitted to giving Griffith prefight instructions that sound awfully ominous in retrospect. However, he never saw the words as anything but necessary for a tough fight like this—and most boxing experts agreed with him.

"Anytime you're inside with this guy," Clancy had warned, "you've got to punch until he either falls or grabs you or the referee stops you."

I never looked at boxing the same way after viewing that fight. It ceased to be just another sport, like baseball or football. I became hyperaware of the risk every fighter took, especially the pros. And I never felt any boxer was totally safe, regardless of their lofty reputation or the comparative weakness of their opponent.

I wanted desperately to talk to Clancy about that fight. There were so many questions that stayed with me over the years. But I had just spoiled a key reporting opportunity in the dressing room and didn't want to screw up another one.

———

Gil Clancy had always been known for his eye for talent. Early on he saw Marvis as potential boxing royalty and secured his first four professional bouts for MSG. Joe, who had recently been inducted into the MSG Hall of Fame, negotiated a $50,000 signing bonus for these initial fights. In addition, he had gotten his son another $5,000 for this debut match.

It was a far cry from the mere hundreds of dollars Joe had received for his first few fights as a pro. And that had been after winning Olympic gold.

The Felt Forum crowd quickly approached the arena's capacity of 5,600 for this special preliminary bout. The opening four-rounder, on a night like this, usually played to mostly empty seats. Once the fight fans settled in, a loud roar greeted Marvis's entourage as it snaked its way toward the ring. Joe Frazier waited, arms crossed, on the ring apron for his son to arrive.

The ex-champ wore the same red silk jacket, with the "Smokin' Joe Gym" insignia, as the other cornermen. He clearly planned to be in Marvis's corner for this pro bout and the ones to come. George Benton was in the corner as well. It remained to be seen who Marvis obeyed when the action heated up.

The ring announcer informed the crowd that it was Marvis Frazier's 20th birthday as soon as he entered the ring. The arena erupted into a boisterous version of "Happy Birthday" with everyone singing and swaying along. The whole thing came across as both spontaneous and joyous—a mass outpouring of affection.

I tried to imagine what Marvis's rather raw opponent thought of that. But moments later something much more intimidating occurred.

Before the fighter introductions, Joe Frazier was brought up to the center of the ring. He was presented to the crowd as "one of the greatest fighters of the 20th century." He received a prolonged standing ovation and shook hands with all the members of the opposing corner.

After veteran referee Johnny LoBianco gave the fighters their instructions, Joe pulled Marvis's opponent aside right there in the ring. He wanted Roger Troupe to know that taking on the Fraziers was serious business.

"My boy is gonna *get* you," the former heavyweight champ said, leaning in to warn Troupe. Joe followed the threat with a long, hard stare. Marvis passively watched the exchange.

The fight was televised, and the broadcasters sat nearby. I was sure they would have some useful observations, but Clancy's comments promised to be more revealing. He began by telling me that the 207-pound, 6'2" Troupe was a lot better than his modest record suggested. The ex–pro football player had particularly long arms, jabbed well, and knew how to push an attack when he saw a weakness.

Clancy rated Troupe as a cut above the typical opponent for a professional boxing debut. He said that was particularly true for a celebrity newcomer like Marvis whom everyone wanted to protect. The veteran trainer warned that Marvis had to be on his game here or pay the price.

Despite Clancy's respect for the former wide receiver, Joe did not seem to see Troupe as a threat. In fact, about 10 months earlier, the ex-champ had made it clear what he thought of any pro football player who traded shoulder pads for boxing gloves. He had been reacting to the transition at the time of Ed "Too Tall" Jones from the gridiron to the ring.

"It's not that easy [to box]," Frazier had said, in a piece published by the *St. Louis Globe-Democrat*. "A boxer can play football or baseball because every youngster played these sports. But not every young man has boxed. I started boxing when I was 16. It took years to learn—how to deliver and protect yourself. I hardly think a pro football player will ever become a boxing champion."

George Benton leaned in to give Marvis his last-second instructions. The young fighter started by looking at his trainer but soon turned away to check his dad's reaction. This struck me as a bad sign. I wondered if George caught the drift in attention as well.

Sure enough, Marvis, frustrated early by Troupe's long arms and persistent jab, ignored Benton's game plan. Instead of boxing, and working his way in close, the kid began to lunge with his punches. He got away with it at first, but Clancy commented that even a novice would eventually take advantage of a mistake like that.

Moments later Marvis responded to Benton's pleas from the corner and mounted a more controlled offensive. He pushed Troupe into the ropes with a series of jabs followed by combinations of tight hooks to the body and face. Clancy flashed a smile and compared the hooks to those thrown by Joe early in his career. All went well until the final minute of the round when Marvis got anxious and started to reach once again.

Troupe caught Frazier midlunge this time with a big overhand right to the face. He pressed the attack and drove Marvis into the corner with an uppercut to the chin that caused his body to sag and jangled his legs. Troupe, hot to end it, followed with two straight rights to the head and barely missed with a lunging right that Marvis ducked. Two more rushed rights grazed Marvis's head as time in the round ran out.

My stomach had dipped wildly at the end of that round as I braced for the worst. Clancy immediately put into words what my body had silently screamed. He admitted that Marvis would have been knocked out if the round had lasted 10 seconds longer or if Troupe had been more patient. The television announcers soon came to the same conclusion.

"The kid looked defenseless there at the end of round one," one of the announcers said.

Things got heated in the Frazier corner after the near knockout. I have no idea what was said, but Marvis soon got back to the Benton approach in the second round. He knocked Troupe down early on with a straight right to the head. But Clancy noted that Troupe's legs were not shaky and Marvis missed doing more damage with several misguided jabs and wild hooks.

Near the end of the round, Marvis rocked his opponent again with a looping overhand right. The punch came at the end of a sequence where Frazier knocked Troupe through the ropes and onto the ring apron. However, it was now Troupe's turn to be saved by the bell as Marvis missed *his* chance to finish him off.

Between rounds Benton was the one in the ring talking to Marvis. However, Joe slapped his son's arm from the apron and yelled his own advice. Marvis was trying hard to listen to George but gave in and turned to hear what his dad had to say as the bell sounded.

Marvis stayed on top of Troupe with hooks to both sides of the body for most of round three. Clancy applauded the kid for scoring consistently inside but worried that he was getting hit too much in the process. He also wanted Marvis to double up on left jabs and hooks and then be ready to land the right when the opening came. Right on cue, the kid began to do just as Clancy suggested.

Marvis's more active hook wore Troupe down in the last minute of the round. Clancy saw that Troupe was starting to drop his hands. Seconds later, Marvis connected with a tight, overhand right and a left hook to the head. Troupe bent over and slouched toward the ropes. Marvis landed another couple of rights to the head and an uppercut flush on the chin. The final sequence drove a dazed Troupe through the ropes, and the referee stopped the fight.

Marvis raised his hands in victory while jumping jackknife-style into the air. Troupe remained on the canvas, under the lower rope. He looked glassy eyed, and unable to get up, as the celebration kicked off around him. The doctor, brought in to check Troupe out, finally helped the woozy fighter to his feet.

Clancy commented on the power Marvis showed with those finishing shots. He seemed immensely relieved and gave a loud "Whew!"

Joe stood in the ring hugging his son and helping him off with his gloves. Soon they were surrounded by the other cornermen and supporters. Amid the joy, I was more fixed on how close Marvis had come to losing his first pro fight, in the first round, against a complete unknown. Joe obviously thought just about the same thing. He eventually pulled Marvis away to the center of the ring and kept shaking his head.

Without knowing Joe's exact words, I got the message. He later shared that message with Maury Allen of the *New York Post.*

"We have a lot to learn," said Joe, about his son fighting like a pro. "It's back to the drawing board."

––––––––––

The television announcer, interviewing Marvis and Joe in the ring, immediately noted Marvis's early troubles. The kid admitted to being anxious at first and to getting caught with a couple of good shots. Joe looked pained by the recounting of his son's first-round woes.

The announcer tried to change Joe's negative mood and draw him into the interview. He made an awkward comparison between Marvis's comeback win and his dad's 1971 victory over Muhammad Ali at Madison Square Garden.

"Joe, you remember those days?" asked the announcer.

Joe didn't bite. He was still fixated on the dangerous lapses he saw in that first round.

"Yeah, John, I go way back, but I don't know how I'm feeling from this [fight] because sometimes you have to go back in the gym and make a lot of changes," said Joe. "Sorry, I got a lot of changes to make on Monday and I won't—"

The announcer, not liking the direction of Joe's comments, abruptly swung the mic back to Marvis. Things seemed to go better for a while. Then Marvis pointed out once again how he "got spanked" in that first round.

Joe scowled and placed a hand around his son's neck as he talked. He was fuming. Suddenly, in the middle of Marvis's on-air comments, Joe interrupted the interview by throwing a big towel over the kid's face. The announcer picked up on Joe's pissed-off vibe and started to shut things down.

"Okay Marvis, we wish you the very best of luck and know you're going to be a great professional. . . . And a very happy birthday to you. I remember you were *this* big, Marvis." The announcer held his hand to his chest and began to back off. "I was with you in those days and I'm happy to be with you now. . . ."

Joe sensed the bum's rush to finish the interview and his part in souring the mood.

"Yeah, I'm not always easy," he said.

"Okay Joe," said the announcer, lowering the mic. "Good to have you. Congratulations."

Joe and Marvis moved somberly off across the ring. Joe had his head down, and Marvis edged away from him. They were not talking. My first instinct was to go congratulate Marvis and put the emphasis on the great finish. One look at Joe's expression convinced me to simply wave as they passed by.

Weeks later, I got the news that Joe was now his son's head trainer. George Benton had been relegated to the role of assistant trainer along with Val Colbert. My first thought was *what a terrible decision.* Joe had the heart of a champion, but George had the wisdom and patience to develop a champion. I knew Marvis would be the one to pay the price for Joe's mistake.

Benton soon decided to leave Marvis's camp. He left the Joe Frazier Gym as well. He never got to complete his mission to turn Marvis Frazier into a truly great, thinking boxer.

––––––––––––

The Fraziers were back at the Felt Forum four weeks later for Marvis's October 10 match against Dennis Rivers. James Shuler, a 21-year-old former top-ranked amateur middleweight, was also on the card. He was another highly touted member of Joe Frazier's growing stable of fighters. According to a *New York Times* piece back then, Joe claimed to be handling nine boxers in all.

Joe talked about "putting his music aside" for a while to concentrate full-time on directing the careers of his young boxers. Several, like Shuler, had met Joe at his North Philadelphia gym. Shuler had been just 12 when they first crossed paths. He had been working out there ever since.

Both Marvis and Shuler won in convincing fashion on this night, and Joe's new career move looked promising. Of course, it helped that Marvis's opponent, despite standing 6'3" and weighing 215, had the same 1–0 pro record. The big exception here was that Rivers's inexperience really showed.

Marvis chased Rivers around the ring in the first round and hit him constantly for two and a half minutes after that. The referee luckily stopped the fight at 2:32 of the second before it got really ugly. Both Marvis and Joe were ecstatic after the win and bragged about being back on track.

"I'm getting better as we go down the road," Marvis told reporters, flashing a grin. "I got him with two right uppercuts at the end. He took some good shots. In fact, I changed position at one point so he wouldn't know where I was working from."

Joe, for his part, lauded his son's dramatic improvement since his first shaky outing. Of course, nobody mentioned that Rivers was a lot less dangerous or aggressive in the ring than Roger Troupe. The outcome was never in doubt.

In the postfight interviews, Joe said Marvis's immediate career plans called for a couple of monthly four-rounders before stepping up to six-round matches in the new year. Almost a month later, that fight schedule fell apart in frightening fashion.

While sparring with Jimmy Young in the North Philly gym, Marvis took a blow to the chin. He fell to the canvas and remained conscious but completely paralyzed for more than 10 minutes. Medical tests later revealed a congenital weakness in the neck—not the "pinched nerve" suspected after the James Broad knockout in the Olympic Trials. According to Marvis's autobiography, a neurosurgeon was brought in to reduce the chance of another incident.

On April 10, 1981, six months after his cakewalk over Rivers, Marvis finally made it back for a match against a minimally talented, inexperienced fighter named Melvin Epps. Marvis pursued the punch-shy Epps around the Felt Forum ring for six uneventful rounds. The surgically repaired neck never got tested in the fight. Even so, Joe took the victory as a confirmation that his son could continue to box for a living.

Just one month later, in May 1981, Joe dramatically raised the level of Marvis's competition. He booked a televised match against the highly regarded, 21–1 Steve Zouski for the main arena at Madison Square Garden. The 27-year-old had started his career with a dozen victories, mostly by knockouts, before suffering his lone loss. The expectation was that he had too much ring experience for the mostly untested Frazier.

Marvis surprised the experts—and most of those in attendance—by dominating the action all through the six-round bout. He eventually prevailed with a TKO in the final round. The fight was stopped after a barrage of Frazier blows went unanswered.

This completed the Fraziers' initial four-fight contract with Gil Clancy and Madison Square Garden. For better or worse, it convinced Joe he was handling Marvis's pro career just fine. The kid was undefeated. It was time to plan the next phase and for his son to continue stepping up.

———————

Joe Frazier's professional career, despite the Olympic gold medal, began with a whole lot less fanfare or support than his son later received. There were no major publicity campaigns for the early matches, and nobody offered to foot the bill for training expenses. And, as noted before, he was paid a lot less prize money as well.

Joe returned from the 1964 Olympics with a damaged left hand, no job, and nobody willing to invest in his pro boxing dreams. The Philadelphia slaughterhouse reneged on giving Joe his old job back. They saw he couldn't manage the work with his injury. The local black businessmen Yank Durham approached for money turned him down. They mostly thought Joe was too small to be successful in a heavyweight division dominated by big guys like Muhammad Ali.

Florence continued to work for a while, doing her share. Joe and his wife were able to scrape by until his hand mended and Yank got him back in the gym. The trainer decided to get Joe some professional experience first and look for long-term financial backing once the victories began to mount up. The plan called for Joe to build a winning record with some easier fights.

Durham went overboard and wound up with a true bum-of-the-month parade. For his first four bouts, Joe fought the dregs of what professional boxing had to offer. Unfortunately, the prize money matched the competition.

Joe supposedly made a paltry $125, from selling complimentary tickets, for his pro debut on August 16, 1965, at Philadelphia's Convention Hall. Joe's opponent, a last-minute stand-in, was Woody Goss. He was a pipefitter by trade. The fight lasted less than two minutes into the first round before it was stopped.

In the second fight, about a month later, Joe went up against a somewhat tougher Mike Bruce. In this bout, Joe showed a weakness in his attack that would haunt him throughout the early part of his career. He exchanged some wicked blows with Bruce in the first round. Then Joe got knocked down in the second. It took a tirade from Durham between rounds to motivate Joe to knock Bruce out in the third.

Morty Holtzer, in one of our conversations, had described Frazier's early problems as a professional. Believe it or not, Joe was not assertive enough in those days. He also had a terrible problem with starting slow.

"Joe was very quiet and unassuming as a [young] pro," said Holtzer, smiling at my surprised reaction. "At first, nobody paid much attention to him [even with the Olympic medal]. Nobody really thought he'd be much good [as a professional]."

"You said he also needed to be more assertive in the ring," I reminded Holtzer.

"Yeah, Joe was the kind of fighter that needed three rounds to warm up— no matter how many minutes [he spent] warming up in the dressing room. He would [often] take a beating the first two or three rounds. But, once he worked up steam, his conditioning and endurance would carry him right over the guy."

Just eight days after rallying against Bruce, Frazier returned to the Philadelphia Convention Hall to knock out the then 12–4 Ray Staples in 2:06 of the second round. After another slow start, Joe really went to town on his lighter opponent. In fact, Staples never won another fight after that, according to BoxRec.

On November 11, 1965, Frazier won his fourth pro fight against the monumentally inept Abe Davis. This time there was no hesitation in getting the job done. Joe knocked him out in the last minute of the first round. Davis, a professional victim throughout his career, never got much better after that. He finished his boxing days with a dismal record of five wins, 27 losses (13 by KO), and one draw.

Both the Staples and Davis bouts came with the same chump-change payouts. Heck, according to Joe, the pushovers were getting more money to risk a beating than he was for meting out the punishment. Yank Durham realized it was once again time to try to find some boxing angels with deep pockets.

Durham put his fighter together with a neighborhood reverend, William Gray, according to a publicity bio Joe provided. Gray helped them reach out in turn to a local businessman, F. Bruce Baldwin. It was Baldwin who finally put together a diversified group of 80 black and white investors. That original group included a department store executive, a former Olympic sculler, and the sportswriter Larry Merchant, among others.

The Cloverlay Inc. official agreement, dated December 16, 1965, called for the investors to purchase shares at $250 each. A few years later, those shares were already valued in excess of $14,000 apiece and rapidly on the rise. The syndicate agreed to give Joe 50 percent of the fight purses off the top. They also provided him with a nominal weekly salary that escalated along with the size of the prize money. Yank got 15 percent, and Cloverlay paid all expenses out of its 35 percent cut.

This deal was similar to the one Cassius Clay made with the Louisville group that bankrolled him when he went pro in 1960. It also closely mirrored Joe's arrangement with his son in their deal with MSG. In that instance, Joe assumed the roles, and percentages, of both trainer and financial backer.

In 1966, once the new agreement kicked in, Cloverlay managed to get Joe only slightly bigger purses at first. However, the regular salary allowed him to train more worry-free, and life at home got easier too. In time, the payoffs started to reflect the boxer's continued success. In the first seven months of that year, Frazier recorded seven victories and none of them came close to going the distance.

On September 21, 1966, in his 12th professional bout, Joe finally stepped up to the big time. He fought a 10-round, main event in Madison Square Garden against a ranked contender. His opponent was the hard-hitting, South American champion Oscar "the Argentine Strong-Boy" Bonavena. It was a fight many boxing experts thought Joe would lose.

Bonavena was about Joe's height but outweighed him by at least 20 pounds of solid muscle. He was also one of the few fighters who could match Joe's strength and punching power. The free-swinging brawler—known for throwing many not-so-legal blows—was coming off a decision over the respected Canadian champion George Chuvalo. With a record of 21–2, most by knockout, Bonavena had also become adept at keeping other bears, like Joe Frazier, from doing damage inside.

Morty Holtzer had worked Frazier's corner for that fight. He recalled that Joe was still plagued by slow starts. He had not yet figured out how to effectively penetrate the defenses of a bruiser like Bonavena. Holtzer laughed at the memory of how Joe had tried to rely on his jab from the opening bell.

"Right from the first round he got clobbered," said Morty, who mimicked Joe's attempt to throw a flurry of jabs. "He tried to box Bonavena, which you can't [do]. In fact, Joe couldn't box anybody. Bonavena, a dirty fighter, was doing everything but kicking him. [Joe] got knocked down in the second round with a right."

Years later, I viewed a videotape of the fight. It showed Frazier dazed by that punch and slow to recover. He went down again later in the second. It was surprising that Joe survived the round.

Holtzer saw the conversation in the corner before the third round as the key to the fight. In fact, he considered it crucial to Frazier's whole boxing success going forward.

"Yank [looked] ready to walk out because Joe was not listening," said Morty, describing the tension in the corner after round two. "We told him to fight inside with short hooks to the body. He [finally] listened and *annihilated* him. He never had to use the right hand because the left was enough. [We] used to call that a Philadelphia punch years ago."

It was true that Joe's heavy, left-hook attack became entrenched as his signature style in this bout. But Morty's take on the denouement of the fight, and how Frazier "annihilated" Bonavena down the stretch, was a gross exaggeration. It ended in a close, mixed decision for Frazier, not a shattering knockout.

Still, considering the early knockdowns in round two, it was a startling turnaround. In addition, the comeback came against a potent, more experienced opponent. After a year as a pro, Joe Frazier boasted a 12–0 record and was poised to become a title contender.

———

Marvis Frazier, after his first four pro victories at MSG, traveled to Las Vegas for two competitive bouts. On August 22, 1981, he took a bruising, six-round unanimous decision against Tony Pulu. The fighter from Tonga, sporting a 19–11–1 record, brought a good deal of experience to the match and made the kid work.

Less than a month later, on September 16, Joe snagged a coveted showcase bout for his son. He wangled him a place on the undercard for the megafight between welterweights Sugar Ray Leonard and Thomas Hearns. It was Marvis's first scheduled eight-round match, but he rose to the occasion and ended it in four. He had Guy "the Rock" Casale, a New Jersey fighter with a 15–2–3 record, in trouble from the third round on.

Joe had Marvis throwing a lot of combinations in the third, and several connected with his opponent's face. Casale's eyes puffed up, and a cut opened on his nose. Later, in the fourth round, Marvis continued to head hunt and wound up breaking the guy's nose. Finally, just before the bell, a crisp right to the head had Casale wobbly, and he decided not to come out for the fifth.

Joe and his boy were 6–0 in the pros and clearly on a roll. Fight experts and fans were starting to believe, and that first shaky match against Roger Troupe seemed a distant memory. The hope was for one more good fight, one more solid win, to finish out the year.

Unfortunately, Marvis lost the rest of 1981 and all of 1982 to a series of medical problems. It began with a viral ear infection about a month after the Casale fight that wasn't properly diagnosed or treated at first. This was followed by a lingering case of hepatitis and months of intensive conditioning to get back into fighting shape. The hepatitis had caused a temporary inflammation of the liver and jaundice. But, luckily, there was no long-term damage.

Joe had his son ease back into the ring with a 10-rounder against a weak opponent. Amos Hayes had a losing record when he faced Marvis on February 8, 1983. And it only got worse after suffering a fifth-round TKO.

One month later, Joe purposely raised the level of competition when he pitted his son against the much more capable Mike Cohen. He also turned the Charleston, South Carolina, match into a kind of family reunion for nearby relatives from his ancestral home. The family festivities certainly lasted a lot longer than the fight. Marvis knocked out the 14–3 Cohen in two rounds.

The next fight Joe Frazier booked was the ultimate revenge match. It was meant to settle an old score that had been eating away at him—and his son— for almost three years. The Fraziers were finally getting another shot at James Broad, the man who had paralyzed Marvis with one punch in the 1980 Olympic Trials. They were also getting a chance to put Marvis up against another undefeated rising star.

The 8–0 Marvis Frazier faced the 12–0 Broad in a nationally televised bout on April 10, 1983, in Atlantic City. That gave Broad, a Wildwood, New Jersey, native, an enormous hometown advantage. It seems Broad had won a whopping 10 of his previous 12 professional fights right there in Atlantic City. The Jersey native also came into the match about 30 pounds heavier.

The commentators for the fight were my old ringside companion Gil Clancy and the great Sugar Ray Leonard. They described an old-fashioned slugfest with Marvis rocking the 228-pound Broad in round two. Broad found an opening and returned the favor in the seventh. Joe had Marvis in close, breathing on his opponent, all the way.

Marvis came out and dominated the ninth round. He did some real damage and looked to be in charge. Broad, surprisingly, almost turned the whole thing around in the 10th and final round. He mounted a furious attack down the stretch that had Marvis struggling to hold on.

Two of the three scorecards gave Marvis a slight 5–4–1 edge. The other came in at a more comfortable 6–3–1. It was a unanimous decision that drew high praise for the Fraziers from both television commentators and other boxing experts in the days that followed.

Joe quickly seized on the victory as a sign that his still inexperienced son was ready to become a serious heavyweight contender. In addition, the old Larry Holmes "promise" of a championship match was always on his mind. He worried that the time to cash in on it might be growing tight. After all, Holmes was closing in on his 34th birthday.

Holmes was also edging closer to Rocky Marciano's record of 49 heavyweight fights without a loss. Joe knew that reaching that milestone might prompt the champ to retire as well.

Manager Joe Frazier became more intent than ever on finding just the right opponent for his son. It had to be someone beatable, but impressive enough to justify a title shot way ahead of schedule.

10

(Mis)managing Marvis

Joe Frazier's search for Marvis's perfect next opponent surprisingly traced back to a pivotal fight in his own boxing career. It took him back to his bout against British champion Joe Bugner on July 2, 1973. Coincidentally, Marvis told me this was the first time he had been allowed to travel overseas with his dad to one of his matches. The fight had served to revitalize Joe's career, at perhaps its lowest point, and left a lasting impression on his son.

"I went to the Bugner fight [at 12] and I was there in London, England, with the guys in the training camp," Marvis had said, in an early chat up in the lair. "All we did was mostly stay in the hotel room because Pop was resting. But I didn't mind. As long as I could stay with him, that was cool."

Yank Durham, and the rest of Joe's management team, had seen the bout as a key test of Joe's immediate standing in the heavyweight ranks and a bellwether for his boxing future. Frazier had suffered his first professional loss to George Foreman just three months before. He was still smarting from the multiple knockdowns and the loss of the title he had secured in the Fight of the Century against Ali. In addition, many in the boxing establishment had been questioning Joe's ability to challenge for another championship after such a devastating loss.

Even Joe admitted that the way he lost to Foreman—in just two rounds—had somewhat shaken his confidence.

A quality win against Bugner had been deemed the key to showing the Foreman loss was just a fluke. Bugner, only 23, was a young rising star at the time with an amazing number of victories for his age. He was 43–5–1 going into the match and consistently ranked as a top 10 contender. However, despite several noteworthy wins, he had probably gained his greatest measure of acclaim for a recent loss. He was fresh off going the distance in a tightly contested 12-rounder with Muhammad Ali.

After Ali had taken the unanimous decision in Las Vegas several months before, he made a point of showing his respect for the man he had just battled. Ali said Bugner was definitely capable of becoming the world heavyweight champion. Later on, Ali's manager Angelo Dundee agreed.

Frazier's fight against the 6'4", 221-pound Brit quickly turned into a vicious 12-round brawl. Bugner, who seemed even taller due to his straight-up stance, scored well from the outside early on with combinations and sharp counterpunching. Joe began leaping forward in the middle rounds to get inside and go to work. This led to him pounding away at Bugner's body and head near the end.

Frazier did his most damage in the 10th round. He had backed Bugner into a neutral corner and then put him down with a typical Smokin' Joe left hook. Bugner surprised Joe by making it to his feet. Then the Brit showed how dangerous he could be by doing some damage of his own.

Many years later, Bugner looked back at the sequence in an interview with *The Ring* about the best fighters he had faced in his extremely long career. He had credited Joe Frazier for having the "best chin."

"He was so tough and I landed everything I had that fight," Bugner had said, referring to the 1973 match. "He dropped me in round 10 with a huge left hook and I remember looking at Andy Smith [my manager] who gave me the signal to get up. I got to my feet and suddenly Joe left himself wide open, and I caught him with a perfect right hand on the button. His legs went from under him and his knee almost touched the canvas."

Bugner's point had been that anyone else he ever fought would have gone down from that blow. But not Joe—not that day. Frazier had survived a sure knockout punch and took the tight decision on points. British referee Harry Gibbs, the sole official for the match, scored it 59¼ for Frazier and 58½ for Bugner. In the British scoring system at the time, the winner of a round gets 5 points and the loser receives 4¾.

Frazier's victory restored his swagger in the ring. It also placed him once again among the elite in the heavyweight division. After London, he hoped to get Foreman to honor the title rematch clause in their previous contract. He was ready to reclaim his title. But Big George refused to honor the deal.

Yank Durham rose to the occasion as both a trainer and manager. He brushed off the Foreman rejection and parlayed the Bugner decision into an even more important bout for Frazier's career. He arranged the rematch against Muhammad Ali at Madison Square Garden instead.

This was just one of the reasons why Joe talked about Durham in such reverent tones. He saw him as the perfect manager—the one who always chose the right match and kept him moving toward the big payday, the title, and greatness. He fancied he could do the same for his son.

Tragically, Yancey Durham suffered a stroke and died a month after Joe's win over Bugner. It was less than six months before the Ali-Frazier II match. The toll of Yank's death on Joe's career going forward was hard to measure. That's when longtime assistant trainer Eddie Futch took over. He was promoted to oversee Joe's preparation for Ali and to make all future decisions in his corner.

In 1983, Joe Frazier decided to pit Marvis, age 22, against the now 33-year-old Joe Bugner. They fought on June 4 in a televised main event from Atlantic City. It turned out to be a lot more than just the rarity of a father and son taking on the same opponent a decade apart.

The savvy veteran brought a 57–9 record to the match with the younger Frazier. That record included wins over the likes of Jimmy Ellis and Henry Cooper. It also now boasted *two* battles that had gone the distance with Muhammad Ali. Bugner's second Ali fight, on June 30, 1975, had been in Kuala Lumpur for the WBA and WBC belts. He had once again pushed Ali all through the bout and had his chances to win in a close decision.

Bugner didn't fight for more than a year after his second loss to Ali. But, still in his midtwenties, he came back to fight Brit Richard Dunn for the European Heavyweight Championship and the British and Commonwealth crowns. He knocked out the highly regarded Dunn in the first round.

Despite the easy win, Bugner fought only one more time—early in 1977 against the tough Ron Lyle—before taking another three years off until August 1980. The now 30-year-old fighter had his ups and down over the next couple of years but scored four straight knockouts in the bouts leading up to the clash with Marvis.

The towering Bugner weighed a hefty 238 pounds for the fight. Marvis barely cleared 200. Many boxing people, including Bugner, went on record saying that Marvis belonged in the new cruiserweight division for boxers from 176 to 195 pounds. Joe never considered that an option. He figured a win against a big man like Bugner would end that argument.

"I never liked really big guys," Joe had said at our first meeting. "I like a small, lanky guy like Ken Norton. Actually, the number one kind of build was the way the Champ [Muhammad Ali] was earlier in his prime. Going up to 220 is not necessary. Look at your really great champions—these guys were never huge. Rocky Marciano was 185. Jack Johnson, Joe Louis, these guys weren't monsters. Primo Carnera and George [Foreman] were the only good big champions I can think of."

Joe Frazier was a loud, consistent voice in his son's ear from the opening bell. He had Marvis in smokin' mode, in close, pressing his opponent all through the 10-round fight. Bugner jolted Marvis at times with a powerful, accurate jab. He also scored with punishing body shots. But Marvis just kept coming at him.

Marvis used his strength in the clinches to counter Bugner's weight. He used his speed to beat his opponent to key spots on the canvas, to cut off the ring when necessary. According to William C. Rhoden's *New York Times* report on the fight the next day, Marvis also peppered him with "quick overhand right punches and leaping left hooks patented by his father."

In a comparison of father and son, Bugner had high praise for Joe as a true "legend." He offered qualified praise for Marvis. He saw him as potentially "a very good fighter" with a strong hook to the body. Unfortunately, Bugner also said the kid seemed "very vulnerable to the right uppercut, and a left jab as well."

Nevertheless, Marvis took the unanimous decision in convincing fashion. It gave him a win on CBS-TV against a well-known, time-tested, respected warrior. As a result, it jumped Marvis up a bit in the heavyweight rankings. It also gave him the small measure of legitimacy his manager felt he needed for that early shot at a title.

Joe Bugner continued to win regularly against top competition after the loss to Marvis. He retired a second time in 1987, at age 37, and miraculously came back for one more long stint eight years after that. Eventually, at 48, Bugner finally won a world title in 1998 against James "Bonecrusher" Smith. It was the somewhat lightly regarded World Boxing Federation (WBF) version of the heavyweight crown. But he had the distinction of becoming the oldest man to ever capture a world championship belt at the time.

Marvis followed *his* big win over Joe Bugner by marrying his high school sweetheart, Daralyn Evon Lucas. He was just shy of his 23rd birthday but considered himself much further along in life than his parents when they took the plunge. In this instance, Marvis knew best. The couple had a strong, loving marriage right from the beginning.

Joe took part in all the family festivities but didn't miss a beat in his role as fight manager. He was more than ready to cash in on the Bugner win, Marvis's 10-0 record, and the Larry Holmes promise. In fact, according to Marvis's autobiography, Joe was already pushing for a World Boxing Council championship fight against Holmes while the newlyweds cruised the Caribbean on their honeymoon.

———

The Holmes-Frazier title match was snakebitten right from the get-go. As soon as Joe and promoter Murad Muhammad announced the November 25, 1983, bout, the WBC refused to sanction it. Challengers for the championship had to be ranked among the top 10 contenders. Marvis, after defeating Joe Bugner, was generously ranked only 11th.

The WBC also mandated that the next title defense for Holmes had to be against the number one contender. That was currently Greg Page, who most boxing people saw as a highly dangerous opponent. In addition, there was already a tacit agreement in place for a Holmes-Page fight through the maneuverings of promoter Don King.

The upshot of all this was that there were still plenty of hurdles to clear before Marvis Frazier and Larry Holmes could step in the ring. What's more, even if Marvis managed to get the fight—and miraculously won—he would *not* be crowned the champion. The WBC ruled the title would be declared vacant instead.

Larry Holmes was initially enticed into the Frazier match by the promise of a staggering $3.1 million payday. He also desired to do everything possible to avoid fighting Greg Page. Holmes didn't want to risk a loss to Page with Rocky Marciano's record for consecutive fights without a defeat looming so close. He obviously saw the still raw Marvis Frazier as the easier opponent.

Holmes decided to defy the WBC and reneged on his earlier deal to fight Page. The WBC countered by saying it would approve a "non-title" fight with Frazier if Holmes could come to terms with Page and Don King. In the end, Holmes agreed to a three-pronged approach to the dilemma. He signed on for a title match first against the 10th-ranked Scott Frank before the November date with the Fraziers. The dreaded Page fight was supposed to take place after the one with Marvis.

The champ quickly disposed of the 20–0–1 Frank on September 10 in Atlantic City. The contest lasted just 1:28 into round five of the scheduled 12-rounder. Holmes easily won on a TKO and retained his WBC crown.

In some of the title bouts leading up to the Frazier dispute, and the Frank fight, Holmes had handled several celebrated, more ominous foes. For instance, he knocked out Leon Spinks, the former undisputed world champion, on June 12, 1981, in the third round. He took out the undefeated Great White Hope, Gerry Cooney, in round 13 a year later. And he prevailed over "Terrible" Tim Witherspoon via a hard-fought split decision on May 20, 1983.

In the days before the champ's match with Marvis, a lot of the talk centered on Holmes's huge size advantage. Holmes was 6'3", with a long 81-inch reach, and a much thicker, more massive 220-pound body. But the real lopsided "tale of the tape" for this fight centered around the experience of the combatants.

Holmes came into the match with a 44–0 professional record that included 31 knockouts. He had won an incredible 16 straight heavyweight title defenses against the best boxers in the world. He had fought a total of 320 pro rounds against opponents with a combined 1,042 fights to their names.

Marvis's professional experience was puny by comparison. He had just 10 pro victories, six by knockouts, against mostly novice competition. He had boxed a mere 54 rounds in the pro ranks. All his opponents combined had amassed just 211 fights—and at least a quarter of those came courtesy of Joe Bugner.

————

The mismatch appeared startling even before a single punch was thrown. Larry Holmes hulked over the comparatively slender Marvis Frazier during the prefight instructions at the Caesars Palace Sports Pavilion in Las Vegas. It looked like some beefy NFL lineman preparing to run over a high school kid. In that moment, as I watched on a prime-time television feed over NBC, I became genuinely afraid for Marvis.

Years later, I watched a YouTube video of the match. It included live commentary from a rather reserved British announcer. All it did was confirm how right my initial fears turned out to be.

Round one began with the champ from Easton, Pennsylvania, flicking away with a long, efficient jab. He seemed to be biding his time, just probing for an opening. He also used his superior bulk and strength to push his opponent into the ropes when needed.

Marvis, inexplicably, started out by standing upright, smack in front of Holmes. He did a nimble job of slipping the constant barrage of jabs for a while. But he was unable to get close enough to the champ to throw any effective punches of his own as the round moved on.

I assumed Joe was calling the shots in the corner. He must have seen this as a good strategy. I just didn't know why. The British announcer didn't see the wisdom in the Frazier fight plan either.

Around the two-minute mark, things were sailing along in acceptable fashion. Marvis wasn't doing any damage, but he kept dodging most of the incoming shots. Then the kid got cocky enough to suddenly drop his hands and taunt the champion. That was when it all fell apart.

Holmes faked a jab and got the expected flinch. He patiently waited a beat, measuring the next punch. A moment later, a powerful overhand right connected to the side of Marvis's head.

Marvis reeled backward and fell in a heap to the canvas. After taking the eight-count, he rose up tentatively on one knee. He then stood on shaky legs.

Holmes, rightly known as "the Easton Assassin," immediately pounced with a speed that belied his size. He backed Marvis into his corner, inches from where Joe hugged the apron. Seven straight rights connected with Marvis's head and jaw as his dad looked on.

Holmes purposely hesitated between blows to give the referee time to step in. Marvis's mouthpiece flew out of the ring after one mighty shot, and Holmes took an even longer pause in his attack. He began waving his right arm, visibly urging referee Mills Lane to stop the fight.

The veteran referee didn't oblige. Holmes continued to whale away on the defenseless challenger. He kept doing his job.

After 15 unanswered blows, Lane momentarily checked Marvis's eyes. He apparently found them okay. He allowed Holmes to deliver four more accurate punches before stopping the fight. It officially ended in 2:57 of round one.

After the referee waved Holmes away, Joe climbed into the ring. He grabbed his son.

"It's all right," Joe said, hugging Marvis. "It's all right."

Joe spoke to reporters a bit later about that moment. They wanted to know what else he had to say to his son.

"I told him I still love him and don't worry," said Joe.

Holmes went over and gave both Marvis and Joe a heartfelt hug. Joe later reported to the press what Larry told him in that emotional moment.

"He said he didn't want to fight no more," said Joe, according to a *New York Times* story the next day. "That he didn't like doing this."

Holmes also told journalists directly about his reluctance to beat up on the son of a friend. He sounded truly upset.

"I didn't want to hurt him," said Larry, in his comments to a reporter for UPI. "He was hurt bad and I didn't want to hurt him anymore. I called the ref in to stop it four or five times before he stepped in. Marvis was taking an awful lot of punishment."

Holmes told UPI that he knew exactly how things would unfold. Nothing in that one-sided round surprised him.

"I said before the fight that Marvis was biting off more than he could chew," said Larry, referring to the challenger's lack of experience. "Fighters like that are made for me. He stood right there in front of me. Those guys are so easy to hit. I couldn't miss him."

If Holmes came off as heartsick over the lopsided contest, remarks to the *New York Times* showed that his trainer was absolutely furious about it. Eddie Futch had been the head trainer in Joe Frazier's corner for the last two fights with Muhammad Ali. He was now in Holmes's corner, but obviously still cared deeply for Marvis and the Frazier family.

"What a ridiculous mismatch," said Futch, criticizing Joe's mistake in rushing to book a title shot that endangered his son. "How could Joe let a kid in with a fighter who has this much experience? I thought Marvis needs at least a year more experience, five or six good fights."

"I never make mistakes," replied Joe, when he heard his old trainer's comments. "I know what I'm doing."

As a fighter, that kind of bravado plausibly helped in surviving a tough stretch in the ring. In a manager, it might have contributed to getting an overmatched fighter killed. Any boxer would rightly be scared if he heard that come out of the mouth of someone who controlled his fate.

Thirty minutes after the fight, Marvis was bruised but luckily appeared to be okay. Referee Mills Lane defended his decision to let the fight continue. He insisted Marvis had "clear eyes" when he had checked them. Lane reminded reporters that Marvis Frazier's corner could have stopped the fight earlier.

Joe's answer to Lane came straight from his warrior heart. But, once again, it wasn't something any boxer ever wanted to hear from his corner.

"I'm not the guy who believes in throwing in the towel," said Joe, who never made a move to stop the beating.

Joe's refusal to act seemed even more callous given his history with Eddie Futch. Remember, Futch was the trainer who threw in the towel before the 15th round of the Thrilla in Manila. Joe had been sitting on his stool between rounds badly beaten, both eyes swollen shut. In arguably the biggest boxing match of all time, Futch had put his fighter's health over his own visions of glory. Joe didn't appear to be able to do the same, even for his own son.

In the aftermath of the Frazier bout, Larry Holmes once again refused to honor his commitment to fight the number one contender Greg Page. The WBC stripped Holmes of his title. However, the newly formed International Boxing Federation (IBF) immediately recognized him as the heavyweight champion.

Marvis Frazier had lingering problems of his own following the public dismantling by Larry Holmes. After a humiliating half-hour press conference, he sank into a heavy depression. In his autobiography, Marvis described how he abruptly escaped to California for a while with his wife and cousin. He confessed to not going back into training for nearly eight months.

Joe Frazier's new strategy now called for his son to go up against one contender after another until Holmes consented to a second fight. He wanted a real title match against Holmes this time around. His plan ignored the fact that there were much less lethal fighters holding versions of the heavyweight crown at the time. He had simply reverted back to his old fighting instincts to get revenge and beat the best. And, of course, Marvis was the one destined to pay the price for his manager's stubbornness.

In order to beat these contenders, Joe borrowed a page from the George Benton training manual. He had Marvis sparring with some of the toughest professionals around. Ironically, some of the worst injuries Marvis endured in his boxing career came at his dad's gym while training.

During his sparring sessions, Marvis suffered a torn retina in his left eye and a detached retina in the right. The latter injury required surgery. It took months to recover and left Marvis with diminished eyesight for the rest of his life.

Michael Spinks was one of the topflight sparring partners Joe brought in to toughen Marvis up. Spinks later beat Larry Holmes twice in a row, in 1985 and again in 1986, to take the heavyweight title. He prevented Holmes from breaking Marciano's all-time undefeated streak. Larry fell one victory short of the record with 48 straight wins.

In one of their sparring matches, Spinks reportedly caught Marvis with a short, powerful punch to the chest. The blow fractured Marvis's sternum. In another training session, the highly ranked heavyweight Pinklon Thomas got Marvis to step back awkwardly. It resulted in a partial rupture of his Achilles tendon. It took several months to heal by Marvis's recollections.

Despite all the setbacks, Joe's plans for success looked pretty good for a while once Marvis recovered. Joe eased his son back into action with a good, old-fashioned cakewalk of a fight. On September 25, 1984, Marvis overwhelmed a 6′5″ stiff named David Starkey in New Jersey. The mismatch lasted 2:50 into the first round. Given Starkey's lame 3–7 record, I had to wonder what took so long.

The next five matches after that were all against top contenders, serious prospects, or future champions. Marvis didn't knock any of these guys out, but he managed to win every decision. That turned out to be more difficult and impressive than it sounds.

The first of these victories came about a month later in a non-title fight against the United States Boxing Association (USBA) cruiserweight champion Bernard Benton. Marvis wasn't able to get down below the weight limit to qualify for a shot at the belt. Still, he controlled the action against a man who would later capture the WBC cruiserweight crown.

Marvis actually swept one official's scorecard 10–0 in the Benton fight. He also received matching scores of 7–2–1 on the other two cards. Years later, looking back, he suggested the true outcome of the bout had been closer to that 10-round shutout than the more moderate scores.

"He was good," Marvis told an interviewer from doghouseboxing.com in 2009, "but I won almost every round."

I always considered that sweep—even if on only one official's card—an amazing feat. It seemed a heck of a lot more difficult, and dominant, to win every round of a main event than to score a first-round knockout. Marvis's loss to James Broad in the Olympic Trials showed that any competitive boxer could luck into a surprise opening and end it with a fortuitous punch. However, there is not enough luck in the world to get through 10 straight winning rounds of boxing without earning it.

Two months later, Marvis finished off 1984 with a December bout against the undefeated Nigerian heavyweight Funso Banjo in London, England. His opponent's name might have sparked some jokes, but the fight was tough and pretty tight for most of the 10 rounds. The Fraziers edged out Banjo in the British single-official scoring system by a tally of 98–97. Coincidentally, the referee for the fight was the same Harry Gibbs who had given Marvis's father the close decision over Joe Bugner in 1973.

Joe Frazier next booked a May 1985 match against the perennial contender James "Quick" Tillis. Most people associated the massive Tillis's nickname with his surprising hand speed rather than his ability to motor around the ring. The Oklahoma-born boxer also got the handle "Cowboy" due to his propensity for wearing an outlandish 10-gallon hat and western costumes. But the natural southpaw had some other eccentric habits that made him seriously dangerous to fight.

Tillis often switched midfight to an "orthodox" stance deemed more appropriate for a righty. He suddenly would go from leading with his right hand, as expected, to pumping powerful jabs or hooks with his left. Quite a few of his opponents were caught off guard and paid the price. This might have explained some of the 27 knockouts in 31 victories Tillis brought to his fight with Marvis.

The five losses on Tillis's record going into that fight told an interesting story of their own. On a high note, more than half of those rare defeats were in championship bouts. However, the way he wound up losing his fights formed a pattern that drove his handlers crazy.

In March 1981, Tillis lost a WBA World Heavyweight Championship match to Mike Weaver. About a year and a half later, he dropped the IBF and USBA titles to the same Greg Page that scared the heck out of Larry Holmes. Tillis also lost a North American Boxing Federation (NABF) heavyweight title fight to Terrible Tim Witherspoon in 1983.

Tillis started strong against Weaver and had him in trouble in the beginning. Unfortunately, he pooped out in the later rounds and wound up falling short in a closely scored unanimous decision. Angelo Dundee, his frustrated manager at the time, begged Tillis to step it up as things slipped away. Dundee ultimately dropped him from his stable of fighters.

In the Page bout, Tillis struck first with a knockdown early on and looked to be in charge. But he soon began to tire and got knocked out in the eighth. A similar scenario unfolded in Quick's fight with Carl "the Truth" Williams— an elimination bout for a shot at a major title. He put Williams down twice in the first round and then ran out of gas later. He lost that decision as well.

Tillis stuck closely to his now familiar script in the fight with Marvis Frazier. The smarter cornerman would have seen it coming and told Marvis to stay away in the opening rounds, make Tillis chase, sap the early energy. Instead, Joe had his fighter in close and exchanging blows.

It almost cost his son the fight. Cowboy predictably caught Marvis with a good shot in the second round that led to a standing eight-count. Given his vaunted knockout power, it could have been a lot worse. As the fight wore on, Tillis faded, as he had in the past, and practically handed the Fraziers the unanimous decision in the final rounds. Marvis won, but Joe made it harder—and riskier—than it should have been.

The 6'5" contender Jose Ribalta boasted an 18–2–1 record, with 12 knockouts, when he faced Marvis Frazier in Atlantic City that September. At just 22 years old, the Cuban boxer was three years younger than Marvis and at least as far along in his quest for a heavyweight title shot. In fact, Ribalta believed he would have been fighting for a crown if he had not been robbed in a recent bout against James Smith.

The Ribalta-Smith fight had ended in a tight split decision. Ribalta thought he had won by a wide margin. The outcome had crushed him at the time, and he never quite got over it.

"The only fight I really shed tears was when I fought James 'Bonecrusher' Smith," said Ribalta in a 2014 interview on *On the Ropes Boxing Radio.* "Because this was my beginning, my first experience of being in a fight and clearly winning the fight and not getting the decision. I really started crying after that fight."

Ribalta's match with Marvis may have prompted more than a few sobs as well. The 10-rounder went down to the wire and ended in a majority decision—two officials going for one fighter and the other calling it a tie. Marvis had the edge on two cards with scores of 6–4 and 5–4–1. The third card had it five rounds apiece.

It was hard to fault Joe's fight plan in this match. Any kind of win against a towering, talented opponent like Ribalta meant doing something right. The Fraziers did seem to earn this victory, and Ribalta didn't complain as vociferously. In Marvis's eyes, the decision should not have been so close, and he said just that in an interview many years later.

In the small, incestuous world of heavyweight contenders, it should have surprised no one that Joe Frazier next scheduled the same James Smith who had just driven Ribalta to tears. Marvis had originally met and beaten Smith in the Golden Gloves when they were both top-ranked amateurs. Now they were experienced pros and Joe saw a win over Bonecrusher as a surefire ticket to a higher ranking for his son and an eventual shot at a heavyweight belt.

The college-educated Smith, a latecomer to boxing in general, didn't turn professional until November 1981. Yet, he had already fought in two tightly contested heavyweight championship bouts by the time he faced off with Marvis on February 23, 1986. His first big fight had been against Larry Holmes in 1984 for the IBF crown. The other one had just taken place in Nevada with Tim Witherspoon for the NABF title. Both fights wound up as losses for Smith, but they announced in graphic style that he had arrived.

Smith's scheduled 15-round bout with Holmes took place about a year after Marvis Frazier's one-round debacle against the champ. Unlike Frazier, the 6'4" Smith had the size, reach (82 inches), and punching power to keep Holmes at a distance while still doing considerable damage himself. Bonecrusher got to Holmes a number of times in the fight and looked to have him in trouble more than once. Later in the grueling match, Smith began to run down, and Larry won on cuts in round 12.

Smith told a UPI reporter that he saw the 10-round main event against Marvis Frazier as a "crossroads fight" in his boxing career. At 32 years old, he had a respectable 15–4 record against some top competition, but he had blown both of his shots at a championship. He wasn't sure how many more chances he would get if he didn't take that one and go on a winning streak. Although Marvis was only 25, his manager also seemed to see this as a make-it-or-break-it opportunity.

Marvis came out at the start of round one dancing and moving. He stuck the jab and had Smith off balance for a while. This was a departure from Joe's insistence that Marvis fight inside like he used to do. Maybe all of George Benton's talk of Marvis not having to fight like a bear had registered after all.

It didn't take long for Joe to prove me wrong. By midway through the round, he had his son down in a Smokin' Joe crouch trying to bore his way in under Smith's long reach. Once inside, Marvis leaned on the older fighter and stayed active. For his part, Smith looked to use his 234 pounds to trap Marvis on the ropes and work the body. It didn't look flashy, but the heavy blows took a toll.

Marvis got in trouble again in the third round before settling down in the fourth. In an effort to fight in close, he once again allowed himself to get pinned on the ropes early in round five. Smith unloaded a series of heavy blows to the body and forced him to cover up.

Joe yelled for his son to get out of there. Marvis finally worked his way free and seemed on the defensive most of the round. Smith acted like he smelled a knockout and kept punching throughout the fifth.

Near the end of round five, Marvis was backing up from an exchange, trying to find some breathing room. Smith landed a sweeping overhand right that put him down. Marvis quickly got to his feet but still seemed shaky at the bell.

Marvis admitted after the fight to being "stunned" by the punch. But he emphasized how quickly he managed to regroup. In truth, Marvis's better performance in the later rounds seemed to be more a product of Smith having punched himself out in that go-for-broke fifth. Bonecrusher was still cornering Marvis on the ropes from time to time but didn't have the energy to make him pay.

In the 10th and final round, Joe obviously thought that his fighter had done enough to be safely ahead on the officials' scorecards. He had Marvis change tactics and go on the run. Smith still wanted to mix it up, but he was too tired to close the gap. The crowd booed the lack of activity.

I had Marvis with just a slight lead at that juncture. It seemed like a terrible gamble to just throw away a round at the finish of a tight fight. That would have been an impossible loss for a manager to explain.

"Pa felt we were comfortably ahead," Marvis told reporters about Joe's avoidance strategy. "He told me just keep moving."

Two of the three final scorecards proved how wrong Joe's assessment of the fight had been. They had Marvis ahead by just a single point in the 10-point must scoring system. One read 97–96 and the other 96–95. The third inexplicably had Marvis winning it by a score of 97–92. I wondered if Joe had filled out that card himself.

This time James Smith was the one who claimed to have been robbed. I didn't agree, but it was open to debate. By the way, Smith met Tim Witherspoon a second time 10 months and four fights later for the WBA Heavyweight Championship. Smith came out pumped and immediately sent the champ to the canvas three times in rapid succession. He won the fight and the title in 2:12 of the first round.

I guess losing the crossroads fight had not ended Smith's chances for a crown. Now the question was, what would winning it do for the Fraziers?

———

James Smith had been ranked eighth by the WBA when he lost to Marvis Frazier. The outcome of that fight, combined with Marvis's other impressive victories of late, suddenly catapulted the Fraziers into the middle of the heavyweight title discussion. Marvis's record had soared to 16–1, and the WBC made him the ninth-ranked contender. The IBF jumped him all the way to number four among its top heavyweights.

Larry Holmes was temporarily out of the championship picture. All manager Joe Frazier needed to do was slow down, scan his options, and carefully choose the right match to keep his son moving toward a title bout. The optimum opponent had to be slightly higher ranked and plausibly beatable. He also had to be the kind of boxer that would allow Marvis to get into a rhythm and likely go the distance. After all, Marvis had only notched seven knockouts since turning pro, and none of them had been against contenders.

Joe's impatience, and desire for a shortcut to the title, unfortunately got the better of him. He opted for the match that would lead directly to a championship fight. Joe signed to have his son fight the number two ranked WBC contender—the fast-rising assassin that everyone else was avoiding. He simply underestimated the danger of putting Marvis in the ring with a young, hungry Mike Tyson.

And, to just give Tyson every advantage possible, Joe agreed to hold the match at the Civic Center in Glens Falls, New York. Mike grew up in the nearby town of Catskill.

Iron Mike, also known as the Baddest Man on the Planet, came into the July 26, 1986, bout with Marvis undefeated. He was 24–0 against fairly elite competition, and an astounding 22 of those fights ended in knockouts. However, even more ominous for the Fraziers, the majority of those wins were first-round knockouts fueled by a fury rarely seen in a boxing ring. He made it clear he would obliterate all who stood in his way.

Tyson had just turned 20 about a month before the fight. He had expressed a much-publicized desire to become the youngest heavyweight champion of all time. That meant he had to beat out Floyd Patterson, who had won the title at 21 years and 11 months. Like everything else Tyson did in the ring, he did it more quickly and violently than people expected. Kid Dynamite, another nickname, reached his goal later in 1986, with more than a year and a half to spare.

Mike Tyson connected with a vicious right uppercut moments after the opening bell. It left Marvis stunned and wobbly. Tyson followed up by driving him into a neutral corner with a jarring combination and finished the job with another uppercut to the chin. Just 30 seconds into the fight, Marvis was lying unconscious on the canvas. The referee didn't even bother to complete the count as the *ABC Wide World of Sports* camera zoomed in for the close-up of the inert body.

"I could have counted to 20 and he wouldn't have gotten up," said referee Joe Cortez, according to BoxRec.com. "Marvis was really out of it. I was more concerned about the safety of the fighter."

In the postfight news conference Tyson verbalized what most boxing people had known for a while. "I'm the best fighter in the world," he declared.

Marvis, for his part, agreed and readily paid homage to the victor's obvious punching power. "Mike, you must have had a sledgehammer," he said, forcing a grin.

Joe, on the other hand, still refused to admit he took Tyson too lightly. Just as with the Larry Holmes match, he never owned up to making a mistake. His postfight comments to Iron Mike sounded more like a challenge coming from a future opponent than the words of a losing manager.

"I'd like to see what he's got myself," said Joe, referring to Tyson's punching power in a *New York Times* report the next day. "What is the guy, an animal? I want to make a date and go down and work with him. I want to check him out myself. I don't believe he can hurt me."

Even before the fight, boxing experts had criticized Joe for booking the Mike Tyson match. They questioned his management skills. Some also questioned whether he saw his fighter in the ring or old Smokin' Joe himself.

Lou Duva, the celebrated manager and trainer, gave the *New York Times* this damning assessment of Frazier about a week before the fight.

"He's a stubborn, opinionated guy," said Duva. "But the question is does he book fighters' matches from here" [a finger pointed to his heart], "or here" [he touched his head]. "Who's fighting the fight: Joe Frazier or his fighter? He'd like them to be as good as Joe Frazier could be. But there's only one Joe Frazier."

In that same article, George Benton chimed in with exactly what went wrong in Marvis Frazier's professional career. It sounded very much like a trainer-poet's ode to what could have been.

"I had him a boxer—a fighter who didn't get hit with a lot of punches," said Benton, recalling the days before Joe pushed him out. "Then, somewhere down the line he became more of a brawler-type fighter."

Unlike Joe, Benton never felt Marvis had to mix it up or eat a lot of leather to be victorious.

Despite the lack of an official announcement, or a recognized meeting of the minds in the Frazier camp, the Tyson hammering had effectively ended Marvis's boxing career. Oh, he went on to fight three more times and won them all. But, by his own account, his heart was no longer in the game.

The ambush by Tyson had sapped much of Marvis's fighting spirit. It had also robbed him of the expectation of bringing another heavyweight crown to the Frazier family. Like the Larry Holmes one-rounder, it was a fight his manager never should have booked.

It took 11 months for Marvis to return to the ring—fighting now more out of obligation than dedication. He fought the capable veteran Tom Fischer at the Hilton in Secaucus, New Jersey. Fischer had a 35–10 record going into the 10-round bout, and he had recently gone the distance in a main event with Leon Spinks. Fischer weighed 217 pounds for the bout, but Marvis nearly matched him at a career-high 214. Ironically, this was around the weight George Benton had originally seen as optimum for Marvis once he grew to maturity.

Marvis used his newfound heft to work effectively in close right from the start. He soon put Fischer down twice from a steady barrage of body shots. Referee Vincent Rainone stopped the contest and awarded Marvis the TKO in 2:47 of round two. The fast, one-sided win reminded boxing people how good Marvis could be. It also demoralized Fischer enough to put him into retirement.

Joe rewarded his son by stepping up the pace of his latest comeback. Two months later, in August 1987, Marvis returned to the Hilton in Secaucus to fight a lightly regarded 6–12–3 Robert Evans. It was not a great sign that Evans went the whole 10 rounds before losing in a lopsided unanimous decision. The match did little for rekindling Marvis's waning enthusiasm. He waited 14 months before willing himself to return for his final professional bout.

"I knew it was my last fight before I took it," confessed Marvis, in a 2016 article for *Boxing Insider*.

It was appropriate that the highly respected 31–2–2 Philipp Brown became the last man Frazier faced in the ring. Brown had won eight straight fights coming into the match and gave Marvis a chance to go out with his head held high. He had also been the opponent in Marvis's amateur coming-out party when he reached national prominence. On March 31, 1979, the undefeated Marvis Frazier had decisioned Brown in his 30th match to claim the National Golden Gloves Championship.

Marvis's quote in the *Washington Post* after that Golden Gloves triumph had an eerie, woebegone ring to it in retrospect.

"I'm not enthused about being a pro," he had said with certainty. "I'm taking a year off for the Olympics, if it is God's will to give me the strength."

Marvis once again went the distance with Philipp Brown on October 12, 1988. He again won the fight in a unanimous decision and had reason to celebrate. The strain of training, and the pain of fighting against fierce pro heavyweights, was finally over. The depression that haunted him in his final years of boxing began to fade. He was free.

I was home in New York, looking after my seven-year-old daughter and her baby sister, when I heard the news. I felt a strange sense of loss for what Marvis could have done, for what Joe wanted for him, for all the years of sacrifice. I also realized how much I had wanted the Fraziers to get their one more championship.

Marvis finished his professional journey with a 19–2 record. When added to his 56–2 amateur mark, it left him with a sensational 75 wins and only four losses for his total boxing career. His only losses in the pros, stunning as they were, came at the hands of two of the greatest heavyweight champions ever. Sadly, these losses have come to define Marvis as a fighter and seem to be all people remember.

Joe Frazier's role in his son's boxing career remained complex from start to finish. Smokin' Joe the brawler gave Marvis the pedigree, work ethic, and inspiration needed to win. Unfortunately, in the end, Joe the manager and trainer deprived Marvis of the patience and fighting style best suited for him to capture a heavyweight crown in the complex world of professional boxing.

I'm convinced that George Benton would have turned Marvis Frazier into the "thinking fighter" he had always envisioned. He would have kept him more on the outside, picking his spots and avoiding unnecessary risk. As a result, he would have kept him healthier and more active—and he would have extended his years in the ring. He would have certainly made better match-making and boxing decisions than Joe.

In the long run, Benton would have had an excellent chance of getting Marvis his championship ring. He might have gotten him his piece of boxing greatness as well.

11

Smokin' Joe and the Ali Wars

When last we checked, Joe Frazier had finished 1966 with that big come-from-behind win over Oscar Bonavena and a clean 12–0 record. He headed into 1967 a more disciplined, dangerous boxer than ever before. Yank Durham still constantly barked instructions in the corner, but his fighter had finally learned to listen.

In the new year, Frazier came out busier and more focused in the earlier rounds. He stayed consistently more active in the middles rounds too and began to efficiently dispatch opponents at a furious rate. The young bear of a boxer also learned to bob, weave, and feint his way through the defenses of taller fighters under the tutelage of assistant trainer Eddie Futch. This made the Smokin' Joe crouch a much more effective stance.

From November 1966 to December 1967, Frazier chalked up seven straight victories against top contenders or wily veterans. Maybe more impressive was the fact that all but one of these triumphs came via knockouts. These respected fighters were falling like tenpins, and Joe threw one strike after another.

The first to go down was Eddie Machen, at 50–8–3, who lasted 22 seconds into round 10 before calling it quits. Two months later, Doug Jones survived only through 2:28 of the sixth before hitting the canvas. He had narrowly lost an earlier decision to Muhammad Ali and seemed confident at first. He likely didn't fully appreciate Joe's power until it was too late.

In April 1967, Frazier took a working vacation in Miami Beach to fight the lean, 6′4″, 205-pound journeyman Jefferson Davis. At 29–11–1, Davis figured to have the experience and size—if not the heft—to give the kid from Philly some trouble. However, Joe no longer had the luxury of sneaking up on opponents with his power. He was now ranked third by the WBA and fourth in *The Ring* magazine standings.

According to an AP report on the fight, Frazier stayed on top of Davis from the start and often had him up against the ropes. He repeatedly scored with left hooks to both the body and the head. In the fifth round, Frazier unleashed a torrent of left hooks right from the bell. He had Davis down twice before the referee put a halt to the assault at 48 seconds into the round. The beating must have made an impression because Davis, only 26 years old, never fought again.

Three weeks later, Frazier ran into a surprisingly resilient George "Scrap Iron" Johnson. From Johnson's performance, it would seem the metal resided more in his chin than his hands. Scrap Iron stayed upright for all 10 rounds before losing a one-sided unanimous decision. *The Ring* magazine found out that Johnson had a special motivation for avoiding the knockout. He had brazenly bet his whole paycheck that he would make it to the final bell.

Frazier's next victim was the popular Canadian champion George Chuvalo. He came out swinging and beat the heck out of Chuvalo for three solid rounds. Somehow the Canuck managed to stay on his feet throughout the onslaught. But the referee mercifully ended the contest just 16 seconds into round four. Chuvalo didn't seem to appreciate the kindness.

It turned out Frazier was the first fighter to stop Chuvalo, despite all the great heavyweights who had tried. In fact, Chuvalo had become the first man to go 15 rounds with Muhammad Ali in a title bout the previous year. Although Ali had denigrated the Canadian before the match, he lauded him as his toughest opponent to date afterward. Chuvalo's pride was not soothed by Ali's belated compliments.

"When it was over, Ali was the guy who went to the hospital pissing blood," said Chuvalo in a later *Irish Times* piece. "Me? I went dancing with my wife. No question I got the best of the deal."

By the way, no one in George Chuvalo's long career *ever* knocked him down—not Ali, Foreman, Patterson, Ellis, or Smokin' Joe.

Frazier's two-round demolition of Tony Doyle in October 1967—the Irishman who had supposedly defeated him as an amateur—has already been chronicled here. That left the muscular Marion Connor as his final opponent of the year. Although he weighed just 180 pounds, Connor had a 30–4 record and the reputation as a hard hitter for a light heavyweight.

Fighting near home in the Boston Garden, Connor took to the offensive from the opening bell. Frazier, momentarily reverting to earlier form, started slowly and likely lost round one. Joe finally turned up the pressure in the second round and weakened Connor with body shots. Sensing it was time for the kill, he went for the knockout in the third.

Marion Connor relived the moment Joe turned out the lights 24 years later for a hometown publication.

"He threw a punch and he missed and went around with the same hand and—Bam!" said Connor, forming a circle with his left hand. "They told me to watch out for his left hand, but they never told me he'd do that."

The powerful roundhouse dropped Connor on the spot, and the referee stopped the fight after 1:40 of the third.

Frazier emerged from his yearlong rampage with a spotless 19–0 record. He was now feared for his knockout power and those punishing body shots. He was also the number-one contender in the heavyweight ranks.

Joe Frazier appeared to be entering his professional boxing prime. Yank Durham and the Cloverlay team decided it was time to seek out the absolute best competition and look for a title shot.

———

Florence Frazier had once told me what it was like to be married to Joe after his 1967 run. She had described her life as the wife of an elite heavyweight boxer. In truth, it didn't sound all that glamorous. From her perspective, Joe's success wasn't always such a good thing.

Florence had said she liked it better in the early days of her husband's career. She had liked it when Joe would "knock guys out" in the first few rounds.

"When the bigger money came, Joe took more punishment and the fights became harder for me to watch," Flo had said, fingers pressed below her lower lip. "If he fought in New York, I would go. But I would stay in the hotel until the fight was over rather than watch. I would wait and listen to the report on television."

That made me wonder exactly when the fights had gotten too rough, too physically abusive for Florence to attend. What fight had represented the tipping point?

"I used to watch the fights live until he fought Bonavena [for the second time] in Philadelphia," Flo had replied, while attending one of her son's AAU matches in 1980. "I also went later on to the first and third Ali fights. During the Ali fights I got in the habit of covering my eyes."

––––––––––

Smokin' Joe's professional prime pretty much coincided with an era in heavyweight boxing I call "the Ali wars." This period began in 1967 when Muhammad Ali was stripped of his heavyweight championships and banished from boxing for refusing the draft. The furor over who got to fight for Ali's crowns, and eventually fill his shoes, sparked the first war. That initial conflict raged on for more than three years—both in and out of the ring.

The second Ali war started once the Greatest was allowed to return to boxing to pursue his lost titles. It began in earnest with the Fight of the Century and thundered through the devastation of the the Thrilla in Manila in 1975. These wars brought on the golden age of heavyweight boxing that featured the likes of Ali, Frazier, and Foreman at first and endured through the 1980s with champions like Holmes and Tyson. These warriors became the measuring stick for all heavyweights to follow and forever changed the landscape of the sport.

Muhammad Ali's last fight before his banishment came on March 27, 1967. At just 25 years old, he was already a global phenomenon. He had been ordered to report for induction into the army a week before the match and refused.

Ali fought Zora Folley, 11 years his senior, at Madison Square Garden. Folley, at 74-7-4, came in as *The Ring* magazine's number-one contender. This was his first championship fight and a reward for taking on the best heavyweights since the 1950s. After the fight, Folley claimed there was no one better than Ali.

"I should know," he had said. "I've fought them all."

Ali scored a seventh-round knockout on the strength of two short rights. It was a stunning turn after what seemed like a lackluster fight in several of the earlier rounds. The first right was so quick, and hard to see, some likened it to the phantom punch that had put away Sonny Liston in 1964. The victory allowed Ali to briefly retain his WBA, WBC, *The Ring*, and lineal titles.

Once Ali's titles were taken away, the WBA decided to hold a heavyweight elimination tournament to determine its next champion. The eight top-ranked fighters, including number-one Joe Frazier, received an invitation to battle it out for the crown. The anemic monetary rewards called for escalating purses that maxed out at only $175,000 for the finalists. A decidedly bigger problem was that the tournament promoter got to keep the ancillary rights to the winner's fights for two years.

Yank Durham and the Cloverlay group opted to blow off the WBA tournament. Frazier's management team naturally cited low prize money and the demand for ancillary rights as the reason for balking. In truth, they preferred to see the lower-ranked contenders knock each other off en route to crowning a best-of-the-rest winner. They figured this would set the scene for the only big-money fight available now that Ali was gone—Joe Frazier versus the survivor champion.

The WBA was enraged by Frazier's refusal to take part in the tournament. It retaliated by dropping him to ninth in the rankings. This made his rejection of the elimination event a moot point in the WBA's eyes. The snub didn't work and soon backfired on the organization.

The New York State Athletic Commission (NYSAC) stepped in to make Frazier their top contender. The plan was to have him fight a heavyweight championship match of their own. When Joe heard the name of his opponent, he was hooked. What more could he want than a shot at his first heavyweight belt and a long-awaited chance for revenge?

————

On March 4, 1968, an undefeated Joe Frazier took on the 23–0 Buster Mathis for the NYSAC title. The combatants were lured into the match by a chance to win a piece of the world heavyweight crown. It also gave them the opportunity to be the first to fight in the just opened, third incarnation of Madison Square Garden. For Frazier, the specter of battering the man who had beaten him twice as an amateur—including at the Olympic Trials—was simply sweet icing on the cake.

The winner of the match would be recognized as the heavyweight champ by New York, Pennsylvania, Texas, Illinois, Maine, and Massachusetts. The prize, and matchup, was momentous enough to draw a then indoor-record crowd for boxing of more than 18,000 fans. The $658,503 in gate receipts was also an indoor record at the time. And the bout was aired via closed-circuit television in 70 cities.

Unfortunately, the excitement of the event inside the Garden was drowned out somewhat by the hundreds of protesters shouting slogans outside. Black power groups had organized demonstrations in support of a wildly popular political martyr known as the Greatest. They were joined by a large contingent of young white protesters who also idolized the exiled champ. All the boxing fans and members of the media had to wade through the throng to get in.

"There is no champion but Muhammad Ali," chanted the demonstrators, the message coming through loud and clear.

With the shadow of Ali looming over the arena, Joe became the aggressor right from the opening bell. He chased the 243-pound Mathis, the heaviest opponent of his pro career, through the first six rounds but had little to show for it. A game Mathis held his own in the exchanges, and the fight remained fairly even.

In the seventh round, Frazier began to step up the ferocity of his body shots. The blows came quicker, harder, and dug more deeply into the flesh around the big man's midsection. Despite a slip that momentarily swept Frazier off his feet, the pace of his attack never waned. The Philly fighter just kept chopping away.

By round 11, the agile giant had slowed dramatically under the pressure of the nonstop punches. He was also bleeding profusely from the nose onto his white shorts. Finally, in the closing minute, Frazier connected with a short, crushing left hook that sent Mathis sprawling across the bottom strand of the ropes. Somehow, he managed to swim through a fog to his feet by the count of nine. But the referee just stopped the beating there.

After the fight, Mathis was asked where the opening came for the thunderous final punch. He struggled with the answer, visibly shaken by the loss. Tears welled up in his eyes as he spoke.

"I pulled back," said Mathis, as reported in the *Pittsburgh Press*. "If you pull back, you get hit. I pulled back."

It was Joe Frazier's first professional championship. It was also the first time Mathis had been knocked down in his career. Frazier and his team were elated in the dressing room. They itched to celebrate the title, the culmination of Joe's boyhood dream. However, that joy was soon tempered by the questions from the media.

The members of the press pretty much took on the attitude of the demonstrators outside the Garden. They questioned whether there could be a true heavyweight champion other than Ali. They wanted to know if Joe felt like the champ with the presence of the undefeated Ali hovering over the arena—and all of the heavyweight division.

Joe didn't respond right away. He seemed at a loss for an answer.

"What do you think?" he finally asked, according to that same *Pittsburgh Press* piece. "What did it look like to you?"

Joe had no more to add. He looked over to Yank Durham for help.

"I'm running out of words, man," he said, deflated by the exchange.

Frazier realized now that banishing Ali from the fight game did not mean he was gone. The Greatest would be the third competitor in the ring for all of Smokin' Joe's title bouts.

―――――――

Joe Frazier's first title defense was set for June, just three months after defeating Mathis. His management team had scheduled the 6'4" Mexican champion Manuel Ramos at MSG. Frazier took his piece of the world heavyweight title seriously and hit training camp in New York's Catskill Mountains with a vengeance. He wanted to be seen as a dominant champion in the Ali mode.

Morty Holtzer, in reminiscing about how fierce Joe had been back then, talked about an interesting problem that arose in that camp. He said the trainers had a terrible time finding willing sparring partners for Joe. Holtzer offered a little anecdote to prove his point.

"One big heavyweight, Roosevelt something, weighed 230 or so, came up to the Concord [Hotel camp] before the Ramos fight," said Morty, warming to his tale. "He walked into the gym and saw Joe hammering the hell out of one of the other sparring partners. I told him to go and change. He said, 'I'm not even going to get undressed.' I asked if he was going to at least stay and have his meal, get carfare home. He said, 'I don't even want to wait for that. I'm going home. I'm not gonna get killed here.'"

Frazier brought that same ferocity to the fight with Ramos. He knew the Mexican was on a 13-match winning streak against mostly top competition and wanted to set the tone early. Joe came out throwing hard from the start. However, in his haste to dominate, he got careless. Ramos staggered him in the first round with a vicious right uppercut.

The 24-year-old Frazier survived the punch and first round on instinct and superior conditioning. He showed his resilience in the second by shaking off the damage done and going on the offensive. He knocked Ramos down twice in the round. After the second trip to the canvas, the challenger struggled to his feet before signaling to the referee that he couldn't go on.

The Frazier camp finished 1968 with an absolutely brutal second match against Oscar Bonavena at the Philadelphia Spectrum. Fight film, articles, and an old conversation with Holtzer made it clear why Florence shied away from watching Joe's matches live after this one. The results were gruesome for both the winner and loser. Joe legitimately beat the heck out of Bonavena, but the Argentine found less than legal ways to do terrible damage as well.

Frazier's 15-round NYSAC title defense on December 10 went the distance with the Philly fighter winning a deservedly lopsided decision. He pummeled his opponent nonstop throughout the contest. Bonavena, renowned for his granite chin, never hit the canvas, but his face and body served as a graphic testament to Frazier's punching power. Joe opened nasty cuts atop both of Oscar's eyes and across the bridge of his nose. And there were raised bruises on his face and body.

Bonavena fought more of a defensive fight—constantly holding back in a peekaboo stance looking for that one knockout shot. As Frazier pressured him along the ropes, Bonavena repeatedly tried to back him off with low blows. The Argentine was warned about hitting below the belt in the third, eighth, 10th, and 12th rounds. Things got so bad that the referee had to penalize the cheap-shot artist by taking away the eighth round.

Marvis Frazier had told me about attending this fight in our initial interview. He had said he was eight years old and realized for the first time that his dad was a "big-time" fighter.

"There was mass confusion," Marvis had recalled. "I really didn't know what was going on. I just realized that everybody was yelling for my father—so, I was yelling for him too. After the fight, I went back with him to the dressing room and there were reporters and fans all around him."

Morty Holtzer, who had worked Joe's corner that night, had given me a much more graphic, emotional depiction of the dressing room scene after the fight. It was a situation any eight-year-old might want to forget.

"Bonavena had hit Joe with 16 or 17 blows beneath the belt," Morty had told me. "We came back to the dressing room after the fight and Joe's balls had blown up terribly. Marvis stood there petting his father's head, kissing him, asking him, 'What can I do?' I started to cry."

———————

Frazier's next NYSAC title defense was against an unknown, unranked, and undefeated Dave Zyglewicz. It took place in the challenger's Houston, Texas, hometown on April 22, 1969. The former Navy Atlantic Fleet champion barely qualified as a heavyweight at 190 pounds. Yet he still boasted 28 wins albeit against mediocre competition.

Zyglewicz had initially been scheduled to fight for the WBA heavyweight crown instead. But reigning champ Jimmy Ellis decided to back out. According to an AP piece, one of Ellis's sparring partners warned him that officials in Texas wouldn't let him win.

The sparring partner had reminded Ellis that everyone associated with the fight down there would be white—except the champ. "You think you're going to knock that boxer out?" Ellis's friend had said. "If you knock him out, they will disqualify you."

Frazier took that challenge and proved Ellis's sparring partner wrong. He came out throwing and soon caught the Texan with a sharp left hook that put him down for an eight-count. Moments later, Zyglewicz was doubled over with a right and a left hook that put him back on the canvas. The match ended in 1:36 of the first round.

"I never felt nobody hit as hard," said Zyglewicz, in the AP postfight report. "He's real fast. I never saw the knockout punch coming."

The bout was not only Zyglewicz's first loss, but also the first time he had been knocked down.

After Joe Frazier danced his Texas two-step on Zyglewicz, he dramatically stepped up the level of the competition two months later. His fourth NYSAC title defense was against the highly ranked, big-fight tested, "Irish" Jerry Quarry. The durable Quarry brought a rock-solid 31–2–4 record to his Madison Square Garden match with Frazier.

Quarry was fresh off a gut-busting, unanimous 12-round decision over Buster Mathis. In that fight, he had Mathis down in the second round and had hurt him continuously with jarring body shots. Quarry had also dropped

Floyd Patterson twice on the way to a mixed-decision win in their WBA elimination tournament bout. And he had barely lost another mixed decision to Jimmy Ellis in the tournament finals for the vacant WBA World Heavyweight Championship.

The ruggedly handsome Quarry was not only formidable in the ring, but also wildly popular with fans. In fact, he had later been named by *The Ring* magazine as the most popular fighter in boxing from 1968 to 1971. The honor had likely been tied to a combination of Ali's banishment, Quarry's string of TV and movie acting credits, and the big-time bouts he had fought in those years. Quarry's popularity served to undercut much of the crowd support that Joe usually enjoyed in New York City.

The bout began with the kind of heated, toe-to-toe action usually reserved for the last moments of a tight battle when the outcome is on the line. Both fighters kept punching away in the first round, neither giving ground, but Quarry connected more and did greater damage. Quarry relied on superior hand speed, combinations, and his ability to counterpunch. Joe kept on the attack all through the round and connected with a few heftier blows.

The Ring, in a recent 50th anniversary article commemorating the fight, analyzed why Frazier "took a shellacking" in that first round. The piece noted that Frazier's bob-and-weave motion usually took time "to synchronize with incoming assaults." It surmised the Philly fighter didn't mind falling behind early on scorecards because once he had his timing down "hell would be unleashed." *The Ring* was impressed enough with both Quarry's and Frazier's initial efforts in the fight to dub round one as the "Round of the Decade."

Frazier settled into a better offensive rhythm in the second round and continued to keep the pressure on. He worked in close with both hands and refused to give Quarry much punching room, according to an AP report the next day. Quarry, for his part, stayed active in those early rounds. He was hoping to catch Frazier with one big blow before fatigue set in.

The fight turned more decisively in Frazier's favor early in the fourth round. That was when he opened a nasty cut around Quarry's right eye. By the end of the round, there was also a puffy mouse under the eye that bled heavily. Quarry pleaded with the doctor not to stop the fight between rounds. Despite's Quarry's reputation as a bleeder, the doctor let him continue.

Frazier swarmed all over Quarry after that—sensing the end was near. Quarry's eye swelled almost shut in the fifth round and took a number of direct hits in the sixth and seventh. Joe pecked away with flurries of accurate jabs and threw in a mix of hooks and quick uppercuts. Quarry fought back valiantly all through those rounds but couldn't mount a substantial attack while trying to protect the eye.

Referee Arthur Mercante finally stopped the fight between the seventh and eighth rounds on the doctor's orders. Joe, comfortably ahead on all three scorecards, was officially awarded a seventh-round TKO. Quarry didn't argue the doctor's decision, but he openly wept. Even though the match lasted nowhere near the scheduled 15 rounds, *The Ring* named it its "1969 Fight of the Year."

Joe Frazier's next fight, a unification match against WBA champion Jimmy Ellis, was truly years in the making. Frazier had to first overcome a reluctant opponent, and a public that refused to accept Ali was gone, while defeating one strong challenger after another. It took an amazing confluence of political pressure, dedication, and persuasion to finally bring a true World Heavyweight Championship fight to fruition.

After winning the WBA tournament for Ali's vacant title in April 1968, Ellis barely beat Floyd Patterson on points that September. Ellis had sustained a broken nose in the first round of that fight, and he took time off to heal afterward. Proposals for title defenses against British champ Henry Cooper and Argentine Gregorio Peralta fell apart over the next several months. And Ellis seemed to consciously avoid taking on Frazier despite his NYSAC crown and string of impressive title defenses.

The public, and boxing governing bodies, began to clamor for a Frazier-Ellis match. Frazier was now 24–0, with 21 knockouts, and seemed a worthwhile successor to the Greatest. When the NYSAC aligned with the WBC, the pressure for a possible undisputed heavyweight title fight soared. The final component for legitimizing the unification bout fell into place when Ali was persuaded to issue a retirement statement. This convinced Nat Fleischer, founder of *The Ring* magazine, to declare the winner his champion as well.

Frazier and Ellis finally met on February 16, 1970, at Madison Square Garden. It had been eight months since Joe had stopped Quarry. Ellis had been out of the ring for nearly a year and a half. Joe outweighed a purposely bulked-up opponent by several pounds and came in as the odds-on favorite to win. But boxing experts had to acknowledge Ellis's speed and lethal right hand. After all, Ellis had knocked Oscar Bonavena down twice with the right and Joe had never come close to putting him on the canvas.

Ellis was managed by Angelo Dundee, who suddenly had a lot more time on his hands with Ali out of the picture. Dundee stirred things up before the bout by saying he wouldn't be surprised if Ellis won by a knockout.

"I'll come out smokin'," Frazier had replied, with a knockout threat of his own.

In the first round, Ellis kept on the move but managed to stop and plant in regular intervals. As a result, he found the distance and power base needed to get off solid combinations. Several of these punches made contact as Frazier predictably charged in. Ellis took round one on most scorecards.

By the middle of the second round, Frazier went into full smokin' mode and pressured Ellis with nonstop left hooks, looping rights, and occasional jabs. He gave Ellis absolutely no punching room or time to catch his breath. Frazier remained at his swarming, body-wrecking best in the third. Ellis wore down in a hurry and never seemed to hurt Frazier, who talked and laughed at times after an exchange.

Frazier turned dead serious in the fourth and put Ellis down twice in the round. The first knockdown came two minutes into the round on a powerful left hook. The second one was just before the bell on another left hook to the jaw. Ellis made it to his feet at the count of nine after the bell. But Dundee decided to throw in the towel before the fifth round began.

After the fight, someone asked Ellis when he had picked up the count.

"At five," Jimmy replied, according to an AP story the next day.

"Both times?" another reporter asked.

"I only went down once," said Ellis, quite seriously.

That was when Ellis's manager broke into the conversation.

"Gentlemen, now you know why I stopped the fight," he said.

Dundee was later asked what he thought of Frazier now—in light of the way he won. People wanted to know if Ali's manager thought Joe deserved to be the champ.

"Joe Frazier tonight would have licked anybody in front of him," said Dundee, in another AP article. "Tonight, he was great."

Frazier was asked what was next for him. With Muhammad Ali gone, there really wasn't much left to accomplish. He had just won the undisputed World

Heavyweight Championship. Frazier had retained the NYSAC crown and won the WBA and WBC belts and *The Ring* title. All the championships that had once belonged to the Greatest had been taken by the 26-year-old from Philadelphia.

"Now *I'm* gonna retire," said Frazier, riffing on the Ali announcement. "I am going to sing rock and roll until that fellow [Muhammad Ali] who wanted to give me a belt [from *The Ring* magazine] wants to fight me."

If the Fight of the Century was Smokin' Joe's greatest victory, the four-round dismantling of Ellis likely ranked a close second.

———————

Joe Frazier's joke about retiring until he could fight Muhammad Ali almost became a reality. He only defended his World Heavyweight Championship once before meeting Ali in their much-anticipated first match.

On November 18, 1970, nine months after taking out Ellis, Frazier stepped into the ring at the Cobo Arena in Detroit against an overmatched Bob Foster. The light heavyweight champ weighed just 188 pounds to Frazier's rock-hard 209. Joe was the prohibitive favorite to win the match. This might have explained the tiny crowd at Cobo willing to pay big bucks for watching live.

The closed-circuit business for the fight was much more impressive. In fact, the closed-circuit TV showing at Madison Square Garden, combined with a live George Foreman–Boone Kirkham match, drew more than 18,000 paying customers. Those New York–Philadelphia Frazier fans were not disappointed.

Frazier was on a bit of a mission. Foster had made the mistake of calling Joe a "dumb" fighter several times during the weeks leading up to the bout. Joe heard the remarks and fumed in silence.

In the first round, Joe tried for a more *cerebral* approach. He didn't throw too many punches. Instead, he seemed content to just move and box with Foster—to gauge the flow of his attack. Maybe Joe thought it made him look like he was thinking his way through the round.

In the second round, Frazier stopped overthinking his approach and concentrated on getting some revenge. He countered a Foster jab with a powerful hook to the chin. Foster went down for a nine-count before shakily rising to his feet. Joe pounced with a vicious hook to the body and another to the head. Foster went down and out—just 49 seconds into the round.

Joe's opponent looked dazed enough to worry even Yank Durham. The trainer ran into the ring and cradled Foster's head in his arms until the doctor came to check him out.

Pat Putnam, from *Sports Illustrated,* had talked to Frazier's assistant trainer, Eddie Futch, before the fight. He wondered how Foster's disparaging comments might impact the fight and Joe's desire for revenge.

"He never reveals his feelings," said Futch, about Joe's prefight demeanor. "But that remark Foster made about being dumb really got to him. He works hard, and he prides himself on being a craftsman. He's too serious about his work to take a remark like that lightly. . . . And when an opponent's mouth gets to Joe, they are in trouble. They had better run—run like thieves."

According to Putnam's *Sports Illustrated* piece, Foster admitted to being totally dazed after both second-round knockdowns. He even owned up to not hearing either count.

"I'm dumb, huh?" Frazier said, when hearing Foster's confession. "Well, he ain't so smart. He fought me, didn't he?"

By the time Joe Frazier had disassembled Foster, Muhammad Ali's comeback was building steam. On August 11, 1970, the City of Atlanta Athletic Commission granted Ali a boxing license while his federal conviction remained under appeal. That cleared the way for Ali's third-round knockout of Jerry Quarry on October 26 of that year.

A September 1970 win in federal court had also pushed the New York State Boxing Commission to reinstate Ali's license. This led to a much more demanding battle against Oscar Bonavena in December. Ali emerged with a gritty but somewhat uninspired TKO in the 15th round. Despite the mediocre reviews for Ali, everyone looked to a much more dynamic performance when he met Frazier for the undisputed World Heavyweight Championship in March 1971.

After his triumph in the Fight of the Century, Joe Frazier received a long list of tributes and honors. But none meant as much to him, or hit so close to home, as the one in Columbia, South Carolina, on April 7. Frazier became the first black man invited to speak to the South Carolina legislature since the post–Civil War Reconstruction era. Quite a reversal for that young, poor kid who had to leave his home state years before to remain safe.

Frazier, flanked by an American flag sandwiched between a Confederate flag and the state flag, began with some humorous remarks about working on farms as a boy. But he ultimately delivered what turned out to be a moving, broad appeal for civil rights activism. Dave Anderson caught the flavor of Frazier's 12-minute speech in his *New York Times* article the next day.

"We must save our people," Joe had said, in the heart of his talk. "I mean white and black. We need to quit thinking who's living next door, who's driving a big car, who's my little daughter going to play with, who is she going to sit next to in school. We don't have time for that."

The standing-room-only crowd, according to Anderson, gave Joe a prolonged ovation at the end of his remarks.

In a luncheon in Joe's honor that followed, different members of the Frazier family got up to speak. The champ's 10-year-old daughter Jacquelyn offered a timely poem.

"Fly [*sic*] like a butterfly, sting like a bee," she said. "Joe Frazier is the only one who can beat Muhammad Ali."

———————

In January 1972, the champ bulked up to 215 pounds for his third World Championship title defense against the 195-pound Terry Daniels in New Orleans. Las Vegas oddsmakers gave Daniels no chance to win and didn't even bother to make a betting line for the contest. They proved prophetic when Frazier ended the fight in 1:47 of the fourth round.

Five months later, Joe Frazier defended his world heavyweight crown again in the unlikely venue of Omaha, Nebraska. His equally unlikely opponent was Ron "the Butcher" Stander from nearby Council Bluffs, Iowa. The local boy came in with a 23–1–1 record and a reputation for withstanding abuse until he found an opening for his knockout punch. His claim to fame was a knockout of the highly respected Earnie Shavers.

In a *New York Times* retrospective on the fight, writer Dan Barry described a first-round blow by the Butcher that "buckled Frazier's knees." Frazier took that as a wake-up call and connected on an uppercut to the jaw that put Stander out on his feet. In the second and third rounds, blood flowed from cuts above Stander's right eye and the bridge of his nose. The referee stopped the fight at the end of the fourth round when he determined the fighter could no longer see.

Barry noted that, going into the fight, not even Stander's wife gave him a reasonable shot at winning. "You don't take a Volkswagen into the Indy 500, unless you know a hell of a shortcut," she had said.

Joe's next title defense, in January 1973, turned into the train wreck known as Frazier-Foreman I. The embarrassing multiple knockdowns ended Joe's winning streak after 29 consecutive victories. It also sent him through a desperate redemption campaign that began with the London decision over Joe Bugner and a dubious loss to Muhammad Ali in their second meeting. But he ultimately fought his way back into title contention with second-time wins over Jerry Quarry and Jimmy Ellis.

Quarry brought a 49–6–4 record into his June 1974 fight with Frazier. He had fought two tough fights against Muhammad Ali, scored victories over George Chuvalo and Ron Lyle, and taken out Earnie Shavers in one round since their last meeting. He saw the fight with Frazier as a stepping-stone to a title match of his own with Foreman.

Joe staggered Quarry at the end of the first round, connected with both hands in the second and third, and dropped him with a shot to the stomach just before the bell in the fourth. He opened nasty cuts over both of Quarry's eyes in the fifth round. Then, when it seemed time to finish him off, Joe visibly backed off. The referee waved the reluctant fighter to continue, and Joe dutifully landed a few more accurate punches before the ref finally stopped the fight.

"Joe was hitting Quarry at will and looking around for somebody to stop the fight," Morty Holtzer had said, when I asked if Joe had ever showed mercy in the ring. "He was pleading with his [Quarry's] corner, 'Someone stop this fight—I don't want to hurt him anymore.' Gil Clancy [Quarry's trainer] finally threw it [the towel] in. Joe always had a little compassion for anybody he fought—even Ali."

Joe's concern for Quarry mimicked the way Larry Holmes reacted years later to a helpless Marvis. Despite the killer instinct most great boxers shared, they tended to more readily differentiate a competitive fight from a one-sided slaughter. They hungered for victory but could more easily afford to show mercy to a beaten opponent.

Joe Frazier's final match before the Thrilla in Manila took place in Melbourne, Australia, against Jimmy Ellis on March 2, 1975. Joe braved the long, frightening flights because a win would reestablish him as the number one

contender for the heavyweight crown. Even better, it meant one more championship match against his nemesis Ali, who had defeated Foreman for the
title in the Rumble in the Jungle just months before. Joe dominated much of
the fight against Ellis and knocked him out in 59 seconds of the ninth round.

"Joe bought his contract back from Cloverlay before the fight in Australia
with Jimmy Ellis," Morty had said, to show me how Joe had been preparing
for his last big-money fight with Ali. "But he gave them [Cloverlay] the Ellis
fight. We [Joe, Yank, and Morty] now had Joe, but Cloverlay by then was
more than just Joe."

————————

The Thrilla in Manila took place at the Philippine Coliseum, in Quezon City,
on October 1, 1975. The fight was held at the strange time of 10:45 a.m. to
go along with the live, closed-circuit television airings around the United
States. No official attendance figures were offered for the match, but spectators filled every aisle and available standing space. And many literally clung
to the rafters.

There was no air-conditioning in the arena, according to an independent.
co.uk article posted September 29, 2005. The humidity and temperature
soared as the venue filled up. By fight time, the air in the arena was jungle hot
and stifling. The bright ring lights made the air between the ropes hotter still.

My impressions of the fight came from many sources but relied most
heavily on the firsthand recollections of Joe, Marvis, and others in the Frazier
camp. The early interviews with the Fraziers had touched on prefight emotions in the dressing room, Marvis's reactions from ringside, and poignant
moments between father and son. Even though Joe was the one taking on Ali,
Marvis recalled the fight as a shared experience.

"Before the last Ali fight, we prayed in the locker room," Marvis had said,
glancing at Joe sitting next to him just outside the lair. "I was 15. . . . I felt a
part of him and the rest of the team that was there getting him together. I felt
like I was his guide leading him into battle."

I asked Joe what his mind-set had been before going into the arena, before
his rubber match with his greatest rival. His answer had come in the form of
a warrior code. It had been a lesson on how to do battle with honor.

"You know this is not just a fight," Joe had said, leaning toward me. "This
is a war. You go out there and pray for victory. There's two men out there and

the better man that day wins. If I lost, I got no hate against anybody. I told Marvis before the fight it's in God's hands."

Marvis had remembered watching the fight from a seat near his father's corner. The progression of the match came across as a terrible roller-coaster ride for the teenager.

"At first, I saw Pop winning all the way," Marvis had said, putting himself in the moment. "But, after a while, his eyes started to get puffy and he started to get hit more than he should. I felt his manager, Eddie Futch, was just in stopping the fight. I felt like I was in there taking the blows. I was trying to move with him and throw punches with him."

I asked Marvis if he had tried to say anything to his dad between rounds.

"I was sitting there saying, 'Give Pop my strength, Lord,'" he had replied. "I wished I could just lie there and be drained—just give him my energy. But things don't work that way."

Marvis then focused on his actions once the fight had ended—with his father sitting beaten and drained on his stool.

"I went into the ring and hugged him, and told him I still loved him. He said, 'I'm sorry Marv.' I said, 'There ain't nothing to worry about. I love you.' It hurts like hell to watch your Pop get beaten up. But I realized, even then, that's part of the game."

Muhammad Ali threw everything he could muster at Frazier in the early rounds in Manila, hoping for a quick resolution. When Joe fought through the onslaught and began to turn the tide in the middle rounds, Ali seemed physically and emotionally deflated for a while. He realized this was going to be the fight of his life.

Both combatants bashed away relentlessly at each other. They kept throwing hard through the blazing heat, blood, pain, and exhaustion for longer than anyone thought possible. At the end of 14 rounds, it was difficult to tell the winner from the loser.

Frazier and Ali later looked back at the fight—especially Joe's performance in those middle rounds—and showed great admiration for each other. Their often-quoted comments, about Ali's ability to take a punch and Joe's resilience, took on biblical proportions.

"Man, I hit him with punches that would bring down the walls of a city," Frazier said, as if preaching to the uninformed. "Lordy, he's great!"

Ali replied with his own reverent tribute. "Joe Frazier is one hell of a man," he said. "If God ever calls me to a holy war, I want Joe Frazier fighting beside me."

In the aftermath of the greatest, most grueling boxing match of all time, both fighters took time to heal. Then, eventually, they each followed their nature in selecting the next match. Frazier, predictably, signed to meet George Foreman the following year. He rushed to fight the one man who had dominated him and knocked him out.

That was typical for Joe Frazier. He aimed to beat the best and always looked for the quickest route back to a championship fight. And, as we know, that ended poorly for him and led to retirement.

Muhammad Ali made the smarter choice. He eased back into the fray by defending his World Heavyweight Championship against Jean-Pierre Coopman in February 1976. The moderate-sized Belgian had a 23–3 record against mostly unranked European boxers. He was considered by most experts as totally undeserving of a title shot. He appeared to have no hope of dethroning the Greatest. Not surprisingly, Coopman was knocked out in five rounds.

In one of our early conversations, I asked Morty Holtzer what had been the most telling tribute Muhammad Ali had ever offered Joe Frazier. He had thought for a while, smiled, and recounted something Ali said at a press conference before the Coopman fight. It had been a response to reporters questioning the validity of his challenger—Coopman's right to fight Ali for a world heavyweight title.

"Three times I fought Joe it was life and death," Ali said, according to Morty. "I deserve an easy one for a change."

It seemed a most fitting way for Ali to honor his fierce, forever rival.

EXTRA ROUNDS

12

Ali and Frazier on the Comeback Trail

Plans for Muhammad Ali's return to the ring began to be bandied about in March 1980. This was just days before Joe and I had first broached the subject up in the lair. However, it wasn't until negotiations with two other champions failed—and choices for preferred fight venues fell apart—that the official contract for Ali's comeback against WBC champion Larry Holmes got put together. It was finally signed on July 17.

The fight quickly became known as "the Last Hurrah." It was set for October 2, 1980, in a temporary outdoor facility on the grounds of Caesar's Palace in Las Vegas. The makeshift arena seated nearly 25,000 people and wound up taking in a then-record live gate of $6 million. Promoter Don King arranged for Ali to get a purse of $8 million and Holmes $6 million, regardless of who walked away with the WBC heavyweight crown and *The Ring* and lineal titles.

The Ali-Holmes bout came at a busy, stressful time for Joe Frazier and his son. It was three weeks after Marvis's shaky professional debut against the ex–football player Roger Troupe and just a week before his second match at Madison Square Garden. Yet Joe was keenly aware of the worldwide attention the championship fight had attracted and the huge payday awaiting Ali. For months now, Joe had stepped up his own training while working with Marvis in the gym.

Joe Frazier, more than most boxing people, understood Ali's decision to fast-track his shot at the heavyweight title and the enormous payday. He knew all too well that it only took one unexpected blow to derail the best of boxing plans. And Joe had learned the hard way that no fight down the line was ever guaranteed.

Still, most boxing experts were shocked that Ali didn't arrange for an easier tune-up bout or two before jumping in with the likes of Larry Holmes. That mistake became even more evident as I watched the airing of the fight along with a record worldwide audience of about 2 billion people. Years later, several more viewings of the bout on YouTube just confirmed that Ali had been totally unprepared to go straight from retirement to fighting an active champion like Holmes in his prime.

Holmes, at 30 years old and 211 pounds, was three years younger and 10 pounds leaner than when he had destroyed Marvis in one round. His record going into the Ali fight was 35–0 with 26 knockouts. He had already successfully defended the WBC title seven times since he had taken it from Ken Norton in 1978. Every single one of those championship bouts ended in a knockout.

Muhammad Ali, at 38, came in at a svelte 217 pounds and boasting a 56–3 record with 37 knockouts from his preretirement days. Although he weighed about the same as in his prime, it still represented a reason for grave concern. Ali had shed about 50 pounds over five feverish months of training to get down to his fighting weight. This had savvy observers worrying about the strength and resilience that had been lost along with the pounds. In addition, Ali had not fought a credible opponent since going up against Joe at the Thrilla in Manila five years before.

Howard Cosell, who called the fight on air, had interviewed both combatants before the event. Ali claimed not to have lost power or stamina from the weight loss. He also minimized the impact of the layoff on his reflexes. Cosell seemed skeptical, which led Ali to predict an unlikely victory by round nine.

Holmes countered with a more credible prediction of his own. He said he would knock out Ali in one to eight rounds. Despite his confidence, there appeared to be little joy or satisfaction in the prospect of dispatching his old friend and idol. He saw it as something he had to do to get the respect he deserved, to be seen as one of the great champions. He described Ali as "the monkey on my back."

In the most poignant moment of the interview, Holmes confessed to Cosell that there was no way to walk away from this fight with what he wanted.

"If I win, they'll say I knocked out an old man," he said.

Holmes looked sharp and methodical in his approach to the fight. From the beginning, he was relentless in his attack and met literally no resistance. Ali's response to fending off the champ's punches seemed sluggish at best. I wondered if Joe felt as heartsick as I did by the way his old rival fared in the first couple of rounds.

The first thing to go in older fighters was their reflexes. They continually got beaten to the punch in an exchange. As a result, many simply became reluctant to attack, try combinations, or even throw a power punch that would open up their defense. Ali acted like the typical over-the-hill boxer from the opening bell. He threw only one punch in the first two rounds while Holmes constantly connected with a jolting, rhythmic jab.

In some of the earlier rounds, Ali got up on his toes to dance around the ring. The enormous crowd responded to the flashes of grace by chanting his name. Unfortunately, Ali seemed unable to throw any effective blows off his movement as he had in his prime.

By the later rounds, the fluid motion stopped. Only Holmes was moving briskly and connecting with his punches at will. The crowd groaned, and I cringed, with every shot that found its mark.

Holmes looked to end things in the ninth round with a crisp uppercut that knocked Ali back against the ropes. When Ali raised his gloves to protect his face, Holmes struck again with a right to the kidney that had the older man in agony. Somehow Ali survived.

By round 10 of the scheduled 12-rounder, Ali was defenseless. He looked lifeless in the ring, and boos alternated with a sad silence. Mercifully, Angelo Dundee stopped the one-sided affair before the 11th round began.

The scorecards screamed support for the trainer's decision. All the officials had Holmes winning every round. In fact, many rounds went to Holmes by a wide margin using the 10-point must system of scoring.

Despite the dominant performance by Holmes, many observers claimed he held back at times out of admiration for Ali. Holmes said they were mistaking a careful approach to the fight for too much concern for an old friend's welfare.

"I love the man," said Holmes, according to a report posted by the *Guardian* years later. "But when the bell rung, I didn't even know his name."

In the postfight televised interview from a jam-packed ring, Holmes came across as much less detached. His emotions welled up and his eyes glistened with tears. He seemed moved by the way history had been turned on its ear. He had gone from the sparring partner for the Greatest to the man who had demolished his old benefactor.

"I did what I had to do," said Holmes, in response to being asked what it was like beating up his idol. "I still love the guy. Can't knock a man for trying."

Holmes was asked if he found it surprising that the fight seemed so easy.

"I thought it would go quicker," Larry admitted before paying his respects to the legend. "Ali is still the baddest man. I always respected the man. He will go down as the greatest of all time."

Fan reaction to the fight wasn't nearly as kind. For instance, the *Guardian* piece got this gruesome take on the demolition of Ali in round 10 from Sylvester "Rocky" Stallone.

"Like watching an autopsy on a man who's still alive," said the actor.

———

As disturbing as it was to watch the Ali-Holmes fight, the medical news that broke sometime afterward seemed even more troubling. It was eventually revealed that the Nevada State Athletic Commission had initially expressed serious concerns about Muhammad Ali's fitness to fight on such a high level. It had mandated that Ali submit to a neurological examination at the Mayo Clinic Sports Medicine in Minneapolis before a ruling could be made on granting a license to box.

Ali was admitted to the Mayo Clinic on July 23 and took part in a battery of neurological tests with Dr. Frank Howard. The results were "shocking," according to the *Telegraph* (UK). The doctor's report said Ali confessed to "tingling in his hands and slurring of his speech." The ex-champ also had a problem with touching his finger to his nose and hopping on one foot with the kind of agility expected.

Surprisingly, Dr. Howard concluded that there were no specific findings to justify prohibiting Ali from fighting. The results of his exams were dutifully sent to the Nevada State Athletic Commission. The report was not made public at the time. Based on that report, Ali received his boxing license in Nevada.

Dr. Ferdie Pacheco, a.k.a. "the Fight Doctor," took care of Ali's medical needs, supposedly free of charge, from 1960 to 1977. In a 2016 interview with the *Mirror* (UK), he admitted to begging Ali to quit boxing for years—starting right after the Thrilla in Manila. He felt that the champ was taking too many punches, sustaining too much damage despite continuing to win.

The beating Ali took at the hands of Earnie Shavers, en route to defending his title in a September 1977 match, was the last straw for Pacheco. The fight went 15 rounds, and the heavy-hitting Shavers kept swinging most of the way. Pacheco wound up giving Ali an ultimatum when it was over—quit the game or go on without him.

"I implored him, 'You have to stop, Champ.' But Ali refused to quit boxing—so I quit Ali," Pacheco said. "It was the hardest decision of my life."

The Fight Doctor had supposedly sent the medical report from the Mayo Clinic to members of Ali's camp before the Holmes fight. But, obviously, nobody saw grounds for calling the match off.

According to another more recent article in *Slate*, Pacheco saw the refusal to stop the Holmes-Ali debacle as downright criminal.

"All the people in this fight should've been arrested," he said. "This fight was an abomination, a crime."

After his disheartening loss to Holmes, Muhammad Ali refused to accept his newfound vulnerability. Ali initially said that he had felt unusually weak and lethargic during the bout. And he claimed to have been inordinately affected by the 100-degree heat in Las Vegas at fight time.

Most people present, including Holmes, took Ali's complaints as a lame excuse. One more aging boxer unable to accept the inevitable. However, a later press conference with Ali's doctor in tow made the ex-champ's take seem more plausible.

Dr. Charles Williams, according to an October 23, 1980, article in *Jet*, confirmed that he had originally prescribed the thyroid drug Thyrolar for Ali in 1978. It was just prior to Ali's two fights with Leon Spinks. The doctor said his patient had suffered from a thyroid deficiency at the time of his diagnosis.

Ali admitted to eventually abusing the drug by taking two pills a day rather than just one, as prescribed. He figured if one pill made him feel stronger, two pills should be better. The article noted that an overdose of Thyrolar resulted in fatigue and a "waste of physical energy." Other side effects from doubling the dose also included weight loss and sensitivity to heat.

"Two weeks before the fight I started to get more tired," said Ali, with Dr. Williams at his side. "I thought it was just because I was nearing the peak of my conditioning. If it's age and I'm finished and washed up, I'll face it. But if it [the loss] was because of the drugs. . . . Healthy I can beat Holmes. I shall return."

———

True to his word, Ali returned to the ring 14 months later on December 11, 1981. However, there was no Larry Holmes involved and no heavyweight title on the line. The nearly 40-year-old legend was matched instead against Trevor Berbick, 27, an up-and-coming contender with a 19–2 record and a world of promise.

Ali had obviously stopped abusing the thyroid medication and brought along one of his doctors to verify it. He even held up a medical report as additional proof prior to the contest. However, the change in regimen had allowed his weight to balloon up to 236 pounds, and he came across as generally more subdued than usual.

Berbick stood 6'2" and weighed a compact 218 pounds for the 10-round match with Ali. The Canadian resident had won his first 11 fights as a professional, 10 by knockout, after representing his native Jamaica in the 1976 Olympics in Montreal. In 1980, he had attracted major attention with a surprise ninth-round knockout of former champion John Tate.

That win over Tate had earned him a shot at the heavyweight crown held by Larry Holmes in April 1981. Berbick lost by a unanimous decision in 15 rounds. Yet he had managed to break Holmes's streak of eight straight title-defense victories via knockout.

The Ali-Berbick fight took place in Nassau and came to be known as "the Drama in Bahama." It headed up an impressive card that included big names like Thomas Hearns, Greg Page, and Scott LeDoux. However, the new company promoting the event was notoriously unorganized and ran into serious financial difficulties. By fight time, the biggest drama in the Queen Elizabeth Sports Centre revolved around whether some boxers—including Berbick—would get all the prize money they were promised.

The fight between Ali and Berbick, on the other hand, offered little suspense right from the beginning. Berbick took on the role of the aggressor in the early rounds and did a good job of pressuring Ali throughout the fight. He landed some solid shots in the first round, controlled most of the second, and pummeled Ali's body all through the third. It quickly became clear that he was too strong, too determined, and just too young for the aging star.

For his part, Ali came across as a slower, immobile, less graceful imitation of his younger self. Before the match he had promised to "dance all night," according to a *New York Times* report the next day. Although Ali rose up on his toes from time to time, there was no movement or dazzling footwork. Instead, he looked like a tired old soldier marching in place.

After being pushed around and bullied in the fourth, Ali finally woke up and showed flashes of the Greatest in the fifth and sixth rounds. He won the fifth by putting together several effective combinations and flustered Berbick with some flurries. At the end of the sixth, he actually had the younger fighter wobbly and praying for the bell.

Berbick ended the Ali uprising in the seventh with a brutal barrage of punches that just kept coming. He landed close to a dozen blows in a row, and the tired, beaten old champ settled in and accepted his fate. The one saving grace was that he managed to go out on his feet and lasted to the final bell.

Of course, the lopsided, unanimous decision surprised no one and the muted crowd took it well. Ali took his final defeat with a measure of grace too.

"I did good for a 40-year-old," Ali told a circle of reporters, in the *New York Times* story. He then referenced the vitality of his opponent as opposed to his own. "I could feel the youth. Age is slipping up on me."

Ali was questioned about coming back for another fight. He didn't give a direct answer at first. But he eventually addressed that question later in a postfight interview reported in the *Telegraph*. He forced himself to face the inevitable.

"Father Time has finally caught up to me and I'm gonna retire," said the three-time heavyweight champion, his speech slightly slurred. "And I don't think I'm gonna wake up next week and change my mind. I came out all right for an old man. We all lose sometimes. We all grow old."

———

After a failed negotiation or two of his own, Joe Frazier finally agreed to a comeback fight. The match took place on December 3, 1981, at the International Amphitheatre in Chicago. It was not-so-coincidentally scheduled just eight days before the Ali-Berbick bout in the Bahamas. As usual, Frazier had one eye on his old rival when making boxing plans.

Frazier, about a month shy of his 38th birthday, signed to fight an un-ranked 30-year-old named Floyd "Jumbo" Cummings. Although ABC-TV covered the match, it was a modest affair compared to Ali's return against Larry Holmes. Only around 6,500 fight fans chose to pay at the gate. There was also no worldwide closed-circuit audience to bank on. I didn't know too many people who watched the original telecast.

Frazier's take for the milestone event amounted to a paltry $85,000—a $73,000 purse and $12,000 for expenses. I could only imagine how hurt Joe must have been, especially in light of the $8 million Ali had earned for his title-fight comeback. Joe's opponent got tipped $10,000 for his services.

Of course, in typical ain't-nothing-but-a-party mode, Joe refused to be-moan the demeaning payday. He tried to put a positive spin on things before the bout.

"I always need money," said Joe, in a *Sports Illustrated* article on the fight. "I love to spend money. I love to party. I have the ability, the energy, the know-how. Why take all that energy and know-how and [just] party with it? Why waste it?"

I never saw evidence of Frazier's opponent addressing his meager pay. He appeared happy to merely be in the ring with the former champ.

The heavily muscled, 6'2", 223-pound Cummings boasted a 17–1 record against middling talent after a little more than two years in the professional ranks. The late start to his career was due to a 12-year prison sentence for murder served at the Stateville Correctional Center in Illinois. Jumbo, a former weight lifter, had found boxing in prison. He said he looked up to Smokin' Joe as his role model.

Frazier's decision to go with a modest opponent, in a low-key bout, was contrary to his usual big-fight, big-payday mantra. Yet he really had no al-ternative. He had to find a predictable, less dangerous tune-up that allowed him to work off the rust after a whopping five-year absence from professional boxing. The proud warrior didn't want to risk looking as helpless as Ali had just a year before. In addition, no titleholder in his right mind was likely to see an upside to giving another rusty old legend a shot after Ali's recent fiasco with Holmes.

When Frazier first announced his plan to get back to fighting, he crowed about turning the heavyweight division on its ear. He envisioned himself becoming a champion again. Other than maybe Holmes, he said he didn't see anyone who could beat him.

For any other boxer of his age, this would have been just willful bravado. It would have been an obvious fabrication for the press to sell some tickets. I didn't think that was true of Joe Frazier. From what I had learned about him, Joe likely believed every word of it.

Nonetheless, the timing of the Frazier comeback—just before Ali's bout with Berbick—reminded me again of Joe's original reason for returning to boxing. He had always pictured another fight with the Greatest and a chance to even the score. If both looked good this week, then an Ali-Frazier IV match became a more respectable, marketable event.

No doubt that same thought had been on Muhammad Ali's mind. He decided to phone Joe from the Bahamas. The call came in just after Joe's prefight weigh-in with Cummings.

"We got to make the old men proud," Ali said, in the *Sports Illustrated* piece.

"I hear you," Joe replied. "I'm gonna hold my end of the deal up."

Ali decided to keep the folksy-old-friend bit going.

"We're old men and we gotta show the world we can do it," Ali said, playing his part.

"Don't call me old," Joe suddenly snapped back.

Frazier was still only able to muster just so much civility when dealing with his longtime tormentor.

———

I watched the fight over and over on a grainy YouTube replay years later. The old film reminded me of key details and thoughts long forgotten. It brought back a flood of memories from my time with the Fraziers.

It was surprising to see Joe Frazier enter the ring first. I figured the plan would be to build anticipation, let the returning legend make a grand entrance. He wore a lush purple-and-white robe and danced in place in the corner. His three-man entourage was led by his son.

In an amazing role reversal, Marvis now served as the key man in his dad's corner. He gave Joe a long, detailed set of prefight instructions. He also stayed in his ear throughout every break between rounds. Ah, that must have been sweet for the kid.

Even better, Joe showed every sign of listening to what his son had to say. Marvis was almost three months into a year-and-a-half illness break after his sixth pro fight. He used a lot of that time to get Joe ready for the comeback. He had become the closest thing to a trainer for his dad.

Joe removed his robe before the bell and loosened up in his corner. There was a thick roll of fat surrounding his midsection that jiggled slightly as he moved. I couldn't help thinking of big Buster Mathis and the way Joe had taunted him, called him "Fat Boy."

Joe weighed in at a hefty 229 pounds. This made him about 10 pounds lighter than the man I saw peel off the plastic sweatshirt up in the lair nearly two years earlier. However, he still remained 20 pounds above peak fighting weight from back in his prime.

In the first round, Joe bobbed up and down and weaved like the old days. However, he missed badly on several lunging hooks. He also tried to stay on top of his opponent and go to the body but got hit too much coming in. Fortunately, the awkward Cummings didn't make a whole lot of solid contact in the round and missed his share of openings too. Joe escaped unscathed.

The same pattern continued in the second round. Joe tried to fight in tight. He missed on hooks while bulling his way in and took some hits in the process. Then, midway through the round, Joe rose up from his Smokin' Joe crouch to connect with a right uppercut flush on the chin.

Oh baby! That's it! I thought to myself, *It's all over!*

But, amazingly, it wasn't over. Jumbo just took a step back and smiled at Joe. This was the biggest revelation of the fight. Joe still managed to move and bob and connect. Unfortunately, his knockout power was gone. It had vanished somewhere between the gym and the road in the five-plus years of eating and singing and just living his life.

Joe charged across the ring to begin round three. He surprised Cummings and connected with his patented left hook. Once again, there was no discernible damage done.

The boxers continued to lean on each other for the rest of round three and through the fourth. Joe usually thrived on the inside, but he got the worst of the in-fighting now. He saved himself by clinching whenever in trouble. Luckily for Joe, Cummings didn't know enough to press his advantages when they arose.

By the end of round four, I feared Joe would tire himself out. I expected him to sink into the same sluggish kind of performance Ali showed for most of his fight with Holmes. I thought of it as the "old-man swoon."

Then, in round five, the fighting angels sang out loud. Smokin' Joe suddenly appeared to be reborn. For one glorious stretch, it all came back.

Early in the round, Joe clobbered Cummings with a tremendous left hook to the head. He hunkered down in his Smokin' Joe stance, bobbed up and down, and connected with several more vintage Frazier hooks. Bam! Bam! Bam! The shots landed one after the other.

Joe snapped Jumbo's head back with a right cross. It made him feel good enough to dramatically lower his gloves. He made a show of taunting his younger opponent. The crowd sprung to life chanting, "Joe! Joe! Joe!"

Later in the round, Joe followed up a jab with another solid hook to the head. Cummings absorbed the shot and just stood his ground. He laughed off Joe's effort. He made a point of showing everyone Joe Frazier couldn't hurt him. The effort seemed forced, unconvincing.

Seconds before the bell, just as Jumbo was starting to believe his own bravado, Joe landed one more crushing left hook. This one did serious damage and shook Jumbo to his core. He was wobbly and definitely not laughing when the bell rang and saved him.

In the sixth and seventh rounds, Joe had his moments and scored with some left hooks. Yet none seemed to sting or stop Cummings from pressing forward. Joe's reflexes, however, seemed better than Ali's and his legs had more life. He basically held his own even if Jumbo never felt the famous Frazier knockout power after that miraculous fifth round.

By the end of the seventh, I stopped worrying about Joe. I took a breath and thought, *This will be okay.* I figured Joe would plod his way to the end without paying a heavy price. Then, if Ali somehow handled Berbick, the old warriors might get a chance to make history with that mythical fourth fight.

My illusions fell apart in round eight. Joe got hit hard and often. It offered a glimpse of what he could face every round with a better opponent.

Cummings landed some uppercuts and stiff shots to the head early on. After trading body shots, he drove Joe into the ropes with a flurry of lefts and rights. Jumbo continued to pummel Joe's head with both hands, leaving the older man's legs weak, eyes puffy, and mouth streaming blood. Joe grabbed his opponent in a fight-saving clinch and held on for his boxing life and dignity.

Both fighters claimed victory in the end. The referee and judges upset both men by scoring it as a virtual tie. The two judges had it even, and the referee had it 46–45 for Cummings. The fight was officially ruled as a draw. It appeared to be the fair outcome.

After the fight, Joe remained true to form. He saw nothing but success, eternal youth, and legendary feats. That perspective on the fight, and his life, held firm into the next day.

"Everything I wanted to do out there, I done it," he said, according to *Sports Illustrated*. "Last night I was just beginning to get back into what I wanted to do. . . . I went the distance. . . . You can't say at 37, 38 I'm old. . . . Anything my boys can do I can do better. And longer. You hear me?"

Joe Frazier finished his tirade by climbing the proverbial mountaintop. He anointed himself superhuman, above the realm of most men.

"I'm one of God's men," he said, the spirit still stirring in his voice. "Separate me from the rest of them. Things that happen to me don't happen to every man."

A while later, once the spirit had a chance to die down, Joe got to see the fight film. He heard what his family had to say. Reality began to set in.

The desire for victory, to be the best, still burned bright in him. But Smokin' Joe admitted the steam in his attack had dissipated, the power in his punches had started to wane. Like his eternal rival, he knew it was time to quit. Joe announced his permanent retirement from the ring.

Epilogue

Ain't Nothing but a Party

In the years after Joe Frazier left the ring, his life and fortunes had their share of dramatic ups and downs. The uneven ride took in his financial situation, health issues, and even personal relationships. Yet his fighting legacy remained unassailable, and he received numerous honors for his boxing success. Along the way his rivalry with Muhammad Ali also took on mythic proportions.

Frazier was enshrined in the prestigious International Boxing Hall of Fame in 1990. This was not to be confused with the World Boxing Hall of Fame that had inducted him years before. *The Ring* magazine tapped Joe as the eighth greatest heavyweight boxer of all time in 1999, and their May 2017 poll still had him in the same position. *Boxing News* also had Joe among their 10 best heavyweights to ever put on the gloves.

Most rundowns of the best heavyweights have had Ali consistently ensconced at the top. The 2017 *Ring* list was no exception. But maybe more telling, for the legacy of both men, has been the effort over the years to fix their place among the greatest sports rivalries.

Without doubt, Ali vs. Frazier has topped just about every list of the best rivalries in boxing history, regardless of weight class. For instance, *Boxing News* ranked Ali-Frazier at number one on their list of "Top-10 Boxing Rivalries of All-Time." They explained their choice this way: "Muhammad Ali vs.

Joe Frazier produced one of the greatest fights of all-time. This heated rivalry between two all-time greats will forever be the benchmark."

The Thrilla in Manila has been widely recognized as the greatest boxing match ever—and the Fight of the Century has been consistently near the top of that list as well. But lately, Frazier-Ali has also been in the running for the title as the greatest individual rivalry in all of sports. And the competition for that has put them among the greatest athletes of all time.

Only a handful of iconic matchups, with combatants who transcend their era, have appeared on just about every list of best individual rivalries. These have included basketball's Magic Johnson and Larry Bird, golf's Arnold Palmer and Jack Nicklaus, John McEnroe and Bjorn Borg of tennis, and, of course, boxing's Joe Frazier and Muhammad Ali. These lists of the all-time greatest individual rivalries have come from traditional outlets like *Sports Illustrated* and the *Los Angeles Times*—as well as edgier websites like Sportster, Total Sportek, Ranker, and Coral.

Ranker, using fan voting to decide its rankings, placed Frazier vs. Ali at the top of its "Greatest Individual Rivalries in Sports History" list. The pair also headed up the Total Sportek list that ranked only the "top 10" rivalries. The criteria for ranking these rivalries usually began with the rare level of competition and the ferocity of their duels. Yet, unlike the other legendary rivalries, only Frazier and Ali kept the antagonistic nature of their relationship intact well into retirement.

————

In his postfighting years, Frazier more and more began to refer to Muhammad Ali by his pre-Muslim name, Cassius Clay. It became symbolic of his lingering animosity toward his old rival. It also captured the way Joe felt about a black man who had attacked him in the harshest of racist terms.

The "slave name," as Ali referred to it, became an easy way to get under the Greatest's cool veneer. Frazier also saw it as a means to remind everyone that he just couldn't forgive the public abuse he had taken from his onetime friend.

Of course, there had been numerous attempts in those years by Ali, and others, to put the feud to rest. In 1988, Frazier met up with Ali at Johnny Tocco's Gym in Las Vegas. They were there—along with George Foreman, Larry Holmes, and Ken Norton—for the filming of a movie titled *Champi-*

ons Forever. Ali, already showing the effects of Parkinson's disease, seemed somewhat slow and stilted in his movements. According to a 2015 *Sports Illustrated* piece, Frazier seized on the moment to make a point.

"Look what's happened to him," Joe said, reported *SI*. "All your talkin', man. I'm faster than you are now. You're damaged goods."

Ali replied, his speech slightly slurred. "I'm faster than you are, Joe." Ali pointed to a heavy bag and suggested a little contest. "Let's see who hits the bag fastest."

Frazier removed his jacket and rapidly fired off a barrage of hook shots. With each punch, he grunted, "Huh! Huh! Huh!" It was an impressive show of speed and power.

Ali kept his jacket on as he squared up in front of the heavy bag and assumed a boxing stance. He copied one of Joe's grunts and bellowed, "Huh!" He had not moved—and had not thrown a punch.

Ali then turned haltingly toward Frazier. "Wanna see it again, Joe?" he asked, a smile spreading across his face.

Everyone burst out laughing. It was typical Ali—just good-natured fun to them. But Joe didn't laugh. He saw it as yet another humiliation at the hands of Ali.

Later, at a lunch for the famous fighters, Holmes and the 290-pound Foreman had to take turns preventing a slightly drunk Frazier from getting at Ali. The frustration for Joe loomed eternal.

In 1989, Joe and Ali were thrown together again. They were invited to be guests of honor at a boxing match in Fayetteville, North Carolina. Ali supposedly wanted to put the past behind them. Joe killed the peace effort before Ali got to say a word. He refused to even be in the same room with his nemesis.

Frazier's resentment toward Ali came to a very public head in 1996. He was upset by the selection of Muhammad Ali as the torchbearer to light the Olympic flame at the opening ceremony in Atlanta. Once again, Ali was destined to be the center of attention for a worldwide audience. And Joe was inexplicably on the sidelines.

Ali was shaking from Parkinson's as he reached to ignite the cauldron, according to a 2011 piece by NPR following Frazier's death. Joe quipped to a nearby reporter that Ali should have fallen into the cauldron. Joe was immediately vilified for his remarks.

Later Frazier tried to put his remarks in context. He wanted them to be seen as the result of years of abuse—and unequal treatment by the media.

"We was fighting," Joe said, in NPR's story. "We was at war. I mean why should he speak all these terrible things about me and then I didn't say anything about him? So, whatever came to my mind and lips, I spit out."

Joe had always seemed most vexed by the dual standards used to judge Ali's words versus his own. He saw Ali as made from Teflon in the public's eye—none of the nasty things he had said or done had stuck to his reputation. Even worse, the media and fans had lauded his impish remarks and cooed about how clever he seemed. They all overlooked the damage done to Joe and his public persona.

The bitter rivalry between Joe Frazier and Muhammad Ali made both men millionaires many times over during their boxing careers. After all, they had literally pioneered the worldwide, closed-circuit superfight phenomenon with the seven-figure purses. Yet, as they moved through retirement, Ali's financial fortunes stayed on the rise while Frazier's fell dramatically.

Frazier's own marketing manager from 1995 on, Darren Prince, believed his client's continued animosity toward Ali contributed to his later money woes. According to a 2006 New York Times piece on Frazier's finances, Prince particularly saw the Olympic remarks and Joe's insistence that he had won all three Ali fights as sore spots with potential sponsors. The marketing man understood Joe's need to fire back after all the hurtful things Ali had said. But he felt Joe sometimes "went too far."

Frazier made the point in his 1996 autobiography that he was quite wealthy at the end of his boxing career. He said the second fight against George Foreman, just prior to retirement in 1976, was never about the money. Yeah, he acknowledged the million-dollar purse he received but claimed he really didn't need the payday.

Joe went on to catalog his real estate holdings at the time. He claimed they included the Philadelphia house, the South Carolina plantation, and major land investments in Bucks County. He also mentioned a large pension earning high interest rates and a trust fund for nearly $400,000.

From there, Frazier gave a long list of vehicles parked inside his mammoth home garage. They included five late-model luxury cars, a vintage auto, a couple of big motorcycles, and three snowmobiles. In the end, he added the powder-blue Cadillac Seville on order for Marvis.

That 2006 *New York Times* article painted a much different picture of Frazier's holdings. It suggested that the legend had squandered the bulk of his money through, well, just being Joe. To me, that was the kindhearted, seat-of-his-pants, fun-loving guy I knew from our time together.

"Joe Frazier has lost a financial fortune through a combination of his own generosity and naïveté, a partying lifestyle and failed business opportunities," the *New York Times* article said.

The reporter, conducting his interview in a more run-down North Philly gym than I remembered, asked Frazier about his financial situation. Joe first replied by jovially saying he had "plenty of money" and noting there was even a roll of "$100 bills in the back of the room." He soon turned serious and second-guessed how he had promoted himself in the past.

"I don't think I handled it right, because I certainly could have gone out more and done better for myself over the years," said Joe. "I could have left the gym a little more to be on the road."

The biggest blow to Frazier's fortune was the money he lost from his 140 acres of land in Bucks County, Pennsylvania. The trust that bought the property from him was supposed to settle the debt in annual payouts. But when the trust went out of business, Joe's checks stopped coming. His daughter Jacquelyn Frazier-Lyde, a lawyer, sued on her father's behalf, but the case was dismissed in 2003.

The *Times* reported that years later, the land became a residential community with an estimated worth of $100 million. None of it went to Joe.

Despite revelations of a fortune lost, nothing shook me more than the report on Frazier's living situation. The 62-year-old ex-champ confessed to residing on his own in an "apartment" just up the stairs from the gym.

"This is my primary residence," he told the newspaper. "Don't matter much. I'm on the road most of the time, anyway."

———

Joe Frazier and his wife Florence divorced in 1985. In his autobiography, Joe described the split as amicable. Given Joe's fun-loving nature and Flo's kind heart, that seemed plausible. But from what I had observed five years earlier, the divorce was also inevitable. Flo had been constantly frustrated by Joe's prolonged absences. She had become more and more outspoken about it in our conversations—albeit in her soft-spoken manner.

In his book, Joe gave his take on what went wrong with the marriage. To his credit, he stepped up and took the blame.

"Hey, I wasn't easy," he admitted. "I know that. I tended to go where I wanted, when I wanted. I was restless in the house. Still, I did the best I could. The proof was in the pudding: The proof was in those kids."

Joe's love for, and dedication to, the family—and especially his kids—was never in question. He took great pride in the accomplishments of all of them. There was evidently a lot to be proud of—and a whole lot of kids to keep track of as well.

Frazier acknowledged fathering 11 children by a number of different women. Of course, he had Marvis, Jacqui, Weatta, Jo-Netta, and Natasha with Florence. According to a *Philadelphia Inquirer* piece after his death, Joe also had a daughter Renae and a son Hector "with another woman during his marriage." And he openly talked about fathering four other sons: Joseph Rubin, Joseph Jordan, Brandon Marcus, and Derek Dennis.

"I have taken responsibility for all of them," he said, in his 1996 book. "My thinking was: If I'm strong enough to make 'em, then I'm strong enough to take 'em as my responsibility."

Besides Marvis, both Hector and Jacqui became high-quality professional boxers. Joe's nephew Rodney Frazier also did quite well in the ring. Joe had a hand in training them all after his retirement. Marvis played a key role in their preparation too.

Hector, fighting under the name Joe Frazier Jr., was a welterweight with an impressive 23–7–4 record from 1983 through 1992. Nineteen of his wins came by way of knockouts. He began his pro career by knocking out his first 12 opponents.

Rodney Frazier, a heavyweight, went 16–4–0 in his relatively short career. However, 12 of those wins were knockouts. He was undefeated at 12–0 until he stepped up in class and lost on a TKO to Philipp Brown—the last man Marvis fought and beat.

Jacqui Frazier-Lyde, a super middleweight, only fought 14 official professional fights from 2000 to 2004. But she won the vacant Women's International Boxing Federation World Light Heavy Title in 2001 and the Global Boxing Union Female World Super Middle Title in 2002. She finished her boxing career with a 13–1 record. She also became the first woman inducted into the Pennsylvania Boxing Hall of Fame.

Jacqui Frazier's only loss came in an extremely close, mixed decision. I'm sure Joe, like some others at ringside, thought his daughter had been robbed. Maybe the hardest part of the loss was that it came at the hands of Muhammad Ali's daughter Laila.

As talented as Jacqui was in the ring, her greatest successes came later in the courtroom. She earned her law degree at Villanova University and went on to a noteworthy career as a lawyer. Jacqui eventually was elevated to municipal court judge in the Philadelphia criminal justice system.

Marvis Frazier, after his retirement from fighting, had his own share of recognition and success. He was inducted into both the Pennsylvania and Philadelphia Boxing Halls of Fame. He was also named to serve in 1992 as a United States boxing coach.

Marvis, as forecasted, took an active role in both the family businesses and the church. After first running the Frazier limousine service for a while, he oversaw his dad's endorsements and card-show bookings. But, eventually, he focused primarily on managing the Joe Frazier Gym and the training program there.

Marvis ran the gym for years and watched it get dragged down as the neighborhood around it declined. Near the end, he nurtured plans for a vastly expanded renovation of the gym to be known as the Frazier Center. Marvis begged his father to keep the gym open and let the grand plans unfold. But Joe became disillusioned and demanded the gym be closed down in March 2008.

In his autobiography, Marvis said he was "devastated" by the decision. Five years later he was still bemoaning his dad's call to close the gym.

"When Pop said, 'Shut it down,' it just killed me," he admitted in an interview. "I never asked for anything from my father. All I wanted was his love. That's all."

In 2013, two years after Joe's death, the Joe Frazier Gym building was named to the National Register of Historic Places.

———

Away from boxing and the gym, Marvis Frazier answered to a higher calling. He became an ordained Pentecostal minister at Faith Temple Church of God where his family worshipped. He also became deeply involved in an organization called Prison Fellowship. It was a ministry that traveled to various penal institutions to work with prisoners and restore families through faith-based reentry programs.

In one of life's great twists, Frazier traveled with the Prison Fellowship to the Plainfield Correctional Facility in Indiana. Former heavyweight champion Mike Tyson, the man who effectively ended Marvis's fighting career, was incarcerated there. According to Marvis's book, Tyson refused to meet with the visitors until he heard that the group included Joe's son. They met and chatted for a while, and then Marvis prayed for the man who had knocked him cold in 30 seconds flat.

Marvis's marriage to his childhood sweetheart, Daralyn, remained strong and loving all through the nineties and into the new millennium. The couple had obviously embraced many of Marvis's early notions about the respect and patience needed to make a relationship work. They had two bright, accomplished daughters together, Tamyra and Tiara.

The girls were teenagers in the spring of 2001 when Daralyn was diagnosed with colon cancer. She died that November. Two years later, Marvis's older daughter, Tamyra, thankfully survived her own battle with cancer.

———

Legendary brawlers like Joe Frazier didn't retire from boxing feeling young and healthy. They left the ring looking old for their age. They also tended to suffer from an array of ailments that went along with their brutal lifestyle. Despite his initial claims to the contrary, Frazier was anything but healthy.

Joe was virtually blind in his left eye. He had taken way too many blows to the face over the years in an attempt to fight in close. Not surprising, he had some troubles seeing out of the right eye too.

The ex-champ also required a series of back surgeries for injuries caused by a car accident. In addition, he suffered from chronic high blood pressure and diabetes. But, in the end, it was the quick-spreading liver cancer that proved to be lethal.

Doctors found the cancer in the latter part of September 2011. Within several weeks, Joe was confined to home hospice care and soon succumbed to the disease. He died on November 7, 2011, at the age of 67.

The heartfelt tributes from luminaries in the boxing world poured in immediately. Oscar De La Hoya, welterweight champ Shane Mosley, former heavyweight titleholder Lennox Lewis, and light heavyweight champion Bernard Hopkins all offered accolades. Floyd Mayweather not only sent kind words and prayers, but also offered to arrange for his financial support team to pay for the funeral.

Muhammad Ali was one of the first of Joe's old opponents to weigh in. Although his words struck just the right note of reverence, there was no apology included. That had supposedly been done indirectly years before.

"The world has lost a great champion," Ali said, reported the *Guardian*. "I will always remember Joe with respect and admiration. My sympathy goes out to his family and loved ones."

Ali had previously apologized to Joe through an interview with the *New York Times*, and later other publications, in Frazier's final years. Initially, Joe had complained that the apology had been to the publication and not him directly. But in the May 2009 issue of *Sports Illustrated*, Joe relented and said he no longer felt the same animosity toward his old rival. While I don't doubt Joe voiced his forgiveness, I'm still convinced he had his fingers crossed behind his back.

George Foreman's remarks after Frazier's death came via an interview with the BBC. They seemed to hit on what would be a recurring theme for all of Joe's renowned former opponents.

"Joe Frazier was the most amazing fighter," he said. "He never stood more than 5'10" but he had every big man in boxing afraid of the little guys. He was such a terror."

Joe Bugner picked up where Foreman left off. Of all the praise heaped on Joe that day, I always thought the former British champ's comments would have pleased him most.

"He weighed about a stone lighter than myself, but he was so courageous and ferocious," said Bugner, in the *Guardian*. "You had to hit him with a sledgehammer to put him away. In 1973, I was 23 years old. I became a man after that fight because I realized you can't go through a career like boxing without seeing and feeling the power of the greats."

———

It was only fitting that an iconic boxer like Joe Frazier had two funerals. One was a celebrity-rich extravaganza at a huge Philadelphia church for Smokin' Joe. The other was an intimate down-home gathering of old friends and relatives on St. Helena Island, South Carolina. It was for the farmer's kid known as Billy Boy.

According to various accounts, Joe's daughter Jacqui was the driving force behind organizing the funeral for the folks from Beaufort County. Approximately 250 people attended the memorial service at Bethesda Christian Fellowship on November 16, 2011. They all had their own memories and stories of the local hero—and those memories filled the space. There was only one thing missing to make the moment complete—the honoree himself.

"I was really hoping to bring my father with me today," said Jacqui to those assembled, reported the *Philadelphia Tribune.* "I was really trying to make sure you had an opportunity to see his face."

The majority of the family had insisted that Joe's remains be kept in Philly for the bigger funeral and the burial to follow. Yet it didn't stop family and friends from remembering all that their Billy had done for them.

"When he came home, we knew he never forgot Beaufort," said Joe's niece Dannette Frazier. "He'd spend three or four days here because he had to visit everybody."

Dannette later recalled how "Uncle Billy" had dropped everything and driven 700 miles from Philadelphia to be with the family when her mother—Joe's sister—died.

"He was legally blind," said Dannette, amazed her uncle had made it in one piece. "He said, 'It was easy. I just looked at the tail lights in front of me.' That's the loving uncle we knew."

Several days earlier, Joe Frazier had been lying in state for a public viewing at the Wells Fargo Center in Philadelphia. Thousands of admirers had filed by to pay their respects. Few had ever met the boxer, but many talked as if they knew him.

The "private" funeral, on November 14, was for the benefit of nearly 4,000 invited guests, a horde of A-list friends, and the world press. They filled the Enon Tabernacle Baptist Church in Frazier's adopted city. Joe's closed white casket was fittingly adorned with his championship belt and a pair of boxing gloves. There was also a blanket over the casket that proclaimed the occupant as "Heavyweight Champion of the World."

The Reverend Jesse Jackson presided over the service, and sports greats like Muhammad Ali, Magic Johnson, and Larry Holmes took their places in the front pews. Ali, accompanied by family members, seemed both frail and emotional throughout.

Reverend Jackson, at one point, urged the mourners to rise and show their love for Frazier one final time. Ali, by several accounts, stood and applauded long and enthusiastically for his fallen rival.

In his eulogy, Jackson lauded Frazier for his rise from "segregation, degradation and disgrace to amazing grace," according to an AP story. But he also bemoaned the fact that a fictitious character like Rocky Balboa received honors denied the all-too-real boxer from Beaufort. There was a statue of Rocky erected outside the Philadelphia Museum of Art—and Joe, the archetypical Philly fighter, deserved one as well.

"Tell them Rocky is fictitious; Joe is reality," said Jackson. "Rocky's fists are frozen in stone. Joe's fists are smokin'. Rocky never faced Ali or Holmes or Foreman. Rocky never tasted his own blood. Champions are made in the ring, not in the movies."

Jackson's words must have hit home. Four years later, a 12-foot bronze statue of Frazier was erected in front of the NBC Sports Arena in South Philly. Joe, in boxing trunks and gloves, had been caught throwing his eternal left hook.

Joe would have loved that.

It has been several decades since my stint in Joe Frazier's inner circle. But I never needed a statue or fight films to feel his presence. The thing I held close over the years was his resilience in the face of disappointment. I relished his refusal to admit loss.

Whenever defeat seemed inevitable, I tried to channel Smokin' Joe's upbeat spirit and hard-won resolve.

I'd recall his raspy laugh that inevitably led to a shrug.

"Ain't nothing but a party," he'd have said, flashing a grin. "Yep, yep, yep, yep."

Bibliography

This book draws heavily on the author's original transcripts of numerous interviews with Joe Frazier and Marvis Frazier and the people around them over several months in 1980, as well as personal observations.

"*ABC Wide World of Sports*—Ali Frazier Studio Brawl." Ringside Videos. Filmed January 26, 1974. Posted October 26, 2016. YouTube video, 1:27:14 (0:56–58:02). https://www.youtube.com/watch?v=2Dh72Os_97c.

"Abe Davis." BoxRec. https://boxrec.com/en/proboxer/10878.

"Ali, Frazier to Collide." Associated Press. *Victoria Advocate*, January 28, 1974. https://news.google.com/newspapers?nid=861&dat=19740128&id=HqlSAAAAIB AJ&sjid=RH8DAAAAIBAJ&pg=5740,4094140&hl=en.

"Ali among 4,000 at Frazier Funeral." Associated Press. *New York Post*, November 14, 2011. https://nypost.com/2011/11/14/ali-among-4000-at-frazier-funeral/.

"Ali Calls Frazier White Man's Champ." Associated Press. *Sarasota Herald-Tribune*, March 2, 1971. https://news.google.com/newspapers?nid=1755&dat=19710302&i d=mjwgAAAAIBAJ&sjid=UmYEAAAAIBAJ&pg=4056,335596&hl=en.

"Ali Reportedly Used Drug to Lose Weight." Associated Press. *Pittsburgh Press*, October 6, 1980. https://news.google.com/newspapers?id=A34fAAAAIBAJ&sjid= C10EAAAAIBAJ&pg=2067,3307959&dq=holmes+ali+thyroid&hl=en.

Anderson, Dave. "Ali Beats Frazier on Decision Here." *New York Times*, January 29, 1974. https://archive.nytimes.com/www.nytimes.com/books/98/10/25/specials/ali-frazier.html.

———. "Ali-Frazier: Opposites Attract." *New York Times*, January 30, 1974. https://timesmachine.nytimes.com/timesmachine/1974/01/30/issue.html.

———. "So. Carolina Legislature Hears Frazier." *New York Times*, April 8, 1971. https://www.nytimes.com/1971/04/08/archives/so-carolina-legislature-hears-frazier.html.

"Another Round for Smokin' Joe." *New York Times*, August 22, 1981. https://www.nytimes.com/1981/08/22/sports/another-round-for-smokin-joe.html?searchResultPosition=1.

Barry, Dan. "After Frazier Kept the Belt, a Long Shot Withstood the Blows." *New York Times*, November 15, 2011. https://www.nytimes.com/2011/11/15/us/the-butcher-and-the-joe-frazier-ron-stander-bout.html.

Berger, Phil. "For Marvis Frazier, Does Father Know Best?" *New York Times*, July 21, 1986. https://www.nytimes.com/1986/07/21/sports/for-marvis-frazier-does-father-know-best.html.

———. "Tyson a Winner over Frazier in 0:30." *New York Times*, July 27, 1986. https://www.nytimes.com/1986/07/27/sports/tyson-a-winner-over-frazier-in-0-30.html.

BN Staff. "Muhammad Ali vs Joe Frazier—the Greatest Rivalry in Sport." *Boxing News*. Accessed March 28, 2020. https://www.boxingnewsonline.net/muhammad-ali-vs-joe-frazier-the-greatest-rivalry-in-sport/.

———. "On This Day Muhammad Ali Fought Joe Frazier in the Greatest Fight of All Time." *Boxing News*, October 1, 1975. https://www.boxingnewsonline.net/muhammad-ali-remembered-the-hardest-fight-of-all-time/.

Borges, Ron. "Frazier's Pain, Anger Remains Years after Trilogy." ESPN.com, October 16, 2007. https://www.espn.com/sports/boxing/news/story?id=3065738.

"Boxing: Ali v Frazier—'It Was Like Death. Closest Thing to Dyin' That I Know Of.'" *Independent*, September 29, 2005. https://www.independent.co.uk/sport/general/boxing-ali-v-frazier-it-was-like-death-closest-thing-to-dyin-that-i-know-of-316051.html.

"Boxing—1985—10 Round Heavyweight Bout—James Tillis vs Marvis Frazier: Dog Commentary." Imasportsphile.com, January 11, 2020. https://imasportsphile.com/boxing-1985-10-round-heavyweight-bout-james-tillis-vs-marvis-frazier-imasportsphile-com/.

Boyle, Robert H. "At the Fair with Fat Buster." *Sports Illustrated*, June 1, 1964. https://vault.si.com/vault/1964/06/01/at-the-fair-with-fat-buster.

Brady, Dave. "Marvis Frazier's Goal Is as Olympian as Pop's." *Washington Post*, April 12, 1979. https://www.washingtonpost.com/archive/sports/1979/04/12/marvis-fraziers-goal-is-as-olympian-as-pops/7822066b-f68b-4837-a923-16ad346408ec/.

"Brewton Plantation." South Carolina Plantations. Accessed May 21, 2019. https://south-carolina-plantations.com/beaufort/brewton.html.

Brown, Gary. "The Monday After: Canton Boxer Recalls Fight vs. Joe Frazier." *Repository*, December 20, 2011. www.cantonrep.com/article/20111220/NEWS/312209920.

Bucktin, Christopher. "Muhammad Ali's Doctor BEGGED Him to Quit Boxing after the Thrilla in Manila." *Mirror*, June 4, 2016. https://www.mirror.co.uk/sport/boxing/muhammad-alis-doctor-begged-him-8116534.

Burnton, Simon. "Muhammad Ali on Joe Frazier: That's One Helluva Man and God Bless Him; Bitter Rivals in and out of the Ring—in Their Own Words." *Guardian*, November 8, 2011. https://www.theguardian.com/sport/2011/nov/08/muhammad-ali-joe-frazier.

Bynum, Russ. "Joe Frazier Remembered in SC Hometown." Associated Press. *Philadelphia Tribune*, November 16, 2011. https://www.phillytrib.com/sports/joe-frazier-remembered-in-sc-hometown/article_a39da93b-63d7-59ff-80dd-a2e5865953f5.html.

"Chris McDonald 'Lost Heavyweight Prospect.'" Discussion in "Classic Boxing Forum." Boxing Forum 24, July 24, 2012. https://www.boxingforum24.com/threads/chris-mcdonald-lost-heavyweight-prospect.419942/.

Daley, Arthur. "Sports of *The Times*." *New York Times*, March 10, 1971. https://www.nytimes.com/1971/03/10/archives/the-mirror-told-a-distressing-tale.html.

"Dave Prater, 50, Dies; Soul Singer of the 60's." Associated Press. *New York Times*, April 13, 1988. https://www.nytimes.com/1988/04/13/obituaries/dave-prater-50-dies-soul-singer-of-the-60-s.html.

Davies, Gareth. "Day When Time Finally Beat Ali." *Telegraph*, December 11, 2006.
https://www.telegraph.co.uk/sport/othersports/boxing/2352160/Day-when-time
-finally-beat-Ali.html.

Doyle, Jack. "Ali, Frazier, Sinatra, et al.,—Boxing & Culture, 1960s–70s."
PopHistoryDig.com. Accessed November 9, 2015. https://www.pophistorydig
.com/topics/muhammad-ali-joe-frazier/.

Drake, Hal. "Frazier Chases German for Boxing Gold Record." *Stars and Stripes*,
October 25, 1964. https://www.stripes.com/news/frazier-chases-german-for
-boxing-gold-medal-1.20961.

"Exam Is Flunked; Title Go Halted." Associated Press. *Spokane Daily Chronicle*,
February 17, 1970. https://news.google.com/newspapers?nid=1338&dat=1970021
7&id=c5BYAAAAIBAJ&sjid=OfgDAAAAIBAJ&pg=6959,367606&hl=en.

Farrell, Barry. "The Killing at the Notorious Mustang Ranch." *New York*, July 26,
1976. https://books.google.com/books?id=b-MCAAAAMBAJ&pg=PA41.

Franklin, Bobby. "Frazier vs Ellis 1970: Jimmy Showed Incredible Courage." *Boxing
over Broadway*, March 21, 2017. https://www.boxingoverbroadway.com/frazier
-vs-ellis-1970/.

Frazier, Joe, and Phil Berger. *Smokin' Joe: The Autobiography of a Heavyweight
Champion of the World, Smokin' Joe Frazier.* New York: Macmillan, 1996.

"Frazier Can't See Too Tall as Boxer." Associated Press. *St. Louis Globe-Democrat*,
November 29, 1979.

"Frazier Heavy Favorite." Associated Press. *Southeast Missourian*, February 16, 1970.
https://news.google.com/newspapers?nid=1893&dat=19700216&id=mWgfAAAA
IBAJ&sjid=5dQEAAAAIBAJ&pg=3119,4197750&hl=en.

"Frazier in Jan. 15 15-Round Title Defense vs. Daniels." Associated Press. *Lewiston
Daily Sun*, November 23, 1971. https://news.google.com/newspapers?id=KZYgAA
AAIBAJ&sjid=KWgFAAAAIBAJ&pg=1026%2C2959776.

"Frazier's Son Is Victor in Olympic Boxing Trials." Associated Press. *New York
Times*, June 18, 1980.

"Frazier Stopped after 21 Seconds." Associated Press. *New York Times*, June 20,
1980.

"Frazier Stops Davis in Fifth." Associated Press. *News-Press*, April 12, 1967.

"Frazier Stops Quarry in 7th." Associated Press, June 24, 1969. https://boxrec.com /media/index.php/Joe_Frazier_vs._Jerry_Quarry_(1st_meeting).

"Frazier Takes Zyglewicz." Associated Press. *Gadsden Times*, April 23, 1969. https:// news.google.com/newspapers?id=-KsfAAAAIBAJ&sjid=x9YEAAAAIBAJ&pg=74 7,3182247&dq=joe+frazier+zyglewicz&hl=en.

Gelston, Dan. "Joe Frazier Funeral Provides Final Salute to Boxing Legend." *Christian Science Monitor*, November 15, 2011. https://www.csmonitor.com/USA/Latest -News-Wires/2011/1115/Joe-Frazier-funeral-provides-final-salute-to-boxing-legend.

"George Benton." BoxRec. https://boxrec.com/media/index.php/George_Benton.

Gigney, George. "Top 10 Boxing Rivalries." *Boxing News*, October 4, 2016. https:// www.boxingnewsonline.net/top-10-boxing-rivalries/.

"Gil Clancy." International Boxing Hall of Fame. March 22, 2010. http://www.ibhof .com/pages/about/inductees/nonparticipant/clancy.html.

Glass, Andrew. "President Carter Orders an Olympic Boycott, March 21, 1980." *Politico*, March 21, 2017. https://www.politico.com/story/2017/03/president -carter-orders-an-olympic-boycott-march-21-1980-236185.

Goldman, Tom. "Remembering Joe Frazier and an Epic Boxing Rivalry." NPR, November 8, 2011. https://www.npr.org/2011/11/08/142123491/boxing-legend -joe-frazier-loses-cancer-battle.

Goldstein, Richard. "Gil Clancy, Boxing Manager and Trainer, Dies at 88." *New York Times*, March 31, 2011. https://www.nytimes.com/2011/04/01 /sports/01clancy.html.

Gray, Tom. "Best I Faced: Joe Bugner." *The Ring*. Accessed December 30, 2019. https://www.ringtv.com/330445-best-ive-faced-joe-bugner/.

——. "'Fight of the Year 1969': The 50 Year Anniversary of Joe Frazier-Jerry Quarry I." *The Ring*, June 23, 1969. https://www.ringtv.com/569049-fight-of-the -year-1969-the-50-year-anniversary-of-joe-frazier-jerry-quarry-i/.

Gregory, Sean. "Joe Frazier, Former Heavyweight Boxing Champ, Dies at 67." *Time*, November 8, 2011. http://content.time.com/time/nation /article/0,8599,2098907,00.html.

Grimsley, Will. "Ali's Back and So Is Boxing." Associated Press. *Eugene Register-Guard*, January 29, 1974. https://news.google.com/newspapers?id=La5VAAAAIB AJ&sjid=P-ADAAAAIBAJ&pg=6483%2C6312837.

Gross, Jane. "Muhammad Ali Club Agrees to a Boycott of Moscow Games." *New York Times*, January 18, 1980.

Hannigan, Dave. "The Tragic Tale of George Chuvalo—Muhammad Ali's Toughest Opponent." *Irish Times*, December 13, 2017. https://www.irishtimes.com/sport /other-sports/the-tragic-tale-of-george-chuvalo-muhammad-ali-s-toughest-opponent-1.3326096.

Hauser, Thomas. "'The Greatest' Is the Greatest." *The Ring*, April 19, 2017. https:// www.ringtv.com/488242-ring-greatest-heavyweight-time/.

——. "The Night When Ali Screamed in Pain; 2 October 1980." *Guardian*, January 7, 2007. https://www.theguardian.com/sport/2007/jan/07/boxing.features.

Hirsley, Michael. "Punches Took Deadly Toll on Quarry." *Chicago Tribune*, January 5, 1999. https://www.chicagotribune.com/news/ct-xpm-1999-01-05-9901050116 -story.html.

Hissner, Ken. "How Good Could Marvis Frazier Have Been If 'Smokin' Joe Didn't Take Over in the Corner?" *Boxing Insider*, October 24, 2016. https://www .boxinginsider.com/columns/good-marvis-frazier-smokin-joe-didnt-take-corner/.

——. "Interview with Rev. Marvis Frazier: From Delivering Knockouts to Delivering Sermons!" Doghouse Boxing. November 28, 2009. http://www .doghouseboxing.com/Ken/Hissner112809.htm.

"Holmes Crunches Frazier." United Press International. *Bryan Times*, November 26, 1983. https://news.google.com/newspapers?nid=799&dat=19631126&id=DrhTAA AAIBAJ&sjid=5ocDAAAAIBAJ&pg=4957,5639417.

"Holmes Takes Out Frazier in First Round." Associated Press. *Ottawa Citizen*, November 26, 1983. https://news.google.com/newspapers?id=RaQyAAAAIBAJ&s jid=P-8FAAAAIBAJ&pg=2803,3084162&dq=larry+holmes+marvis+frazier&hl=e.

"Jacqui Frazier-Lyde." BoxRec. https://boxrec.com/en/proboxer/15511.

"James Broad." BoxRec. https://boxrec.com/en/proboxer/611.

"James Smith." BoxRec. https://boxrec.com/en/proboxer/563.

"Joe Frazier." BoxRec. https://boxrec.com/media/index.php/Joe_Frazier.

"Joe Frazier Jr." BoxRec. https://boxrec.com/en/proboxer/3105.

"Joe Frazier Net Worth." Celebrity Net Worth. Accessed October 4, 2019. https://www.celebritynetworth.com/richest-athletes/richest-boxers/joe-frazier-net-worth/.

"Joe Frazier Remembered at Home." Associated Press, November 16, 2011. https://www.espn.com/boxing/story/_/id/7241658/joe-frazier-former-heavyweight-champ-remembered-south-carolina.

"Joe Frazier vs. Floyd Cummings." BoxRec. Last modified December 2, 2014. https://boxrec.com/media/index.php/Joe_Frazier_vs._Floyd_Cummings.

"Joe Frazier vs. Jimmy Ellis." BoxRec. Last modified March 25, 2016. https://boxrec.com/media/index.php/Joe_Frazier_vs._Jimmy_Ellis.

"Joseph Frazier | 1944–2011 | Obituary." Marshel's Wright-Donaldson Home for Funerals, November 16, 2011. https://www.marshelswrightdonaldson.com/obituary/1314291.

"Jose Ribalta." BoxRec. https://boxrec.com/en/proboxer/557.

"Jose Ribalta." *On the Ropes Boxing Radio*, January 27, 2014. Interview, 22:56. https://www.google.com/search?q=boxing+radio+interview+jose+ribalta+january+27%2C+2014&oq=boxing+radio+interview+jose+ribalta+january+27%2C+2014&aqs=chrome..69i57.29825j0j7&sourceid=chrome&ie=UTF-8.

"Jose Ribalta vs. Marvis Frazier." BoxRec: Bout, September 11, 1985. https://boxrec.com/en/event/21174/30748.

Junod, Tom. "The Master: George Benton Has a Lifetime's Worth of Boxing Wisdom." *Sports Illustrated*, November 2, 1992. https://vault.si.com/vault/1992/11/02/the-master-george-benton-has-a-lifetimes-worth-of-boxing-wisdom-that-he-imparts-to-the-worlds-best-fighters.

Katz, Michael. "Holmes Stops Frazier in First." *New York Times*, November 26, 1983. https://www.nytimes.com/1983/11/26/sports/holmes-stops-frazier-in-first.html.

Kram, Mark. "Ali in a World of His Own." *Sports Illustrated*, February 26, 1973. https://vault.si.com/vault/1973/02/26/ali-in-a-world-of-his-own.

"Larry Holmes vs. Marvis Frazier (1983)." Filmed November 25, 1983. Posted August 9, 2012. YouTube video, 14:04. https://www.youtube.com/watch?v=zRrvu-PXYzY.

"Larry Holmes vs. Muhammad Ali." BoxRec. Accessed December 6, 2018. https://
   boxrec.com/media/index.php/Larry_Holmes_vs._Muhammad_Ali.

Levin, Josh. "The Time Muhammad Ali Stopped a Man from Leaping to His Death."
   Slate, June 4, 2016. https://slate.com/culture/2016/06/the-time-muhammad-ali
   -stopped-a-man-from-leaping-to-his-death.html.

Mallozzi, Vincent. "Fire Still Burns inside Smokin' Joe Frazier." New York Times,
   October 18, 2006. https://www.nytimes.com/2006/10/18/sports
   /othersports/18frazier.html?searchResultPosition=1.

"Marvis Frazier." BoxRec. https://boxrec.com/en/proboxer/519.

"Marvis Frazier Rebounded from a Fifth-Round Knockdown . . ." Los Angeles Times,
   February 24, 1986. https://www.latimes.com/archives/la-xpm-1986-02-24-sp
   -11557-story.html.

"Marvis Frazier Wins 6th, Stops Casale after Four." Washington Post, September
   17, 1981. https://www.washingtonpost.com/archive/sports/1981/09/17/marvis
   -frazier-wins-6th-stops-casale-after-four/27f5ed79-8a50-4c86-a38c-e88fb530e9a7/.

McIlvanney, Hugh. "When the Mountain Came to Muhammad." Guardian,
   March 9, 1971. https://www.theguardian.com/sport/2011/nov/08/joe-frazier
   -muhammad-ali-1971.

"Mike Tyson vs. Marvis Frazier (1986)." BoxRec. Accessed November 24, 2018.
   https://boxrec.com/media/index.php/Mike_Tyson_vs._Marvis_Frazier.

"Mitch Green." BoxRec. https://boxrec.com/media/index.php/Mitch_Green.

Moody, Erin. "Beaufort Remembers Native Son Smokin' Joe Frazier." Beaufort
   Gazette, November 9, 2011. https://www.islandpacket.com/news/local
   /community/beaufort-news/article33443178.html.

Moore, Thad. "Joe and Marvis Frazier: A Package Deal." Boxing.com, August 9,
   2016. http://archive.boxing.media/joe_and_marvis_frazier_a_package_deal.html.

"Muhammad Ali Leads Tribute to the Late Joe Frazier." Associated Press. Guardian,
   November 8, 2011. https://www.theguardian.com/sport/2011/nov/08
   /muhammad-ali-tribute-joe-frazier.

"Muhammad Ali's Boxing Record." Associated Press. Fox News, June 4, 2016.
   https://www.foxnews.com/sports/muhammad-alis-boxing-record-56-wins-5
   -losses-37-knockouts.

"Muhammad Ali vs. Joe Frazier II." Ringside Videos. Filmed January 28, 1974, Madison Square Garden, New York, NY. *ABC Wide World of Sports* broadcast. Posted October 31, 2016. YouTube video, 57:13. https://www.youtube.com /watch?v=AmyOllzWNHo.

"Muhammad Ali vs. Zora Folley." BoxRec. Last modified March 11, 2016. https:// boxrec.com/media/index.php/Muhammad_Ali_vs._Zora_Folley.

Murray, William D. "Heavyweight James 'Bonecrusher' Smith Battled Marvis Frazier to a . . ." United Press International Archives, February 23, 1986. https:// www.upi.com/Archives/1986/02/23/Heavyweight-James-Bonecrusher-Smith -battled-Marvis-Frazier-to-a/5370509518800/.

Nack, William. "A Sad Show for Smokeless Joe." *Sports Illustrated*, December 14, 1981. https://vault.si.com/vault/1981/12/14/a-sad-show-for-smokeless-joe-after-a -5-12-year-layoff-37-year-old-joe-frazier-returned-to-the-ring-to-fight-please -say-it-isnt-so-joe-jumbo-cummings.

———. "Twenty-Five Years Later, Ali and Frazier Are Still Slugging It Out." *Sports Illustrated*, September 24, 2015. Originally appeared in the September 30, 1996 issue. https://www.si.com/boxing/2015/09/24/muhammad-ali-joe-frazier-william -nack-si-vault.

"1986-05-03 Mike Tyson–James Tillis." ESPN Classic. Filmed May 3, 1986. Posted January 21, 2011. YouTube video, 46:34. https://www.youtube.com/watch?v=z5 _E51vOuqM.

"No One Left for Frazier; Ellis Destroyed Rapidly." Associated Press. *Spokane Daily Chronicle*, February 17, 1970. https://news.google.com/newspapers?nid=1338&dat= 19700217&id=c5BYAAAAIBAJ&sjid=OfgDAAAAIBAJ&pg=6959,367606&hl=en.

Nordyke, Kimberly. "Boxing Legend Joe Frazier, Who Inspired Iconic 'Rocky' Scenes, Dies at Age 67." *Hollywood Reporter*, November 7, 2011. https://www .hollywoodreporter.com/news/boxer-joe-frazier-muhammad-ali-rocky-258563.

Pepe, Phil. "Every Day Is Father's Day in Life of Marvis Frazier." *Daily News*, June 15, 1980.

"Philipp Brown." BoxRec. https://boxrec.com/en/proboxer/1725.

Phillips, Angus. "Cummings, Frazier Draw." *Washington Post*, December 4, 1981. https://www.washingtonpost.com/archive/sports/1981/12/04/cummings-frazier -draw/05043b5d-443c-4d8e-9065-1821ffa59810/.

Potter, Jamie, and Marvis Frazier. *Meet Marvis Frazier: The Story of the Son of Smokin' Joe.* Otego, NY: Gopher Graphics, 2013.

Putnam, Pat. "One Round of Boxing Was More Than Enough." *Sports Illustrated,* November 30, 1970. https://vault.si.com/vault/1970/11/30/one-round-of-boxing -was-more-than-enough.

Rafael, Dan. "George Benton Dies at 78." ESPN.com, September 21, 2011. https:// www.espn.com/boxing/story/_/id/7001072/george-benton-dies-was-legendary -philadelphia-boxer-trainer.

"Ray Staples." BoxRec. https://boxrec.com/en/proboxer/10877.

Retired Boxers Foundation, Inc. "TOMORROW'S CHAMPIONS: Chris McDonald." Facebook, May 5, 2013. https://www.facebook.com /retiredboxersfoundation/photos/tomorrows-champions-chris-mcdonaldwe -know-the-least-about-chris-mcdonald-he-had-/10151580357029621/.

Rhoden, William C. "Frazier Defeats Bugner." *New York Times,* June 5, 1983. https://www.nytimes.com/1983/06/05/sports/frazier-defeats-bugner.html.

"Ring Magazine Fight of the Year [1945–2019]." BoxRec. Accessed December 23, 2019. https://boxrec.com/media/index.php/Ring_Magazine_Fight_of_the_Year.

"Rodney Frazier." BoxRec. https://boxrec.com/en/proboxer/16080.

Saraceno, Jon. "Q&A with Ferdie Pacheco, Muhammad Ali's Longtime Doctor and Corner Man." *USA Today,* June 4, 2016. https://www.usatoday.com/story/sports /boxing/2016/06/04/muhammad-ali-ferdie-pacheco-interview/85352836/.

Schuyler, Ed, Jr. "Holmes Facing 3 Title Bouts." Associated Press. *Ottawa Citizen,* August 16, 1983. https://news.google.com/newspapers?id=8K MyAAAAIBAJ&sjid=Bu8FAAAAIBAJ&pg=1379,2360852&dq=marvis -frazier+greg+page+2.55&hl=en.

Seekins, Briggs. "Ranking Muhammad Ali's 10 Greatest Lines of Trash Talk." Bleacher Report, June 13, 2016. https://bleacherreport.com/articles/2645884 -ranking-muhammad-alis-10-greatest-lines-of-trash-talk.

SI Staff. "The Next Stop Is Costa Rica." *Sports Illustrated,* March 1, 1976. https:// vault.si.com/vault/1976/03/01/the-next-stop-is-costa-rica.

Smith, Red. "Once More, from Memory This Time." *New York Times,* January 29, 1974. http://movies2.nytimes.com/books/98/10/25/specials/ali-memory.html.

"Smokin' Joe Sees Marvis KOd in 21 Seconds." *New York Post*, June 20, 1980.

"South Carolina Native 'Smokin' Joe' Frazier Dies after Fight with Cancer." WACH Fox News Center, November 8, 2011. https://wach.com/news/local/sc-native -smokin-joe-frazier-dies-after-fight-with-cancer.

Stan Ward Boxing. "Meet Stan Ward." Accessed February 19, 2019. http://www .stanwardboxing.com/about-coach/.

Steinberg, Don. "Final Bell for Philly Legend." *Philadelphia Inquirer*, November 8, 2011. https://www.inquirer.com/philly/sports/boxing/20111108_Final_bell_for _Philly_legend.html.

——. "Frazier and Spectrum Arena a Pair of Philly Institutions." ESPN.com, October 17, 2007. https://www.espn.com/sports/boxing/news/story?id=3064971.

"'Terrible' Tim Witherspoon vs. James 'Bonecrusher' Smith in a Heavyweight Fight." Filmed June 15, 1985. Posted November 21, 2011. YouTube video, 13:27. https://www.youtube.com/watch?v=KNrVOprlscg.

"Title to Frazier's Son." Associated Press. *New York Times*, May 12, 1980.

"Tony Doyle." BoxRec. https://boxrec.com/media/index.php?title=Tony _Doyle&printable=yes.

"Tony Pulu." BoxRec. https://boxrec.com/en/proboxer/22658.

"Tyson Says Hello, Goodby to Frazier in Round 1." Associated Press. *Los Angeles Times*, July 27, 1986. https://www.latimes.com/archives/la-xpm-1986-07-27-sp -1691-story.html.

Vecsey, George. "Berbick Defeats Ali on Decision." *New York Times*, December 12, 1981. https://www.nytimes.com/1981/12/12/sports/berbick-defeats-ali-on -decision.html?searchResultPosition=1.

Waldron, Travis. "Remembering Joe Frazier for Who He Was, Not Who He Wasn't." Think Progress, November 8, 2011. https://archive.thinkprogress.org /remembering-joe-frazier-for-who-he-was-not-who-he-wasnt-8971ed5c194d/.

Winderman, Ira. "Bonecrusher Means Business." *Sun-Sentinel*, March 3, 1987. https://www.sun-sentinel.com/news/fl-xpm-1987-03-03-8701140028-story.html.

Wolff, Leslie R. "Remembering Smokin' Joe Frazier, a True Champion." *Philadelphia Business Journal*, June 9, 2016. https://www.bizjournals.com /philadelphia/blog/guest-comment/2016/06/remembering-smokin-joe-frazier-a- true-champion.html.

Index

About the Author

Glenn Lewis is founding director of the BA degree in journalism at York College, CUNY, and a founding professor of print journalism at the Craig Newmark Graduate School of Journalism at CUNY. The veteran journalist and author has written about sports, health, media, and societal trends. He has waited four decades to write about his time with the iconic heavyweight champion Joe Frazier. Lewis has also been an on-air media and journalism expert for a major TV news outlet. He lives in New York City with his wife and has two grown daughters.